Property of
FAMILY OF FAITH
LIBRARY

W9-BJR-837

From Thought
to Word

As part of Houghton Mifflin's ongoing
commitment to the environment, this text has been
printed on recycled paper.

Family of Faith Library

From Thought to Word

Ann Kesslen
El Camino College

Kate Collins
El Camino College

Houghton Mifflin Company   Boston   New York

Senior Sponsoring Editor: Mary Jo Southern
Senior Associate Editor: Ellen Darion
Editorial Assistant: Danielle Richardson
Project Editor: Tamela Ambush
Senior Production/Design Coordinator: Jennifer Meyer Dare
Senior Manufacturing Coordinator: Priscilla Bailey
Senior Marketing Manager: Nancy Lyman

Cover Design: Harold Burch, Harold Burch Design, New York City
Cover Image: Photonica © Kenvin Lyman

Copyright © 2001 by Houghton Mifflin Company. All rights reserved.

No part of this work may be reproduced or transmitted in any form or by any means, electronic or mechanical, including photocopying and recording, or by any information storage or retrieval system without the prior written permission of Houghton Mifflin Company unless such copying is expressly permitted by federal copyright law. Address inquiries to College Permissions, Houghton Mifflin Company, 222 Berkeley Street, Boston, MA 02116-3764.

Printed in U.S.A.

Library of Congress Catalog Card Number: 99-71976

ISBN: 0-395-89962-1

1 2 3 4 5 6 7 8 9-DOC-05 04 02 01 00

contents

From *Thought to Word* is a structural approach to academic writing at the developmental level. To write without structure is to pour one's ideas into an ocean; they flow everywhere. Without form or structure to hold them to their purpose, ideas never become an essay, and writing an academic essay is what your students *want* to master. Consequently, *From Thought to Word* uses only the grammatical and rhetorical principles that show your students how to respond to assignments across the curriculum. After all, most college students do not take writing classes to "find their voices" or train for careers as professional writers. They simply want to succeed in college.

Content and Organization

From Thought to Word consists of sixteen chapters, each one presenting a different step in the writing process that takes a student from understanding the assignment through responding to the assignment with paragraphs and then essays. The steps are cumulative, and each step pairs a grammatical principle with a corresponding rhetorical principle within the same chapter.

Before beginning the first chapter, students write a "starter" essay, against which they can measure their progress throughout the writing process. "A Very Necessary Introduction" then provides them with an overview of the academic writing process: choosing a topic, narrowing the focus of that topic, structuring a response to the topic, developing that response, and editing for style and mechanics.

Section One, "Understanding Assignments," consists of three chapters devoted to the roles of verbs, nouns and pronouns, and modifiers in assignments to teach students how the language of the assignment directs the response.

Section Two, "Responding to Assignments," consists of six chapters devoted to structuring and developing a single-paragraph response to an assignment.

Section Three, "Refining Style," consists of two chapters devoted to effective word choice and sentence patterns in a student's writing.

Section Four, "Editing," consists of two chapters devoted to correcting errors in structure and development in a student's writing.

Section Five, "Writing Essays," consists of three chapters devoted to extending the structure of a paragraph into that of an essay, extending the support for a paragraph into support for an essay, and then writing the summary essay, a necessary skill for college-level courses.

Special Features

- Need-to-Know Grammar

Rather than presenting snippets of grammar in the same chapter with writing instruction and calling that an "integrated approach," *From Thought to Word* is the first text that finds the *common principle* underlying each grammatical element taught with its corresponding rhetorical element, thus presenting the first truly integrated approach to both. Therefore, this text includes only the grammar principles relevant to the students' writing, instead of overwhelming the students with extraneous grammar concepts. If students do not *see* the connection between grammar and writing in the text, then there will be no connection between them in their own writing.

- Building-Block Structure

From Thought to Word teaches students how to construct a response to an assignment, first in a paragraph and then in an essay, building up from a skeletal structure to a fully developed and edited paper by using specific techniques and models. These are followed by exercises that give students a chance to practice each technique. In other words, students master parts before putting them together in a whole essay. This building-block approach *makes success repeatable* because students use the same building blocks for each assignment. Only the contexts and questions that prompt the students' writing change. This approach gives students control of their academic success.

- Review Questions

At the end of each chapter, easy-to-answer questions and page references to the answers give students another chance to *review and internalize the key concepts,* which are boldfaced in that chapter. This review parallels the recursive nature of writing itself.

- Extensive Writing Exercises

Like the writing instruction itself, the writing exercises at the end of each chapter and in each Section Review are cumulative. The writing exercises themselves represent a wide variety of academic disciplines and highlight what is important in world music, art, literature, history, economics, science, and sports, thus giving students a *mini-course in cultural literacy.*

The students address the earliest writing exercises with skeletal responses and develop those responses further with the skills they learn in each successive chapter. The directions to these cumulative exercises provide students with a checklist of skills that is an organized method for rewriting assignments. Consequently, students check their progress and improve their skills all the way through the writing process, because *repetition reinforces learning.*

- Looking Back and Looking Forward

Each chapter ends with this section, which summarizes the main grammatical and rhetorical principles of the chapter and previews the next step in the writing process. This *summary-preview* helps students see how each of the small building blocks fits into the larger structure of the writing process and product.

- Adaptability

Although *From Thought to Word* presents a structural approach, which is cumulative, the building-block process is still *adaptable to different teaching styles and needs.* First, the teacher can resequence some chapters, because the grammar instruction is integrally related to the writing concept in each chapter. Thus the teacher and students can use a chapter out of sequence because that chapter is self-contained. Second, writing exercises and assignments can be assigned as individual or collaborative projects. Finally, selected exercises within and following the chapters may be included or eliminated at the teacher's discretion in order to speed up or slow down the rate at which students cover material.

The adaptability of *From Thought to Word* makes it an equally effective choice for *all* composition instructors, regardless of whether they teach writing via a structural approach, by rhetorical modes, or with a portfolio system.

Because of its need-to-know grammar, building-block structure, review questions, extensive writing exercises, summary-preview sections, and adaptability, *From Thought to Word* is suitable for ESL classes, business-writing classes, and college board review classes, as well as developmental college English classes.

Acknowledgments

Our most profound thanks go to the people who guided *From Thought to Word* from proposal to publication: Mary Jo Southern, who believed in and took a chance on a completely new concept; Ellen Darion, who helped us through the writing and—especially—the rewriting processes; Tamela Ambush, who steered us through the maze of production; Danielle Richardson and Katie O'Sullivan, who provided the technical support; and Randall Adams, who believed in and encouraged the early incarnation of this textbook.

We would also like to thank the following reviewers, who contributed constructive suggestions for *From Thought to Word:*

Cathryn Amdahl, *Harrisburg Area Community College*
Kathleen S. Britton, *Florence-Darlington Technical College*
Bobbie R. Coleman, *Antelope Valley College and Moorpark College*
Elaine DelVecchio, *Norwalk Community-Technical College*
Diane LeBow, *Canada College*
Joseph E. Lee, *Horry-Georgetown Technical College*
Jim Murphy, *Southern Illinois University at Edwardsville*
Karen Patty-Graham, *Southern Illinois University at Edwardsville*
Kathleen Rice, *Ivy Tech State College*
Carolyn Russell, *Rio Hondo College*
Dale G. Yerpe, *Jamestown Community College*
Sam Zahran, *Fayetteville Technical Community College*

A "STARTER" ESSAY

You may never have written an essay before, but writing one now will give you and your instructor a place for you to start the writing process. This essay that you are about to write will help your instructor find out what you know and what you need to learn about writing for college. In Chapter One, you will begin writing single paragraphs. After you learn the writing and editing skills in Chapters One through Thirteen, you will return to this "starter" essay and rewrite it, using all that you have learned about paragraphs and essays. When you do rewrite this essay for the Writing Exercises in Chapters Fourteen and Fifteen, you will be able to see how far you have progressed in your writing.

Although you may not fully understand the directions for writing this essay, the more you have to learn in this class, the greater the progress you will see in your writing when you work with this essay again in Chapters Fourteen and Fifteen, so try to have fun writing the essay.

DIRECTIONS: Write a four-paragraph essay about a good friend's or relative's most annoying habit. Think of a paragraph as a collection of sentences that are all about one idea.

Your first paragraph should introduce your friend or relative and his or her annoying habit, and your last paragraph should make a final statement about how annoying this habit is. Each of the two paragraphs between your introduction and conclusion should describe a different situation in which this annoying habit shows up. Writing this essay may take you an entire class period.

When you have finished writing your essay, reread it carefully. Make sure that there are no words missing so that all your sentences make sense. Trust your instincts: If a sentence "sounds" funny to you, try writing it a different way. Finally, if you think a word might be misspelled, look it up in a dictionary.

Circle the item that doesn't belong in each list:

1. fajitas	tablecloth	sushi	crepes	curry
2. king	president	prime minister	dictator	Boy Scout
3. crucifix	Islam	Shinto	Catholicism	Judaism
4. carburetor	valves	plugs	stop sign	fan belt
5. diamond	pearl	necklace	emerald	ruby

How did you choose your answers? Did you think that a tablecloth is not a food, a Boy Scout is not the head of a government, a crucifix is not a religion, a stop sign is not part of a car, and a necklace is not a gemstone? In other words, did you see what the similar items in each list had in common so that you could eliminate the one that did not belong? The process you have just performed is **critical thinking.**

Critical Thinking: An Overview of the Writing Process

Suppose for a minute that you walk into your American history class on the first day of the semester and your professor hands you a course outline that says your semester grade will be based on three assignments: a midterm exam, a final exam, and a term paper on the Civil War. You are pretty sure you can learn the material for the two exams, but the paper has you worried. Do you

a. drop the class?

b. look for a different class section to transfer into?

c. ask the instructor for an extra credit assignment to offset the term paper?

d. use the critical thinking skills you will find in this book to write a term paper you can be proud of?

If you chose (d), you will have made the first of many good choices in the writing process. Thinking critically to make appropriate choices, as you did in the exercise above, is the basis of all good writing.

Choosing Your Topic

You must begin making choices as soon as you get an assignment. First you choose a topic. Then you **focus** on that topic. Focusing is a process of choosing what to leave out and what to keep in your paper. If, for example, your teacher has assigned a paper on the Civil War, you will realize when you do some reading that you cannot possibly write about the whole war because it is just too big a topic. Instead you could focus your paper on the causes of the Civil War, or on a battle, or on a hero. What other topics could you choose to focus on?

If you choose to write about a battle, you will should read about several battles before making your selection. You might ask yourself which one was the most exciting or which one made the biggest difference in the outcome of the war. What are some of the other reasons you might choose one battle over another? You should have a reason for your choice. This reason will help you stick with your topic rather than stray to other battles or even other topics, such as heroes. This is an example of focusing, or sticking with your topic.

Narrowing Your Focus

Once you have chosen your topic, the battle you will write about, you must repeat the process of focusing so that you can write about the parts of the battle in an organized way. You might write about the causes of the battle and then their effects, or you might concentrate on the weapons used, like cannons, muskets, bayonets, and sabers. What are some other parts of a battle you could write about? You must realize when you choose your parts which ones go together and which do not. For instance, you would not include a discussion of cannons if you have chosen to write about the causes of the battle. The choices you make about a topic and how to break it down will provide you with a plan for developing and later supporting your topic with examples.

Structuring Your Paragraphs and Essays

Every academic paper has a beginning, a middle, and an end. The beginning is an **introduction** to your topic, whether it is a single sentence or a whole paragraph. You write an introduction because your reader needs to know what your topic is and what you plan to say about it. The middle is the **main body** of your paper, whether it is several sentences or several paragraphs. You write a main body because your reader needs evidence that what you say in your introduction is true. The end of your paper is the **conclusion,** whether it is a single sentence or a whole paragraph. You write a conclusion because it is your last chance to convince your reader why your topic is important. The introduction, main body, and conclusion are the **structure** of your essay.

Developing Your Topic

Since the main body of your paper is where you set out evidence to support your topic, you must develop that evidence adequately. You have a number of ways you can develop the details of your topic. For example, if the details you want to describe are weapons, you can make your description of the weapons come alive by emphasizing sights or sounds or smells, or you can accomplish the same thing by comparing an unfamiliar detail with something familiar. You might choose to compare the thickness of the smoke from all the cannons and muskets to the heavy smog that hangs over Los Angeles in summer. Will you make your descriptions suspenseful? shocking? sad? What your reader feels is the results of the words you choose and the way you put those words together in sentences. What else can you make your reader feel with your language choices? The details you choose provide the **development** of your topic.

Developing Your Style

As you develop your topic in the main body of your paper, the words you choose and the ways you put those words in sentences reflect your individual **style.** For example, if you were writing about the tremendous loss of life at the Battle of Gettysburg, you would write that many soldiers "died" or were "killed"; you would not write that many soldiers "croaked" or were "blown away" because these word choices are slang and do not belong in a college paper.

With practice, you will learn that all your various choices send you off in specific directions; therefore, you need to review your choices for *focus, structure, development,* and *style* all the way through the writing process to make sure you are continuing in the same direction because each choice affects others. If you change one part, you will need to change others as a result so that your paper will have unity. For example, after you've chosen to write about a particular battle in the Civil War, you might find yourself going into great detail about the life of a famous general in that battle. Then you must remind yourself that your focus is the battle, not the life of one of the heroes in that battle; however, if you are really more interested in a particular hero at that point, you can go back and change your focus to heroes.

Editing Your Writing

Writing is a process of discovery: discovering what you like, what you want to say about it, how you want to say it, and, finally, whether or not you have accomplished these goals. Making sure that all your choices are consistent with each other is **editing.** As a result of your editing, you will have to revise and rewrite your papers.

Looking Back and Looking Forward

Critical thinking leads to sound choices; sound choices give you the security of knowing your paper makes sense because every part of it is logically related to every other part. *From Thought to Word* will teach you how to write single-paragraph papers and then college essays, which are made up of many paragraphs. Once you have mastered single-paragraph papers, the transition to writing multi-paragraph college papers is relatively easy, for the elements are the same in both, and so is the process.

The structure, which results from your focus on a topic; the development, which builds support for your topic; the style, which produces the desired response from your reader; and the editing, which draws all these elements together and makes them work as a unified whole, all come from critical thinking. To sum up, critical thinking affects what you say and how you say it.

Understanding Assignments

Chapter one

Verbs and Assignments

Before you can write a paper, you must understand what your assignment is asking you to do. This means understanding what particular words are doing in a sentence. In English there are eight kinds of words called **parts of speech.** Each part of speech does something different from the other parts of speech. If you understand what each part of speech does in a sentence, you will find it easier to understand your assignment since an assignment is generally expressed in a sentence. Remember, you can recognize the parts of speech by <u>what they do</u> in a sentence. You will begin by learning about *verbs* because they are usually the first part of your assignment.

Verbs

There are two kinds of verbs:

1. **action verbs**
2. **condition verbs**

Action Verbs

EXAMPLE: <u>Describe</u> what a turbine <u>does</u>.

In this example, notice the words *describe* and *does* express action, so they are called *action verbs.* Most of the verbs in English are action verbs. Here are some you will recognize:

tell	run	write	solve	climb
laugh	trust	read	avoid	ski
lie	revise	register	complain	introduce

Exercise One **Identifying Action Verbs**

DIRECTIONS In the following sentences, underline the action verbs. Remember that a sentence may have more than one verb.

MODEL Tell what you do when you revise an essay.

1. Describe how you winterize a house.

2. Eliminate and replace the contraction in the sentence *You aren't your brother's keeper.*

3. Review the sentences that contain active verbs.

4. Harmony results when two or more complimentary notes occur at the same time.

5. Archers aim their arrows slightly above the bull's-eye.

Condition Verbs

EXAMPLE: How is a hurricane different from a tornado?

In this example, notice that the *is* tells you that there is a condition that exists now and may always exist, and that condition is the existence of a difference between a hurricane and a tornado. Since this word expresses a condition, it is called a *condition verb.* Some condition verbs have more than one word. The condition verbs you are most likely to find in assignments are

am	is	are
was	were	
will be	will have been	
could be	could have been	
would be	would have been	
should be	should have been	
ought to be	ought to have been	
appear/appears	appear(s) to be	appear(s) to have been
seem/seems	seem(s) to be	seem(s) to have been

Exercise Two **Identifying Condition Verbs**

DIRECTIONS In the following sentences, underline the condition verbs. Remember that some condition verbs are made up of more than one word, and some sentences may have more than one condition verb.

MODEL   Who <u>was</u> Groucho Marx?

1. Where is the Magna Carta?

2. Who seems like the best candidate in the mayoral election, and why is he or she most qualified?

3. Who should be responsible for a teenager's behavior when he or she breaks the law?

4. What will be the effect of digital electronics on the television industry?

5. Where are palm trees native to?

Verbs with More Than One Word

Some words that come before or after the main verb are considered part of that verb. Words that come before an action or condition verb that are part of that verb are called **helping verbs.** In the list of condition verbs, several have helping verbs. For instance, *will be* contains the helping verb *will,* and *would have been* contains the helping verbs *would have.* What are the helping verbs in *should have been?*

Action verbs can also have helping verbs. For instance, in the sentence *Tell about the ways you can survive a night lost in the woods in winter,* the helping verb *can* expresses part of the action and is, therefore, part of the verb *can survive.*

Sometimes a word that follows an action verb is also part of the activity you are being asked to perform in an assignment. In that case, also, the extra word is considered part of the verb. For instance, in the previous assignment, *Tell about the ways you can survive a night lost in the woods in winter,* the whole activity you are being asked to perform is to *tell about,* not just *tell.* Therefore, the whole verb is *tell about.* The word *about* is often part of an action verb when it follows that verb.

Exercise Three   **Identifying Verbs**

DIRECTIONS   For each of the following assignments, identify the complete verbs.

MODEL   Tell about a time when you made a painful decision.

Verbs: <u>tell about, made</u>

1. Describe the ways a farmer is like an athlete.

    Verbs: _____

2. Tell about a time you may have insulted someone.

    Verbs: _____

3. Analyze the way a dentist performs a root canal.

    Verbs: _____

4. Discuss the effects of fetal alcohol syndrome.

    Verb: _____

5. Why is physical contact necessary to mental health?

    Verb: _____

Exercise Four | **Classifying Verbs**

DIRECTIONS | Identify each of the verbs from Exercise Three as either an action verb or a condition verb. You will find six action verbs and two condition verbs.

Exercise Five | **Supplying Verbs**

DIRECTIONS | For each of the following assignments, supply either an action or condition verb that makes sense. Remember there are words that sometimes come before or after a verb that are part of that verb.

MODEL | _____ [action verb] two ways you can _____ [action verb] a single-paragraph paper.

ANSWER | Describe _____ [action verb] two ways you can develop _____ [action verb] a

single-paragraph paper.

1. Why _____ [condition verb] Hitler's forces successful in overcoming Poland at the beginning of World War II?

2. _____ [action verb] the things you _____ [action verb] to transfer from one college to another.

3. _____ [action verb] the biological functions of the parts of a flower.

4. What _____ [condition verb] the process for applying for a small business loan?

5. What _____ [condition verb] the symptoms of the common cold?

The Role of Verbs in an Assignment

As you may have noticed in the previous exercises, assignments may be given in two forms: a **question** or a **command.** For instance, you might be asked *What is the life cycle of an amphibian?* or told *Trace the life cycle of an amphibian.*

Questions

If your assignment is a question, it will begin with a **key question word** like *who, what, where, when, why, how,* or *how much,* followed by a condition verb like *is, are, was,* or *were.* Although both questions and commands call for the same response, it will be easier for you to respond to assignments in future chapters if you turn questions into commands. In the last example, you can see that to make a command out of the question *What is the life cycle of an amphibian?,* all you need to do is replace *What is* with an action verb, like *Trace.*

Exercise Six	**Turning Questions into Commands**
DIRECTIONS	For each item below, change the words at the beginning to form a command by using the action verb *describe.*
MODEL	Question: What is a mentor?
	Command: <u>Describe what a mentor is.</u>

1. Question: How do you tune a piano?

   Command: _____

2. Question: What is the job of a queen bee?

   Command: _____

3. Question: What is the history of African Americans in the United States?

   Command: _____

4. Question: Why do ocean tides change?

   Command: _____

5. Question: How do you make dim sum?

   Command: _____

Commands

When your assignment is a command, it may also begin with a variety of action verbs like *tell about* a favorite person, place, or thing; *compare and/or contrast* several things; *discuss* the causes and/or effects of a condition or event; *tell about* an important time in history or your own life; *explain* how something works; *classify* items into groups; or *define* what something is.

No matter what language your assignment begins with, it is really telling you to describe. *Describe* is an action verb. In every paper, you describe what is asked for in order to help the reader see it your way. For instance, if your assignment tells you *Explain how to make dim sum,* you must describe all of the ingredients as well as the steps you take to put them together. If your description is clear, your reader can follow your directions and end up with dim sum for dinner.

Each action verb that is used as a command tells you to describe something a little differently from every other command. For instance, *Trace the suffragette movement in the United States* asks you to describe the suffragette movement differently from *Analyze the suffragette movement in the United States.* The first assignment requires you to describe how the movement began and changed over the years, while the second assignment asks you to describe the various parts of the movement and their functions.

The following is a list of commands commonly used in assignments and the kinds of description they ask for.

Analyze	Describe how the <u>various parts or elements</u> of something <u>work</u>
Compare	Describe the <u>similarities</u> between
Contrast	Describe the <u>differences</u> between
Clarify	Describe the <u>confusing parts or elements</u> to avoid confusion
Classify	Describe the <u>categories</u> into which you place things
Define	Describe the <u>characteristics</u> of something that give it its identity
Describe	Describe <u>what something</u> looks, sounds, smells, feels, and tastes like
Discuss	Describe in the <u>way the assignment indicates</u> (for example, *Discuss the effects of . . .* tells you to describe *(continued)*

	effects, while *Discuss the reasons for* . . . tells you to describe causes)
Evaluate	Describe the good and bad points of
Explain	Describe how something works or the reasons for
Summarize	Describe only the main points
Tell about	See *Describe* and *Discuss*
Tell how	Describe the way something works or is done
Trace	Describe the history of

Did you notice that some of the commands ask you to do similar things? For instance, *Describe, Tell about, Discuss,* and sometimes *Define* may be used interchangeably; the same is true of *Explain* and *Tell how.* Why can't you use *Clarify* and *Contrast* interchangeably?

Since some verbs express action and your assignment tells you to perform an action, it is important to understand that verbs are the key to understanding assignments.

Prewriting

Chapter Two and Chapter Three will show you that there is more to understanding an assignment than what you have learned in this chapter, but because the Writing Exercises at the end of this chapter ask you to produce a paragraph, you will need to know some techniques for coming up with ideas to write about in the Writing Exercises. The further you go in the writing process, the more focused your techniques for generating ideas will become. Specifically, in Chapter Four you will learn how to ask focusing questions to find a topic, and in Chapter Six you will use focusing questions again as you build the structure of your paragraph. You can think of these questions as **focused brainstorming** because they keep your thinking focused on your assignment. For now, however, your brainstorming for ideas can take two simple forms:

1. listing

2. clustering

Listing

When you have a day off from work or school and have a lot of chores to accomplish, some of you may make a list of those chores so you will not forget to do any of them. All of these chores might come under the heading of *Chores to Do Today*. You would not put your family picnic on this list because it is not a *chore*; it is recreation. Likewise, you would not include your doctor's appointment for tomorrow on this list because it is not a chore *to do today*. The heading *Chores to Do Today* helps you decide what belongs on your list and what does not. **Listing** uses your assignment as a heading and asks you to come up with as many ideas as you can that fit the assignment.

Exercise Seven   **Listing**

DIRECTIONS   For each of the following assignments, make a list of all the ideas you might include in a paragraph responding to the assignment.

MODEL   Assignment: Describe your Saturday activities.

List:

make pancakes for breakfast	get bike from repair shop
wash dishes	check e-mail
empty wastebaskets	weed garden
take Fido for nailclipping	get Mohawk haircut
mow lawn	type history paper
pay utility bills	make caramel apples for Halloween
do laundry	pay credit card bills

1. Assignment: Describe the benefits of a college education.

   List:

2. Assignment: Describe ways to take a vacation without leaving home.

   List:

3. Assignment: Tell what you would do if you won the Lottery.

   List:

Clustering

In the model for Exercise Seven, do you see any items on the list that might go together? For example, do you see that *weed garden* and *mow lawn* go together because they are both gardening chores? Do you also notice that *make caramel apples for Halloween* and *make pancakes for breakfast* go together because they involve cooking?

Putting together items on your list that are similar is called **clustering.**

Exercise Eight **Clustering**

DIRECTIONS For each of the assignments from Exercise Seven, cluster your responses and name what they have in common. For now, do not worry if some items do not belong to a cluster.

MODEL Assignment: Describe your Saturday activities.

Clusters:

wash dishes
empty wastebaskets } cleaning
do laundry

pay utility bills
pay credit card bills } paying bills

make caramel apples
make pancakes for breakfast } cooking

check e-mail
type history paper } working on computer

weed garden
mow lawn } gardening

take Fido for nailclipping
get Mohawk haircut
get bike from repair shop } running errands

1. Assignment: Describe the benefits of a college education.

   Clusters:

2. Assignment: Describe ways to take a vacation without leaving home.

   Clusters:

3. Assignment: Tell what you would do if you won the Lottery.

   Clusters:

Review Questions

Answer the following questions to help you review the material you have covered in this chapter.

1. What are the eight kinds of words in English called? (p. 9)

   _____

2. What will knowing the parts of speech help you understand? (p. 9)

   _____

3. How do you recognize parts of speech in a sentence? (p. 9)

   _____

4. What part of speech is usually in the first part of your assignment? (p. 9)

   _____

5. What are the two kinds of verbs called? (p. 9) _____

   _____

6. Words that are part of the action of the main verb and come <u>before</u> it are called
   _____. (p. 11)

7. What is one word that sometimes comes after the main verb and is part of it?
   _____. (p. 11)

8. What two forms can assignments take? (p. 13) _____

   _____

9. When your assignment is a question, how does it begin? (p. 13)

   _____

10. What action is every assignment really telling you to do? (p. 14)

    _____

11. What are two commands that can be used interchangeably? (p. 15)

    _____ and _____

12. What are two commands that cannot be used interchangeably? (p. 15)

    _____ and _____

13. What are two simple forms of brainstorming? (p. 15)

    _____ and _____

Writing Exercises

I. Filling in Verbs

In the following paragraph, all the verbs are missing. Some of the verbs that are missing should be action verbs, and some should be condition verbs; some are single words, and some are more than one word. Fill in the missing verbs so that the paragraph makes sense. Then try it a second time, using different verbs.

Many people _____ spiders both fascinating and frightening because they _____ ingenious in the ways they _____ themselves from discovery, _____ their young from predators, and _____ their prey. First, most spiders _____ themselves in their homes. For instance, some spiders _____ webs from the silk they _____, and then they _____ themselves in the middle. Also, the Trapdoor Spider _____ a burrow underground, complete with a door. Second, spiders _____ their young from predators in different ways. For instance, the Wolf Spider _____ her egg sac with her, and when her young _____, she _____ them around with her until they _____ for themselves. The true water spider _____ the eggs of its young when it _____ them in a dome of waterproof silk, which it _____ to the stem of a plant under water. Finally, many spiders _____ distinctive ways of catching their prey. For instance, the Raft Spider of Europe _____ tiny boats of leaves and twigs, which he _____ on a pond when he _____ water insects. Some spiders _____ webs, but they _____ not _____ in them. Instead, they _____ a trapline from the web to a nearby den. When an insect _____ by and _____ into the web, the spider _____ this be-

cause the trapline —————————. Then he ————————— to the
web and ————————— his prey. Spiders ————————— ad-
mirable craftsmen, but it ————————— easy to see why spiders
————————— many people.

II. Writing a Paragraph with Appropriate Verbs

Study the preceding paragraph about spiders. Notice that the first sentence introduces the subject and says three things about it. Then the rest of the paragraph gives
examples of those three things. Choose two of the following topics and brainstorm
for ideas, making lists and then clustering the ideas in those lists. Finally, write a
paragraph about each topic like the one on spiders. Be sure to pay special attention
to the verbs you choose.

1. Describe how your family pet is special.

2. Tell why a college subject is either difficult or easy for you.

3. Explain why the bathroom is the most dangerous room in the house.

4. Describe the parking problems on your campus.

5. Describe how to play your favorite sport.

Looking Back and Looking Forward

Now that you understand that all assignments tell you to describe something, you
are ready to consider what your assignment is telling you to describe. In the next
chapter, you will learn about nouns, which are used to express the subject matter of
the assignment.

Chapter two

Nouns/ Pronouns and Assignments

In Chapter One, you learned to recognize the verbs in an assignment that tell you to describe something. Now you will learn about the words that tell you what your assignment tells you to describe. These words are nouns and the words that replace them, pronouns.

Nouns

Nouns name a *person, place,* or *thing.*

EXAMPLES: Characterize America's most influential <u>politician.</u>
Describe the <u>Kremlin</u>.
Define <u>democracy</u>.

Exercise One | **Identifying Nouns**

DIRECTIONS | In the following assignments, identify each noun, and tell whether it names a person, place, or thing.

MODEL | Describe the effects of radiation.

Nouns: <u>effects</u>　　　　　　　(thing)

<u>radiation</u>　　　　　(thing)

1. Trace the development of trade unions in England, and discuss the ways they were important to the economy.

Nouns: —————————— (　　　)

—————————— (　　　)

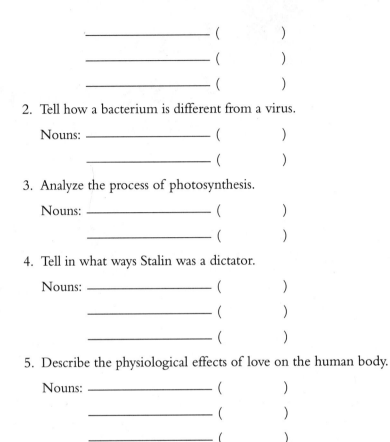

_____ (   )

_____ (   )

_____ (   )

2. Tell how a bacterium is different from a virus.

    Nouns: _____ (   )

    _____ (   )

3. Analyze the process of photosynthesis.

    Nouns: _____ (   )

    _____ (   )

4. Tell in what ways Stalin was a dictator.

    Nouns: _____ (   )

    _____ (   )

    _____ (   )

5. Describe the physiological effects of love on the human body.

    Nouns: _____ (   )

    _____ (   )

    _____ (   )

Proper Nouns and Common Nouns

What characteristics did you notice about the nouns in the three examples before Exercise One? Did you see that one is capitalized? Why? The word *Kremlin* is capitalized because it is a noun that names a specific place. Nouns that name specific persons, specific places, or specific things are called **proper nouns,** and nouns that name general persons, general places, or general things, like *politician,* are called **common nouns.** Proper nouns are capitalized, and common nouns are not.

Exercise Two   **Placing Nouns in Categories:
Proper Nouns or Common Nouns**

Directions   Place each of the fifteen nouns you identified in Exercise One into its correct category. You will find two proper nouns and thirteen common nouns.

Supplying Common and Proper Nouns

DIRECTIONS For each of the following assignments, fill in the blank with either a common or proper noun that makes sense. Remember that proper nouns must be capitalized.

1. Tell how _____ multiply.

2. Contrast military _____ with civilian _____.

3. Discuss the _____ of the famous _____, _____ _____.

4. Tell how to use a _____.

5. Why is a _____ hard to find?

Concrete Nouns and Abstract Nouns

In the examples preceding Exercise One, did you notice anything else about the nouns in addition to two being common and one being proper? How are the *Kremlin* and *democracy* different? Although you can see evidence of democracy in your lives, you cannot see democracy itself. On the other hand, you can see the *Kremlin* and a *politician*. Nouns that you can experience through your senses of sight, hearing, touch, taste, and smell are called **concrete nouns,** and nouns that you cannot experience through your senses are called **abstract nouns.**

Identifying Concrete and Abstract Nouns

DIRECTIONS Place each of the fifteen nouns you identified in Exercise One into its correct category: concrete or abstract. Notice that a proper or a common noun will also be either concrete or abstract. You should find eight concrete nouns and seven abstract nouns.

Supplying Concrete and Abstract Nouns

DIRECTIONS For each of the following assignments, supply a concrete or abstract noun that makes sense where indicated.

MODEL Describe an ethnic _____ [concrete noun].

ANSWER Describe an ethnic _meal_____ [concrete noun].

1. How is _____ [abstract noun] different from _____ [abstract noun]?

2. How is a _____ [concrete noun] different from a _____ [concrete noun]?

3. Describe how to solve a _____ [abstract noun].

4. Discuss the major _____ [concrete noun] in the human _____ [concrete noun].

5. Describe where to put the _____ [concrete noun] when building a _____ [concrete noun].

Verbal Nouns

Sometimes words that do not look like nouns really are because they do what a noun does. For instance, in the assignment *Contrast lying and exaggerating,* the words *lying* and *exaggerating* sound like verbs because they suggest action, but they are really activities, and activities are things, which makes them nouns. Words like these are called **gerunds.** Gerunds are nouns that always have an *ing* ending.

Similarly, consider the assignment *Describe what you must do to win a scholarship.* The words *to win*—like *lying* and *exaggerating*—also sound like a verb, but in this sentence they are used together as a noun because they express an activity, which is a thing. Words like these are called **infinitives.** Infinitives are formed by *to* plus an action verb, and they may be used as several other parts of speech in addition to nouns.

The reason that gerunds and infinitives can be mistaken for verbs is that they actually have verbs in them. For instance, the verb in *lying* is *lie.* What are the verbs in *exaggerating* and *to win?* Because gerunds and infinitives are built from verbs, they are called **verbals.** Verbals are words that <u>contain</u> verbs but are never used as verbs.

Exercise Six **Identifying Verbals**

DIRECTIONS   In the following assignments, find the verbals, and identify each as either a gerund or an infinitive.

MODEL   Contrast composing a photograph with composing an essay.

Verbals: <u>composing</u>   Type: <u>gerund</u>

1. Discuss how politicians try to win votes in an election.

    Verbal: _____   Type: _____

2. Explain the physical benefits of weight training.

    Verbal: _____   Type: _____

3. Describe how retailers can attempt to prevent customers from shoplifting.

    Verbal: _____   Type: _____

    Verbal: _____   Type: _____

4. What are the signs of global warming?

   Verbal: _____   Type: _____

5. Describe appropriate landscaping for a desert home.

   Verbal: _____   Type: _____

Exercise Seven **Supplying Verbals**

DIRECTIONS   For each of the following assignments, fill in the blanks with either a gerund or an infinitive that makes sense.

1. Discuss the aerodynamic principles of _____.

2. How can a debater convince a judge _____ with him?

3. Describe the steps in _____ a suit in a fashion design course.

4. What flaws do you check for when _____ an English paper?

5. Describe the responsibilities involved in _____ a television show.

Common Noun Endings

In addition to verbals, some other nouns contain verbs, but you can recognize them as nouns by their common noun endings *ment, ance* or *ence,* and *tion* or *ion.* Can you pick out the verbs in the following nouns?

continuance _____

development _____

existence _____

exaggeration _____

entertainment _____

digestion _____

suggestion _____

acquaintance _____

government _____

performance _____

Pronouns

While nouns name persons, places, or things, there is another part of speech that refers to these same persons, places, or things without naming them. This part of speech is **pronouns,** and these words can be used like nouns in an assignment.

Pronouns stand in for nouns. In fact, in the word *pronoun,* the Latin prefix *pro* means *for,* so the word *pronoun* literally means *for the noun.*

Pronouns can be used in many different situations. They can refer to a specific person; they can refer to people in general; they can show ownership; they can point at a word they are referring to or back to a word they are related to; and they can show emphasis. These are the different kinds of pronouns:

1. personal pronouns

2. indefinite pronouns

3. possessive pronouns

4. demonstrative pronouns

5. relative pronouns

6. intensive and reflexive pronouns

What do you notice about the following paragraph?

Barbara went on an archeology trip. Barbara took along several tools. First, Barbara packed a small pickaxe for breaking rocks. Next, Barbara packed a small spoon-like instrument for digging. Finally, Barbara packed a soft brush for clearing away debris from bones. Barbara was well prepared for the trip.

Why does this paragraph sound unnatural? If you rewrote this paragraph, what word would you replace in several instances? What word would you replace it with? If you said you would replace the noun *Barbara* several times with *she,* you already know that pronouns make a paragraph sound less stiff and repetitive. Would your rewritten paragraph look like this?

Barbara went on an archeology trip. <u>She</u> took along several tools. First, Barbara packed a small pickaxe for breaking rocks. Next, <u>she</u> packed a small spoon-like instrument for digging. Finally, <u>she</u> packed a soft brush for clearing away debris from bones. Barbara was well prepared for the trip.

Personal Pronouns

Pronouns that take the place of specific nouns are called **personal pronouns.** For instance, in the assignment *Trace the career of the Russian choreographer Diaghilev, and tell how he influenced the world of ballet,* the personal pronoun *he* stands in for the specific noun "Diaghilev." All of the personal pronouns are

I	you	he	she	it	we	they
me		him	her		us	them

Exercise Eight ## Using Personal Pronouns

DIRECTIONS   In the following paragraph, replace the underlined nouns with personal pronouns so that the paragraph does not sound repetitive and stiff.

> Many colleges have writing center tutors that can help a student in several ways. First, <u>tutors</u> can help come up with ideas for content that are relevant to the assignment. Next, <u>tutors</u> help organize these ideas into the first draft of an essay. Then the tutors help edit <u>the essay</u> for content, organization, development, and grammar. When the tutors and the student finish working together, the final essay is complete.

Indefinite Pronouns

Pronouns that take the place of general nouns are called **indefinite pronouns.** For instance, in the assignment *An agoraphobe is <u>someone</u> who is afraid of open spaces; describe what a phobia is,* the indefinite pronoun *someone* stands for the general noun *agoraphobe.* Some of the common indefinite pronouns are

anybody	everybody	nobody	somebody	one
anyone	everyone	no one	someone	
anything	everything	nothing	something	

Even though some of these pronouns look as if they refer to a group of people, they are <u>all singular.</u> For instance, *everyone* means *every <u>single</u> one.*

Exercise Nine ## Using Indefinite Pronouns

DIRECTIONS   What indefinite pronouns would stand for the following words?

1. all the students _____

2. none of the students _____

3. any of the students _____

4. a student _____

5. some student _____

Possessive Pronouns

Pronouns that show ownership are called **possessive pronouns.** For instance, in the assignment *If you were told to choose one favorite possession, what would your choice say about your psychological make-up?,* the possessive pronoun *your* shows ownership of both the *choice* and the *psychological make-up.* All of the possessive pronouns are

my	our	your	their	her	his	its
mine	ours	yours	theirs	hers		

Exercise Ten

Using Possessive Pronouns

DIRECTIONS   In the following assignments, replace some of the nouns with appropriate possessive pronouns.

MODEL   Describe how to rescue a drowning swimmer without the swimmer's cooperation.

Revised: *Describe how to rescue a drowning swimmer without his cooperation.*

1. Granite is an igneous rock. Describe granite's mineral composition.

   Revised: _____.

2. A "cosmology" is a particular worldview. Describe the cosmology you believe in.

   Revised: _____.

3. Howard Hawks and Preston Sturges were directors famous for screwball comedies. Contrast Hawks's and Sturges's film techniques.

   Revised: _____.

4. Amelia Earhart disappeared on a flight around the world in 1937. What historical theory do you favor to explain Amelia Earhart's disappearance?

   Revised: _____?

5. Human beings and primates are similar not only biologically but also sociologically. Compare human beings' and primates' similarities.

   Revised: _____.

Demonstrative Pronouns

Pronouns that point at nouns are called **demonstrative pronouns.** For instance, in the assignment *Color, texture, and taste are the characteristics a chef considers when creating a great dish; describe <u>these</u> characteristics in Hungarian goulash,* the demonstrative pronoun *these* points at the characteristics of *color, texture,* and *taste,* which have just been mentioned. All the demonstrative pronouns are

this	that
these	those

It might help you to remember that *this* and *these* point to nouns that are close enough to touch, while *that* and *those* refer to nouns that must be pointed at from a distance.

Exercise Eleven

Using Demonstrative Pronouns

DIRECTIONS   For the following assignments, fill in the blanks with the appropriate demonstrative pronouns.

1. Hearsay is a type of evidence. Explain why _____ type of evidence is usually not admitted in court.

2. Describe _____ characteristics that distinguish the polka from the schottische.

3. The Sicilian Defense is a famous chess strategy. Describe _____ strategy in detail.

4. Many science fiction writers introduced devices in their fiction that later became part of our culture. Describe some of _____ devices.

5. Public morality can be different from private morality. Develop examples that define one of _____ types of morality.

Relative Pronouns

Pronouns that point back to a word they are related to are called **relative pronouns.** For instance, in the assignment *Describe a person <u>who</u> is a genuine hero,* the relative pronoun *who* is related to the noun *person.* All the relative pronouns are

who	whom	which	that

The pronoun *which* never refers to people.

Using Relative Pronouns

DIRECTIONS In the following assignments, fill in the blanks with the appropriate relative pronouns.

1. Describe a method of tracking credits and debits _____ is suitable for a business with multiple sites.

2. Contrast two schools of thought _____ represent two different types of medicine.

3. Describe an actor _____ symbolizes lost innocence.

4. Describe two methods _____ are used for applying color to jewelry.

5. Describe the features _____ are known about quarks.

Intensive and Reflexive Pronouns

Pronouns that emphasize the noun or pronoun they refer to are called **intensive pronouns.** For instance, in the assignment *Although President Richard M. Nixon pointed the finger of blame for the Watergate cover-up at his subordinates, it was he himself who was responsible for the cover-up; defend this opinion,* the intensive pronoun *himself* emphasizes the *he* who is really to blame.

Other pronouns that are used for emphasis are called **reflexive pronouns.** For instance, in the assignment *Describe how Benedict Arnold distinguished himself during the Revolutionary War,* the reflexive pronoun *himself* emphasizes the noun *Benedict Arnold.*

The same pronouns are used as intensive and reflexive pronouns.

myself	yourself	himself	herself	itself
	ourselves	themselves		

Using Intensive and Reflexive Pronouns

DIRECTIONS In the following paragraph, fill in the blanks with the appropriate intensive and reflexive pronouns.

Embryology is a science that examines the growth process of life _____. The science begins with an examination of the tiniest cells which reproduce _____ to form tissue. Tissues then grow to form _____ into organs, and organs combine _____ to build the body _____. K. E. von Baer is called *the father of modern embryology* because he took it upon _____ to disprove old theories of cell development. He showed how all tissues and organs form _____ from cell layers.

The Role of Nouns and Pronouns in an Assignment

In an assignment, nouns or pronouns that follow a verb generally tell you the broad subject you will describe. When a noun or pronoun does this, it is called a **direct object** of the verb because it receives the verb's action. For instance, in the assignment *Define migration,* the action verb *Define* is telling you to describe the noun *migration,* which is the direct object of the verb. Likewise, consider the assignment *The achievements of Frederick Douglass, who rose from slavery to become a famous abolitionist and journalist in the second half of the nineteenth century, are legendary; describe <u>them</u>.* In this assignment, the pronoun *them,* which stands for the noun *achievements,* is the direct object of the verb *describe.*

Direct objects answer the question *Who?* or *What?* after the verb. In other words, *migration* is the direct object of the verb *Define* because it answers the question *Define <u>what?</u>,* and *them* is the direct object of the verb *describe* because it answers the same question. When you find the verb in your assignment, you must look for the direct object of that verb by asking the question *who?* or *what?* <u>after</u> the verb in order to find what you will write about.

Exercise Fourteen ## Identifying Direct Objects

DIRECTIONS   In each of the following assignments, find the direct object of the action verb.

MODEL   Contrast tundra and taiga.

Direct objects: <u>tundra, taiga</u>

1. Explain symbiosis.

   Direct object: _____

2. Design a model airplane.

   Direct object: _____

3. Summarize *Of Mice and Men*.

Direct object: _____

4. Define *sociopath*.

Direct object: _____

5. Many geological formations are created by water. Classify them.

Direct object: _____

Exercise Fifteen   **Supplying Direct Objects**

DIRECTIONS   Complete the following assignments by filling in the direct objects.

1. Discuss _____.

2. Compare _____ and _____.

3. Fruitflies display distinctive mating behavior. Describe _____.

4. Describe the _____ for a criminal trial.

5. Fire drills require several safety procedures. Describe _____.

Review Questions

Answer the following questions to help you review the material you have covered in this chapter.

1. Words that tell you what your assignment asks you to describe are what parts of speech? (p. 21)

_____ and _____

2. What three things does a noun name? (p. 21)

a _____, a _____, or a _____

3. What do proper nouns name? (p. 22)

a _____ _____, a _____ _____,

or a _____ _____

4. What do common nouns name? (p. 22)

a _____ _____, a _____ _____,

or a _____ _____

5. Which nouns are capitalized? (p. 22) _____

6. Nouns you can experience through your senses are called _____ nouns. (p. 23)

7. Nouns you cannot experience through your senses are called _____ nouns. (p. 23)

8. The kind of nouns that express activities rather than action are called _____ and _____. (p. 24)

9. What kind of ending does a gerund have? (p. 24) _____

10. How do you form an infinitive? (p. 24) _____

11. What are gerunds and infinitives called? (p. 24) _____

    Why? _____

12. What are three common endings for nouns which are not gerunds and infinitives but which still contain verbs? (p. 25)

    _____, _____, and _____

13. What stands for a noun? (p. 26) _____

14. What are pronouns that take the place of specific nouns called? (p. 27)

    _____

15. What do indefinite pronouns do? (p. 27) _____

    _____

16. Even though some indefinite pronouns sound like they refer to many people or things, they are really all _____. (p. 27)

17. What do possessive pronouns show? (p. 28) _____

18. What are pronouns that point at nouns called? (p. 29) _____

19. What are the four relative pronouns? (p. 29) _____

    _____ _____ _____

20. Two kinds of pronouns that emphasize are _____ and _____. (p. 30)

21. What does a direct object do? (p. 31) _____

22. What questions can a direct object answer after the verb? (p. 31)

    _____? or _____?

Writing Exercises

I. Writing with Nouns

In the following paragraph, all the nouns are missing. Some of the nouns you put in should be common, some should be proper, some should be concrete, and some should be abstract. Remember that abstract and concrete nouns can also be common or proper.

In addition, some nouns will be in the form of gerunds and some in the form of infinitives. Fill in the missing nouns so that the paragraph makes sense.

_____ say that man's best _____ is the _____. There are many _____ for this _____. _____ can be loyal, affectionate, playful, and helpful. First, _____ like _____ and _____ are known to be loyal. They will protect their _____ against any _____. Second, _____ are especially affectionate. They love _____ and _____ canine _____. Third, _____ are playful. _____ and _____ are their favorite _____. Finally, _____ even help _____ perform _____. Specifically, that's what seeing-eye _____ do. Without _____, our _____ would be poorer.

II. Placing Nouns in Categories

Classify the twenty-five nouns in Writing Exercise I as common, proper, concrete, abstract, gerunds, and infinitives.

III. Filling in Pronouns

In the following paragraph, all the pronouns are missing. Fill in the blanks with the appropriate personal, indefinite, possessive, demonstrative, relative, intensive, and reflexive pronouns.

Science and mythology offer different explanations for the natural phenomenon _____ call an echo. Science tells _____ when a person makes a sound _____ bounces off a flat surface, _____ sound returns to _____ in the form of an echo. Since the original sound waves lose strength during _____ trip back, the echo cannot be heard until the original sound has ceased. _____ is why a person hears only the final syllable of the call. On the other hand, mythology tells _____ a nymph named Echo fell in love with a selfish man named Narcissus, _____ loved only _____. Because _____ could not return Echo's love, _____ pined away until only _____ voice was left. _____ had only enough strength to repeat the last sound of any call _____ heard. _____ of the two explanations do you prefer?

IV. Placing Pronouns in Categories

Classify the sixteen pronouns you used in Writing Exercise III as personal, indefinite, possessive, demonstrative, relative, intensive, or reflexive.

V. Writing with Appropriate Nouns and Pronouns

Study the paragraph in Writing Exercise III on echoes. Notice that the first sentence tells us what the paragraph is about, and the rest of the paragraph gives us two explanations of the topic. Choose two of the topics below and brainstorm for ideas, making lists and then clustering the ideas in those lists. Finally, write a paragraph on each one like the one on the echo. Pay special attention to the nouns and pronouns you choose.

1. Describe two ways you could explain death to a child.

2. Describe several ways a computer can make your life easier.

3. Describe the two most important qualities of your ideal mate.

4. Examine both your and your parents' ideas of punishment.

5. Invent two different explanations for rainbows.

Looking Back and Looking Forward

In this chapter, you have learned how to find what you will write about in an assignment. In the next chapter, you will look at words that modify what you will write about so you can focus your response accurately.

Chapter three

Modifiers and Assignments

In the last two chapters, you saw how verbs in an assignment tell you what to do, while nouns and pronouns tell you what to do it to. In this chapter, you will learn how some words called **modifiers** can help verbs, nouns, and pronouns, as well as other words in your assignment, be more precise by describing them. The two parts of speech that act as modifiers are *adjectives* and *adverbs*.

Adjectives

Adjectives modify nouns and pronouns by adding size, shape, color, degree, intensity, number, and any other characteristic that describes or limits.

EXAMPLES: 1. Describe how the media covered a <u>recent</u> scandal.

2. President John Fitzgerald Kennedy was popular with many people, but he also had many enemies. Discuss why some people thought he was <u>dangerous</u>.

In the first example, *recent* is an adjective that modifies the noun *scandal*. This modifier helps you choose a scandal to write about by limiting when it occurred. For instance, you may know about a sex scandal involving a Hollywood personality that happened a year ago and a murder-for-hire scheme involving a local politician's family that happened last month. For this assignment, the modifier *recent* tells you that the murder-for-hire scandal is the more appropriate choice.

In the second example, there are several adjectives that modify nouns, but the adjective *dangerous* is the only one that modifies a pronoun. Can you tell which one? The adjective *dangerous* limits your response to the assignment by telling you what to describe. In other words, different people remember President Kennedy in different ways. Some feel he was heroic, some feel he was immoral, and some feel he was diplomatic; however, the modifier *dangerous* limits your description of President Kennedy's behavior to only those things he did that people thought were dangerous.

Like nouns and pronouns, adjectives have certain characteristics that make it easy for you to recognize them. First of all, their placement is helpful. Most adjectives come right before nouns or right after condition verbs. Second, adjectives answer one of three questions: *which one?, how many?,* or *what kind?* Third, many adjectives have the same endings. For instance, *ous, able, al, er, est, ic,* and *y* are common endings for adjectives, as you can see in the words *adulterous, bearable, eternal, bolder, boldest, realistic,* and *furry.*

Exercise One ## Identifying Adjectives

DIRECTIONS In the following assignments, find the adjectives and the words they modify. You will find that sometimes more than one adjective modifies a single noun or pronoun.

MODEL Describe the design flaw in the "unsinkable" *Titanic.*

Adjective: *design* _____   Word modified: flaw _____

Adjective: *unsinkable* _____   Word modified: *Titanic* _____

1. What are the timeless qualities of rock music?

    Adjective: _____ Word modified: _____

    Adjective: _____ Word modified: _____

2. Napoleon Bonaparte has been described as being cunning and crazy. Give examples of his behavior that support both qualities.

    Adjective: _____ Word modified: _____

    Adjective: _____ Word modified: _____

    Adjective: _____ Word modified: _____

3. What are the structural elements of a technical report that comes at the end of the fiscal year?

    Adjective: _____ Word modified: _____

    Adjective: _____ Word modified: _____

    Adjective: _____ Word modified: _____

4. Describe the geological process that produces meander scars.

    Adjective: _____ Word modified: _____

    Adjective: _____ Word modified: _____

5. Discuss how certain food products can cause severe allergic reactions in some humans.

Adjective: _____ Word modified: _____

Adjective: _____ Word modified: _____

Adjective: _____ Word modified: _____

Adjective: _____ Word modified: _____

Adjective: _____ Word modified: _____

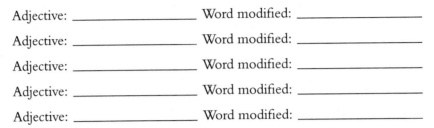

Exercise Two | **Supplying Adjectives**

DIRECTIONS | In the following assignments, fill in each blank with an adjective that makes sense.

1. Contrast _____ methods of teaching a _____ language.

2. Discuss the _____ reasons for _____ surgery.

3. Explain the _____ theory that _____ foods are actually _____ for _____ problems.

4. Tell how to produce a _____ adaptation of a _____ play.

5. Discuss the _____ flaws of the _____ program to provide food for _____ people.

Participles

In Chapter Two, you learned about two kinds of nouns that can be mistaken for verbs because they have verbs in them. Do you remember what those two verbals are called? Here is a third verbal: This one is called a **participle.** Even though participles contain verbs, participles are adjectives. There are two kinds of participles.

A **present participle** has an *ing* ending. For instance, in *spinning wheel,* the word *spinning* is a present participle. What verb does it contain? What noun does it describe?

A **past participle** usually has an *ed, n,* or *t* ending. For instance, *stewed tomatoes, known criminal,* and *bent twig* all have past participles. What are they, and what verbs do they contain? What nouns do they describe?

Exercise Three **Identifying Participles**

DIRECTIONS In the following assignments, find the participles, and identify them as either present or past. Remember that present participles end in *ing*, and past participles usually end in *ed, n,* or *t.*

MODEL Discuss why moving water is usually drinkable and standing water is not.

Participle: moving   Type: present

Participle: standing   Type: present

1. What technological advances made talking movies possible?

   Participle: _____ Type: _____

2. What are the long-term health effects of dyed hair?

   Participle: _____ Type: _____

3. What are the advantages of taking your car to a trained mechanic for a tune-up rather than doing it yourself?

   Participle: _____ Type: _____

4. Describe what a restraining order does.

   Participle: _____ Type: _____

5. Contrast the effects of torn ligaments with those of a broken bone.

   Participle: _____ Type: _____

   Participle: _____ Type: _____

Exercise Four **Supplying Participles**

DIRECTIONS For the following assignments, fill in each blank with either a present participle or past participle that makes sense.

1. What are the duties of the _____ monarch of Great Britain?

2. Discuss the food value of store-_____ bread.

3. Describe the chemical composition of what we call a _____ star.

4. Compare a _____-point mortgage to a balloon-payment mortgage.

5. What are the stylistic differences between _____ communication and _____ communication?

Adverbs

Adverbs modify *verbs, adjectives,* and other *adverbs.*

EXAMPLES: 1. Explain <u>fully</u> the process of cross-pollination.

2. What factors can contribute to producing an infant whose birth weight is <u>too</u> low?

3. Compare the characteristics of experiences reported by people who have <u>very</u> nearly died.

In the first example, *fully* is an adverb that modifies the verb *Explain.* This modifier tells you that you must go into depth in your answer. For instance, instead of discussing insects and mammals as contributors to the process, you must be more specific in discussing the particular insects and mammals, such as bees and bats, as well as their specific contributions.

In the second example, *too* is an adverb that modifies the adjective *low.* Without this modifier, the assignment would mean something different. It would be telling you to consider the reasons for a low birth weight; however, the modifier *too* tells you that the baby's birth weight is <u>so</u> low it jeopardizes his or her life. Consequently, in this assignment you need to describe the degree of particular causes. For instance, instead of discussing the mother's drinking during pregnancy, you may have to consider <u>how much</u> she drank on a daily basis.

In the third example, *very* is an adverb that modifies the adverb *nearly.* This modifier emphasizes <u>how</u> close to death these people came.

Adverbs have two characteristics that help you recognize them. First, they can answer one of several questions: *when?, where?, why?, how?,* or *how much?* Second, many of them end with *ly,* like *badly.*

Exercise Five | **Identifying Adverbs**

DIRECTIONS | In the following assignments, find the adverbs and the words they modify.

MODEL | Describe the more severe symptoms of menopause.

Adverb: <u>more</u>   Word modified: <u>severe</u>

1. Describe fully the internal combustion engine.

   Adverb: _____ Word modified: _____

2. Discuss how several words in English are often misused.

   Adverb: _____ Word modified: _____

Adverb: _____ Word modified: _____

3. Automobile accidents are usually caused by human error. Discuss several examples analytically.

Adverb: _____ Word modified: _____

Adverb: _____ Word modified: _____

4. Trace the westward expansion of American settlers in the nineteenth century. Accurately represent the conflicting interests of the settlers and Native Americans.

Adverb: _____ Word modified: _____

5. Discuss briefly the notetaking techniques that are most helpful in college.

Adverb: _____ Word modified: _____

Adverb: _____ Word modified: _____

Exercise Six **Identifying Modified Words**

DIRECTIONS Identify each of the eight words modified in Exercise Five as either a verb, an adjective, or an adverb.

1. Word modified _____ Part of speech _____

2. Word modified _____ Part of speech _____

3. Word modified _____ Part of speech _____

4. Word modified _____ Part of speech _____

5. Word modified _____ Part of speech _____

6. Word modified _____ Part of speech _____

7. Word modified _____ Part of speech _____

8. Word modified _____ Part of speech _____

Exercise Seven **Supplying Adverbs**

DIRECTIONS In the following assignments, fill in each blank with an adverb that makes sense.

1. Explain _____ the effects of prolonged exposure to violence in children's television programs.

2. In what ways are field hockey and lacrosse _____ different?

3. Discuss the reason President Franklin D. Roosevelt _____ withheld vital information from the American people about Pearl Harbor prior to our involvement in World War II.

4. Compare the ways Pope John Paul II and the Dalai Lama _____ lead their followers.

5. What are the reasons that mountain gorillas are _____ extinct?

Groups of Words as Modifiers

So far, you have learned about single words that work as modifiers. Sometimes, a group of words may work together in an assignment as a single modifier. There are two kinds of groups of words that act as modifiers:

1. modifiers that begin with relative pronouns

2. modifiers that begin with prepositions

Modifiers That Begin with Relative Pronouns

When your subject matter is a common noun, the most helpful adjective is usually a group of words that begins with a **relative pronoun** like *who, whom, that,* or *which*. For instance, your assignment might say, *Describe a person who was a bad advisor to a national leader.* Without the adjective *who was a bad advisor to a national leader,* you would have a difficult time choosing which person to write about, but this group of words, like all adjectives, limits your choices. You would not choose to write about Elvis Presley or your favorite aunt, but you might choose Rasputin, G. Gordon Liddy, or Oliver Cromwell, all of whom were bad advisors to national leaders.

Can you tell why the whole group of words *who was a bad advisor to a national leader* is an adjective? What word does this group of words modify?

Exercise Eight

DIRECTIONS

Identifying Adjectives That Begin with Relative Pronouns

You may find more than one adjective in each of the following assignments. Identify <u>only</u> the adjectives that begin with relative pronouns. Remember that the relative pronouns are *who, whom, that,* and *which*.

MODEL   Assignment: Describe a heating method that is fueled by a source of power other than electricity.

Adjective: <u>that is fueled by a source of power other than electricity</u>

1. Trace an economic trend that led to the American stock market crash of 1929.

   Adjective: _____

2. Describe a technique which is characteristic of Impressionistic art.

   Adjective: _____

3. Describe a procedure that a nurse in training is expected to perform on a patient.

   Adjective: _____

4. Describe a maneuver which is useful for defensive driving.

   Adjective: _____

5. Describe a teenaged singer who influenced country music.

   Adjective: _____

Exercise Nine — Explaining How Adjectives That Begin with a Relative Pronoun Change Assignments

DIRECTIONS   In Exercise Eight, you found groups of words that modify the subject of each assignment. In order to explain how those modifiers change the assignments, tell what subject you would be responding to in each assignment if you did not have those modifiers.

1. Unmodified subject: _____

2. Unmodified subject: _____

3. Unmodified subject: _____

4. Unmodified subject: _____

5. Unmodified subject: _____

Exercise Ten — Supplying Adjectives That Begin with Relative Pronouns

DIRECTIONS   In the following assignments, fill in each blank with a group of words that begins with a relative pronoun and modifies the assignment.

1. Describe an animal _____.

2. Examine a document _____.

3. Trace a medical trend _____.

4. Summarize a film _____.

5. Discuss a child-rearing theory _____.

Modifiers That Begin with a Preposition

Sometimes a verb or a noun can be modified by a group of words that begins with a **preposition.** Usually a preposition is a word that shows direction, like the following common prepositions:

above	around	beside	in	off	past	under
across	at	between	inside	on	through	up
against	behind	beyond	into	outside	to	upon
along	below	down	near	over	toward	within
among	beneath	from				

However, a few prepositions do not express a direction, like the following prepositions:

about	by	for	since	with
after	during	like	until	without
before	except	of		

Whether they express direction or not, all modifiers that begin with prepositions are followed by a noun or a pronoun. Sometimes there is a small word like *a, an,* or *the* between the preposition and the noun or pronoun. Consider the following modifiers that begin with a preposition:

around the bend	over the hill	under the weather
without it	by them	up the creek

The noun or pronoun in this kind of modifier is called the *object of the preposition,* and because it is an object, that noun or pronoun cannot be the subject of a sentence.

The modifier beginning with a preposition can be an adjective or an adverb. Consider this assignment:

Analyze in outline form the breakup of the former Soviet Union.

Can you see that the two modifiers beginning with prepositions in this assignment are *in outline form* and *of the former Soviet Union?* Which of these modifiers answers the adverb question *How?* Which of these modifiers answers the adjective question *Which one?* Did you see that *in outline form* must be an adverb because it answers the adverb question and limits the command *Analyze* by telling you <u>how</u> to analyze? Did you also notice that *of the former Soviet Union* must be an adjective because it answers the adjective question and limits the subject of the assignment by telling you <u>which</u> breakup to analyze?

Exercise Eleven　**Identifying Adjectives and Adverbs That Begin with Prepositions**

DIRECTIONS　You may find more than one modifier in each of the following assignments. Identify <u>only</u> the adjectives and adverbs that begin with a preposition. You may want to refer to the list of prepositions.

MODEL　Assignment: In a brief paragraph, classify the major effects of global warming.

Modifier: <u>of global warming</u>　　Type: <u>adjective</u>

Modifier: <u>in a brief paragraph</u>　　Type: <u>adverb</u>

1. Trace the Reconstruction Era population shift from rural areas.

   Modifier: _____　　Type: _____

2. Describe in twenty-five words or less your philosophy of life.

   Modifier: _____　　Type: _____

   Modifier: _____　　Type: _____

3. Explain photosynthesis in oak trees.

   Modifier: _____　　Type: _____

4. List three main reasons for divorce among couples whose children are grown.

   Modifier: _____　　Type: _____

   Modifier: _____　　Type: _____

5. Describe with specific examples the role of multiculturalism in education.

   Modifier: _____　　Type: _____

   Modifier: _____　　Type: _____

   Modifier: _____　　Type: _____

Did you notice in Assignments 4 and 5 in Exercise Eleven that two modifiers beginning with prepositions followed each other immediately? Did you see that the second modifier in each of those assignments describes the noun in the first modifier?

Exercise Twelve ## Explaining How Modifiers That Begin with Prepositions Change Assignments

DIRECTIONS   In Exercise Eleven, you found groups of words that began with a preposition and modified either the subject of an assignment or the directions in that assignment. Fill in the subject and the commands you would be responding to in each assignment if you did not have those modifiers.

1. Unmodified subject: _____

2. Unmodified command: _____ Unmodified subject: _____

3. Unmodified subject: _____

4. Unmodified subject: _____ Unmodified subject: _____

5. Unmodified command: _____ Unmodified subject: _____

Exercise Thirteen ## Supplying Modifiers That Begin with Prepositions

DIRECTIONS   In each assignment, fill in each blank with a group of words that begins with a preposition.

1. Describe _____ the process _____.

2. _____, categorize the types _____.

3. Investigate the significant properties _____.

4. Contrast white collar crime _____.

5. _____, discuss the origins _____.

The Role of Modifiers in Assignments

When you think about the kinds of modifiers you have learned in this chapter, you will realize that each modifies a different part of the assignment. Adjectives modify the subject of your assignment, while adverbs usually modify the command. Can you tell which of the two modifiers usually has a bigger effect on your assignment? Consider the assignment *Briefly describe virtual reality.* Did you identify the adverb *briefly* and the adjective *virtual?* Which one is the more powerful modifier? The adverb *briefly* tells you how detailed your response should be, but it doesn't change the subject you will be describing. On the other hand, the adjective *virtual* does change your subject because *reality* is a very different thing from *virtual reality.*

Review Questions

Answer the following questions to help you review the material you have covered in this chapter.

1. What two parts of speech act as modifiers? (p. 36)

    _____   _____

2. Give two of the characteristics that adjectives add to nouns and pronouns to describe or limit them. (p. 36)

    _____   _____

3. Where are adjectives usually placed in an assignment? (p. 37)

    _____   _____

4. What three questions can adjectives answer? (p. 37)

    _____   _____   _____

5. Give three common endings for adjectives. (p. 37)

    _____   _____   _____

6. What kind of verbal is used as an adjective and has an *ing* ending? (p. 38)

    _____

7. What are the endings for a past participle? (p. 38)

    _____   _____   _____

8. What three parts of speech can an adverb modify? (p. 40)

    _____   _____   _____

9. What are three of the questions adverbs can answer? (p. 40)

    _____   _____   _____

10. What is the most common adverb ending? (p. 40) ———————————

11. Groups of words working as an adjective usually begin with one of what two parts of speech? (p. 42)

    ——————————— and ———————————

12. What are three relative pronouns? (p. 42)

    —————————— —————————— ——————————

13. What two parts of speech can modifiers that begin with prepositions be? (p. 44)

    ——————————— and ———————————

14. What part of your assignment is usually modified by an adjective? (p. 46)

    —————————————————————————————————————

15. What part of your assignment is usually modified by an adverb? (p. 46)

    —————————————————————————————————————

16. Which of the two modifiers has a greater effect on your assignment? (p. 47)

    —————————————————————————————————————

    Why? —————————————————————————————————————

Writing Exercises

I. Filling in Modifiers

In the following paragraph, all of the modifiers are missing. Some of them are adjectives, and some are adverbs; some of the adjectives are single words, and some are groups of words. The long blank lines are for adjectives beginning with relative pronouns, and the broken blank lines are for modifiers that begin with prepositions. Fill in the missing modifiers so that the paragraph makes sense. Then try it a second time, using different modifiers.

Before you buy a house, you should check out ——————————— things.

———————, you should look ——————— ——————— ——————————. Flush

the toilets, and run the taps to determine that there are no leaks

———————————————————. It helps to bring a ———————————

plumber to see that the house has _____ pipes, not

_____ pipes. _____, you should check the _____ sys-

tem _____ _____ _____. Check the _____ box

_____. See that _____ the circuits are _____. You should

_____ examine the wires; they should not be

_____. _____, you should examine the roof. Leaks

_____ can damage the drywall as well as short out the circuits.

Check for _____ gutters; there should be no leaves or

_____ debris _____. It is important to re-

alize that the parts _____ _____ _____ you can see can

cause you _____ trouble than the parts _____.

II. Writing a Paragraph with Appropriate Modifiers

Study the paragraph in Writing Exercise I above about checking out a house before buying it. Notice that the first sentence tells you to check a number of things before buying a house, and the rest of the paragraph describes those things specifically. Choose two of the topics below and brainstorm for ideas, making lists and then clustering the ideas in those lists. Finally, write a paragraph about each like the one on buying a house. Pay special attention to the modifiers you choose.

1. Describe the stages of giving birth.

2. Discuss some ways of purifying water.

3. Describe some ways of celebrating a graduation.

4. Describe some ways of ending a relationship.

5. Discuss sources of information for a class paper.

Looking Back and Looking Forward

In the three chapters of this first section, you have learned how to understand your assignment by the kinds of language used in the various parts of it. In the next section, you will learn how to respond to your assignments. Chapter Four will show you how to narrow your subject to a topic.

Section one review   *Understanding Assignments*

Remember what you have learned in the first three chapters about verbs, nouns and pronouns, and modifiers, and how they are used in assignments. First, analyze Assignments 1 to 5 according to the following guidelines, and then respond to the assignment. You don't have to number your responses or put them in any particular order, as long as they make sense together.

- Explain what kind of description the command is asking for.

- Identify the direct object of the command, which is your subject.

- Explain how any modifiers affect the subject and make it different from an unmodified subject.

- Choose one assignment and respond to it.

Assignments:

1. Contrast two blockbuster movies of the 1990s.

2. Tell how to plan a surprise party.

3. Describe a fictional character that you would like to be.

4. Compare your two favorite relatives.

5. Describe an ad on television that irritates you.

Responding to Assignments

Chapter four

Narrowing Subjects to Topics

In the first section, you learned how to understand your assignment by identifying the command (action verb), the subject (noun or pronoun), and any modifiers (adjectives or adverbs) that affect the subject or command. In this section, you will see that the subject is often too broad to write about as a whole, so you must distinguish between the subject of an assignment and the topic you choose to write about. Then you will learn how to divide that topic into parts to write about and put those parts together into a whole paragraph. Just as giving your car a tune-up involves working with its various parts, responding to your assignments involves working with wholes and parts. Understanding wholes and parts will help you learn how to find a topic from your assignment. For instance, in the assignment *Describe justice,* you might choose to focus on frontier justice as your topic. It is smaller than the whole subject *justice.* In fact, it is a part of the whole subject.

The following exercises will help you develop the kind of critical thinking necessary to make appropriate choices based upon recognizing wholes and parts.

Exercise One   **Wholes and Parts**

DIRECTIONS   Circle the whole in each list.

1. Bora Bora   Mackinac   Santa Catalina   islands   Manhattan

2. novel   characters   setting   plot   tone

3. Nigeria   Libya   Tanzania   Sudan   Africa

4. AIDS   measles   diseases   pneumonia   leprosy

5. solitaire   card games   bridge   Old Maid   gin rummy

More Wholes and Parts

DIRECTIONS   Supply the wholes based on the parts that are given.

MODEL   The Battle of Fredericksburg   The Battle of Gettysburg
The Battle of Antietam   The Battle of Bull Run

whole = Civil War battles

1. jai alai   soccer   skiing   cricket   bowling

    whole = _____

2. English   algebra   chemistry   biology   Latin

    whole = _____

3. novels   short stories   poems   plays   essays

    whole = _____

4. Mojave   Sahara   Gobi   Sonoran   the Australian Outback

    whole = _____

5. jacks   marbles   checkers   hide and seek   hopscotch

    whole = _____

Even More Wholes and Parts

DIRECTIONS   For each whole, add three more parts that go with the two already given.

1. whole = exercises

    jogging   rowing _____ _____ _____

2. whole = dances

    polka   Texas two-step _____ _____ _____

3. whole = sweets

    churros   fudge _____ _____ _____

4. whole = film directors

    Woody Allen   Spike Lee _____ _____ _____

5. whole = states in the former Soviet Union

    Latvia   Georgia _____ _____ _____

Levels of Generality

When you break down a whole into its parts, you are going from broad to narrow. Broad and narrow are **levels of generality.** You will use these levels of generality when you find a topic from the subject of your assignment. In the beginning of this chapter, you saw that tuning up an automobile involves working with its parts. These parts include its engine, headlights, and tires. Is it possible for these parts to be wholes at the same time? Does an engine have parts? If you know that the carburetor, the valves, and the spark plugs are parts of an engine, you can see that an engine can indeed be a whole because it contains parts. When would you think of an engine as a whole? When would you think of it as a part? Each time you break down a part of a whole into even smaller parts, you are moving to a new level of generality—a narrower one.

Just as you can break a whole into parts, you can also break an assignment into several possible topics if you think of the subject as a whole and then break it down into its parts. Sometimes, a part can be an example of a whole. For instance, if your assignment asks you to describe an automobile with superior engineering, *an automobile with superior engineering* is really a category that contains several examples that could be topics. You might choose as your topic a Mercedes-Benz, a Jaguar, or a Volvo, all of which are generally considered to be examples of automobiles with superior engineering.

Narrowing Topics by Asking Questions

In Chapter One you came up with ideas to write a paragraph in response to an assignment by using simple brainstorming involving lists and clusters. Now you will use another kind of brainstorming to narrow the subject of your assignment to a topic. Narrowing down the subject of your assignment to possible topics is easy if you ask **focusing questions** that begin with a **key question word:**

Who? What? Which one(s)? When? Where? Why? How? How much?

These words begin focusing questions because they help you narrow your focus whenever necessary in the writing process. To form the rest of a focusing question, you refer to the subject of your assignment. For instance, to get from *an automobile with superior engineering* to *Jaguar,* you had to ask yourself <u>*What*</u> *is an automobile with superior engineering?*

Since the subject of your assignment comes from your teacher, it is usually broad enough to allow every student in the class to choose a particular part of it that interests him or her as a topic. In this way, an assignment is a partnership between the teacher and the student.

Exercise Four

Focusing Questions

DIRECTIONS   Each of the following assignments is followed by the key question word in a focusing question that is most useful in narrowing down the subject to a topic. Apply that word to the subject to form a focusing question.

MODEL   Assignment: Describe a psychological condition.

Key question word: What?

Focusing question: *What <u>psychological condition</u>?*

1. Assignment: Tell about a difficult choice you made that you are proud of.

    Key question word: What?

    Focusing question: *What* _____?

2. Assignment: Describe somebody who inspired you when you were in elementary school.

    Key question word: Who?

    Focusing question: *Who* _____?

3. Assignment: Discuss an important tradition in your family.

Key question word: What?

Focusing question: *What* _____?

4. Assignment: Describe a popular diet.

Key question word: Which one?

Focusing question: *Which one* _____?

5. Assignment: Discuss one method of communication.

Key question word: What?

Focusing question: *What* _____?

Exercise Five   **Narrowing Subjects to Topics**

DIRECTIONS   For each of the following assignments, identify the subject that is the direct object of the command. Then ask the appropriate focusing question to narrow the subject to several possible topics. Your topics will probably differ from other students' topics.

MODEL   Assignment: Describe a current fashion trend.

Subject: *a current fashion trend*

Focusing question: *What current fashion trend?*

Topics: *the grunge look*

       the retro look

1. Assignment: Describe a type of ethnic music.

Subject: _____

Focusing question: _____?

Topics: _____

_____

2. Assignment: Describe a relaxing vacation.

Subject: _____

Focusing question: _____?

Topics: _____

_____

3. Assignment: Describe an emotional occasion.

   Subject: _____

   Focusing question: _____ ?

   Topics: _____

   _____

4. Assignment: Describe a kind of marine life.

   Subject: _____

   Focusing question: _____ ?

   Topics: _____

   _____

5. Assignment: Compare two computer software programs.

   Subject: _____

   Focusing question: _____ ?

   Topics: _____

   _____

Using Modifiers to Find a Topic

As you learned in Chapter Three, sometimes the subject in your assignment contains a modifier (adjective or adverb), and that modifier helps you narrow the subject to a topic. For instance, if your assignment says, *Describe someone who made a significant contribution to American literature,* the subject is *someone,* and the modifier *who made a significant contribution to American literature* helps you narrow the *someone* to an example that can be your topic, like Toni Morrison.

Modifiers can occur anywhere in the assignment, but the modifiers that help you narrow the subject to a topic will occur right before or right after the subject. For instance, your assignment might say, *Describe a devastating natural phenomenon.* In this assignment, the subject is *natural phenomenon,* and the modifier *devastating* helps you look for a particular kind of natural phenomenon, one that can do a lot of damage, like an earthquake. When you ask your focusing question, be sure to include the modifier in order to keep your focus on the subject, or you might come up with an inappropriate topic. In other words, your focusing question for the first example above would be *Who made a <u>significant</u> contribution to American literature?*, not just *Who made a contribution to American literature?* Likewise, your focusing question for the second example would be *What <u>devastating</u> natural phenomenon?*, not just *What natural phenomenon?*

<table>
<tr><td>Exercise Six</td><td>

Using Modifiers to Find a Topic

</td></tr>
<tr><td>Directions</td><td>For each of the following assignments, circle the subject, and underline the word or words that are the important modifiers that will help you choose a topic.</td></tr>
<tr><td>Model</td><td>Assignment: Describe (a person) <u>who changed the course of history on the North American continent.</u></td></tr>
</table>

1. Assignment: Compare two obsolete kinds of transportation.

2. Assignment: Discuss the effects of an earthquake that happens under the ocean.

3. Assignment: Describe a celebration from a country that is not your own.

4. Assignment: Define *repressed hostility.*

5. Assignment: Tell about a place that has belonged to different nations.

The preceding exercises show you that some assignments need to be narrowed down. For instance, in Assignment 1, the subject *two obsolete kinds of transportation* is a whole that is too broad to write about. You need to ask the focusing question *Which ones?* in order to narrow the subject to a topic like *horse-drawn buggies* and *Model T Fords.*

However, sometimes the subject of an assignment is already narrow enough to be your topic. In other words, it has already answered a focusing question beginning with one of the key question words: *who?, what?, which one(s)?, when?, where?, why?, how?,* or *how much?* For example, in Assignment 4, if you ask *which one?* of the subject *repressed hostility,* you will see that it is already a topic because *repressed hostility* is a part of the whole *hostility.* When you cannot find a narrower part of your subject, you already have a topic.

Subject and Topics

Some of the following assignments contain subjects that are already narrow enough to be topics, and some assignments are still too broad. For each assignment, use what you know about parts and wholes to identify the topic if it is there or to come up with one if it is not there. If the direct object is just a broad subject, you will be able to narrow it to one of several possible topics by asking a focusing question. However, if you ask a focusing question and cannot find an answer that is narrower than the subject of the assignment, the direct object is already a topic.

Assignment: Describe the process of forest regeneration after a fire.

Direct object: the process of forest regeneration after a fire

Focusing question: What process?

Topic: the process of forest regeneration after a fire

1. Assignment: Describe a high school regulation.

   Direct object: _____

   Focusing question: _____?

   Topic: _____

2. Assignment: Describe Neanderthal Man.

   Direct object: _____

   Focusing question: _____?

   Topic: _____

3. Assignment: Discuss a devastating man-made ecological disaster.

   Direct object: _____

   Focusing question: _____?

   Topic: _____

4. Assignment: Tell how to develop a photograph.

   Direct object: _____

   Focusing question: _____?

   Topic: _____

5. Assignment: Explain a car repair process.

   Direct object: _____

Focusing question: _____ ?

Topic: _____

To prove whether you have already narrowed the subject of an assignment you should be able to look at a topic and see the broader subject it came from.

Topics Back to Assignments

For each of the following topics, ask an appropriate focusing question to find what the topic is either a part of or an example of. To do this, ask *What is the topic a part of?* or *What is the topic an example of?* Then add the words *Describe* or *Tell about* to your answer, and you will have found the assignment.

MODEL Topic: a relative's wedding

Focusing question: What is a wedding an example of?

Answer: a family celebration

Assignment: Describe a family celebration.

1. Topic: child-proofing a home

   Focusing question: _____ ?

   Answer: _____

   Assignment: _____

2. Topic: the Boston Tea Party

   Focusing question: _____ ?

   Answer: _____

   Assignment: _____

3. Topic: Queen Elizabeth II

   Focusing question: _____ ?

   Answer: _____

   Assignment: _____

4. Topic: bedwetting

   Focusing question: _____ ?

   Answer: _____

   Assignment: _____

5. Topic: making a chocolate cake that you eat when you are sad

Focusing question: _____ ?

Answer: _____

Assignment: _____

   Now you are ready to put together all you have learned in this chapter in order to focus the subject of your assignment on a topic, which is the first step in responding to an assignment.

Exercise Nine **Putting It All Together**

Directions   For each of the following assignments,

1. identify the subject;

2. identify any modifiers that affect the subject;

3. ask the appropriate focusing question to narrow the subject to a topic;

4. fill in the answer; and

5. rewrite the original assignment, substituting the topic for the subject.

Model   Assignment: Trace the stages in the life of an amphibian.

Subject: the stages in the life of an amphibian

Modifier: none

Focusing question: What amphibian?

Answer: frog

Topic: Trace the stages in the life of a frog.

1. Assignment: Describe a labor-saving invention.

Subject: _____

Modifier(s): _____

Focusing question: _____ ?

Answer: _____

Topic: _____

2. Assignment: Analyze a volatile substance.

   Subject: _____

   Modifier(s): _____

   Focusing question: _____?

   Answer: _____

   Topic: _____

3. Assignment: Compare two fattening desserts.

   Subject: _____

   Modifier(s): _____

   Focusing question: _____?

   Answer: _____

   Topic: _____

4. Assignment: Tell about a distressing time in your life.

   Subject: _____

   Modifier(s): _____

   Focusing question: _____?

   Answer: _____

   Topic: _____

5. Assignment: Tell how to make a work of art.

   Subject: _____

   Modifier(s): _____

   Focusing question: _____?

   Answer: _____

   Topic: _____

Review Questions

Answer the following questions to help you review the material you have covered in this chapter.

1. To narrow your assignment, you must recognize _____ and _____. (p. 53)

2. You can think of the subject of your assignment as a whole. What is the part of the subject you write about called? (p. 53) _____

3. When you look at wholes, which are broad, and parts, which are narrower, you are looking at two _____ _____ _____. (p. 55)

4. Sometimes the topic can be an _____ of the subject. (p. 55)

5. What are the key question words that begin focusing questions? (p. 56)

   _____?

   _____?

   _____?

   _____?

   _____?

   _____?

   _____?

   _____?

6. When do you use focusing questions? (p. 56)

   _____

7. What do some assignments have that help you narrow the subject to a topic? (p. 58)

   _____

8. How do you know when you have found your topic? (p. 59)

   _____

Writing **Exercises**

I. Writing Paragraphs with Focus

Choose one of the following assignments and use focused brainstorming by asking the appropriate focusing question to narrow the subject to possible topics. Next, choose one of those topics to write about. After you have your topic, ask focusing questions about that topic to give you raw material for a paragraph. To help you plan your paragraph, look again at the paragraphs on spiders in Chapter One, echoes in Chapter Two, and buying a house in Chapter Three as models. Finally, write a paragraph on your topic.

1. Explain a biological change that occurs in the human body.

2. Describe an outfit you might wear that would make your parents cringe.

3. Compare two pieces of art you love.

4. Tell about a time in history during which you would like to have lived.

5. Describe an item you own that expresses your personality.

6. Explain how to fix an appliance that you find essential.

7. Contrast your grandparents' music with your music.

8. Discuss a safety procedure for work.

9. Describe someone who is a *knockout*.

10. Describe a gift you will always treasure.

II. Revising Paragraphs with Focus

This exercise introduces you to revising, which, as you remember from *A Very Necessary Introduction,* is a process that goes on at the same time as the writing process. You will use the paragraphs you wrote for the Writing Exercises in the first three chapters for this exercise. Then, as you learn more about writing a paragraph, you will continue to revise these paragraphs.

Look back at the paragraphs you wrote for Writing Exercise II in Chapter One, Writing Exercise V in Chapter Two, and Writing Exercise II in Chapter Three. Use focused brainstorming to check the focus in the first sentence of each paragraph by asking the correct focusing question of the subject in the assignment to determine if the topic in your first sentence is appropriate. Revise these first sentences if necessary. Then rewrite the rest of each paragraph to support each revised topic sentence.

Looking Back and Looking Forward

In this chapter, you learned how to move from the subject of your assignment to a topic by recognizing parts and wholes and by asking focusing questions. In the next chapter, you will begin building a structure for your response to your topic.

Chapter five

Creating Topic Sentences

In the last chapter, you learned how to find a topic from the subject of your assignment. In this chapter, you will learn how to introduce that topic in your paragraph with a topic sentence. A sentence is a group of words with a particular purpose. In order to understand topic sentences, you need to understand how groups of words behave in a sentence.

Sentences

A group of words that is a **sentence** has three characteristics: a subject, a verb, and a complete thought that makes sense by itself. A sentence might express a statement or a question or a command. As you will remember from Chapter One, most assignments are in the form of a command, like *Discuss the effects of sunlight deprivation on humans.* Notice that the punctuation that comes at the end of a command is a period. Some assignments are questions which you need to change to commands, like *What are the effects of sunlight deprivation on humans?* Notice that the punctuation that comes at the end of a question is a question mark. The sentences you write in response to an assignment will usually be statements, like *The effects of sunlight deprivation on humans can be both mental and physical.* Notice that the punctuation that comes at the end of a statement is a period.

There can be a difference between the subject of the assignment and the subject of a sentence that is not an assignment. When you think of what words do in sentences, you remember that the subject of an assignment is the direct object of the command or action verb. It answers the focusing question *who?* or *what?* <u>after</u> the verb. In the preceding assignment, *Discuss the effects of sunlight deprivation on humans,* the subject of the assignment, *the effects of sunlight deprivation on humans,* answers the focusing question *Discuss <u>what</u>?*

The subject of a sentence is something different. You can usually find the subject of a sentence by asking a focusing question <u>before</u> the verb. Your answer will always be a noun or a pronoun. For instance, in the assignment *Discuss the effects of sunlight deprivation on humans,* the subject *you* answers the focusing question <u>*Who should discuss?*</u> Even though the pronoun *you* isn't written in the assignment, it is implied. In fact, the subject of all commands is the pronoun *you* because when you give a command, you are addressing a person you call *you.*

Since the sentences you use to respond to your assignments occur as statements rather than commands, their subjects will actually appear in the sentence. For instance, in the sentence *The effects of sunlight deprivation on humans are both mental and physical,* the subject *The effects of sunlight deprivation on humans* answers the question <u>*What*</u> *are both mental and physical?* Remember, it is easy to identify the subject of a sentence if you find the verb first and then ask the focusing question beginning with one of the key words *who* or *what* before that verb.

If there is no verb, there cannot be a subject because verbs and subjects need each other. Without a verb and a subject a group of words cannot make sense. Do not be confused by nouns and pronouns in a group of words that is not a sentence. In the absence of a verb, a noun or pronoun is only a potential subject. There may be other nouns and pronouns in a sentence that are not subjects. As you learned near the end of Chapter Two, nouns and pronouns that answer the questions *Who?* or *What?* <u>after</u> action verbs are direct objects.

<u>Exercise One</u>

Analyzing Sentences

DIRECTIONS For each of the following sentences, identify the verb, and write the focusing question you would ask to find the subject. Remember that a focusing question begins with a key question word and then repeats the verb. Finally, identify the subject.

MODEL Most people have several kinds of fears.

Verb: <u>have</u>

Focusing question: <u>Who have?</u>

Subject: <u>Most people</u>

1. My best friend and my worst enemy have a lot in common.

   Verb: _____

   Focusing question: _____?

   Subject: _____

2. Describe an environmental hazard.

   Verb: _____

Focusing question: _____?

Subject: _____

3. Writing a paper is challenging.

Verb: _____

Focusing question: _____?

Subject: _____

4. Discuss a particular legal procedure.

Verb: _____

Focusing question: _____?

Subject: _____

5. My last doctor's appointment was painless.

Verb: _____

Focusing question: _____?

Subject: _____

Fragments

A group of words that is missing either a subject or a verb or a complete thought cannot be a sentence. We call a group of words like this a **fragment** because it is only a piece of a sentence. You should avoid fragments in your writing because they make your writing unclear to the reader.

Exercise Two | ## Sentences and Fragments

DIRECTIONS | Identify each of the following group of words as either a sentence or a fragment. For each fragment, tell which of the three characteristics of a sentence is missing. Remember that some fragments are missing more than one characteristic. In other words, if a group of words has no verb, it cannot have a subject; consequently, it cannot express a complete thought either.

MODEL | The rain forests of Brazil.

Sentence or fragment: _fragment_ _____

Missing part(s): _verb, subject, complete thought_ _____

1. Compare the properties of aluminum and tin.

    Sentence or fragment: _____

    Missing part(s): _____

2. Describe a religious service.

    Sentence or fragment: _____

    Missing part(s): _____

3. When pain is debilitating.

    Sentence or fragment: _____

    Missing part(s): _____

4. The sound of an orchestra tuning up.

    Sentence or fragment: _____

    Missing part(s): _____

5. Nuclear fission is an explosive process.

    Sentence or fragment: _____

    Missing part(s): _____

Clauses

A group of words that is a **clause** has at least two of the same characteristics as a sentence, a <u>verb</u>, and a <u>subject</u>. Sometimes a clause is a sentence. When this happens, the clause also expresses a complete thought that makes sense. This kind of clause is called an **independent clause** because it doesn't need anything else to be a complete sentence; therefore, it is independent. For instance, *Monitor lizards can be dangerous pets* is an independent clause. Did you identify *Monitor lizards* as the subject? What two words are the verb? Do the words in this clause express a complete thought that makes sense? Now you can see that this independent clause is also a sentence.

On the other hand, when a group of words has a verb and subject but does not express a complete thought, it is called a **dependent clause** because it must depend on an independent clause to complete its thought. For instance, *Because they are unpredictable* is a dependent clause. What is the subject? What is the verb?

At the beginning of the dependent clause is a word that makes it dependent. If we remove the word *Because*, we would have an independent clause that could stand by itself as a sentence. However, if we keep the word *Because,* we will have to join this dependent clause to an independent clause, like *Monitor lizards can be dangerous pets;* otherwise, the dependent clause is a fragment because it does not express a complete thought.

Another kind of dependent word is the relative pronoun you learned about in Chapter Two. A clause that begins with a relative pronoun is dependent upon the noun that pronoun is related to in an independent clause in order to make sense. For instance, in the sentence *Jonas Salk, who pioneered the use of live viruses in vaccines, helped end the polio epidemic of the 1950s,* the dependent clause *who pioneered the use of live viruses in vaccines* does not express a complete thought. Even though it contains a subject, the relative pronoun *who,* and an action verb, *pioneered,* it does not make sense unless it becomes part of the independent clause that contains the noun to which *who* is related, *Jonas Salk.* In this kind of dependent clause, you cannot simply remove the dependent word *who* to make a complete sentence. You must join this kind of dependent clause to an independent clause. When you do this, the relative pronoun clause acts as an adjective, as you learned in Chapter Three.

A dependent clause that is not joined to an independent clause is a fragment because it lacks one of the characteristics of a sentence, a complete thought. Remember, you want to avoid fragments in your own writing.

We can put the first kind of dependent clause either before or after the independent clause to make a sentence. For instance, we can say, *Because they are unpredictable, Monitor lizards can be dangerous pets,* or we can say, *Monitor lizards can be dangerous pets because they are unpredictable.* The second kind of dependent clause, the one that begins with a relative pronoun, must be placed directly after the word in the independent clause it is related to.

| Exercise Three | **Identifying Independent and Dependent Clauses** |

DIRECTIONS   Identify each of the following groups of words as either an independent or a dependent clause. Then identify the dependent word in each dependent clause.

MODEL   When stars explode.

Clause: <u>dependent</u>

Dependent word: <u>When</u>

1. Most scientists believe in the "Big Bang" theory of creation.

    Clause: _____

    Dependent word: _____

2. Which completes the cycle.

    Clause: _____

Dependent word: _____

3. Because glaciers move very slowly.

Clause: _____

Dependent word: _____

4. That are the characteristics of a cad.

Clause: _____

Dependent word: _____

5. Although hair stylists must be state-certified.

Clause: _____

Dependent word: _____

Exercise Four Completing Dependent Clauses

DIRECTIONS   Complete each of the dependent clauses in the left column by matching it with an appropriate independent clause in the right column so that the resulting sentence makes sense.

Dependent Clauses	*Independent Clauses*
1. When alligators hatch,	a. firefighters often set backdrafts.
2. Although each one is different,	b. some people avoid tomatoes.
3. When winds are favorable,	c. the reptiles' mothers carry them to water.
4. Since diamonds are so precious,	d. most snowflakes have six sides.
5. Because nightshade vegetables can be toxic to arthritis sufferers,	e. jewelers work on them carefully.

Exercise Five Completing More Dependent Clauses

DIRECTIONS   Make a sentence out of each of the following dependent clauses either by writing an independent clause to go with it that makes sense or by eliminating the dependent word if eliminating it doesn't change the meaning of the clause. Remember that some dependent clauses can go either before or after the independent clause, while other dependent clauses must be placed beside the word each is related to in the independent clause.

MODEL   Dependent clause: who cannot live independently

Sentence: Parasites, who cannot live independently, require a host organism.

1. Dependent clause: when primates reach maturity

   Sentence: _____.

2. Dependent clause: which is the result of auto exhaust and industrial pollution

   Sentence: _____.

3. Dependent clause: who was a star of early television

   Sentence: _____.

4. Dependent clause: when a person has strong feelings for someone else

   Sentence: _____.

5. Dependent clause: because department stores experience a great deal of theft by employees

   Sentence: _____.

Phrases

A group of words that has none of the characteristics of a sentence and acts as a single part of speech is called a **phrase.**

Types of Phrases

Most phrases can be identified by the first word of the phrase. If the first word of a phrase is a helping verb, then the whole phrase is a **verb phrase,** like _had been smiling._ If the first word of the phrase is a present or past participle, then the whole phrase is a **participial phrase,** like _hanging_ by a thread or _surrounded_ by fire. If the first word of the phrase is a gerund, then the whole phrase is a **gerund phrase,** like _windsurfing_ in the Bahamas. If the first word of the phrase is an infinitive, then the whole phrase is an **infinitive phrase,** like _to win_ by cheating. If the first word of the phrase is a preposition, then the whole phrase is a **prepositional phrase,** like _in the barn._

   Look again at the preceding examples for participial, gerund, and infinitive phrases. Were you confused by the prepositional phrases _by a thread, by fire, in the Bahamas,_ and _by cheating?_ In each case, the prepositional phrase comes right after a participle, gerund, or infinitive. When you identify prepositional phrases, always check the word before the prepositional phrase to be sure that it is not a participle, a gerund, or an infinitive. If it is, then the whole phrase becomes a participial, gerund, or infinitive phrase.

Labeling Types of Phrases

DIRECTIONS   Find all the phrases in each of the following sentences, and identify each one as either verb, participial, gerund, infinitive, or prepositional.

MODEL   Discuss the ways in which birds migrating to warm climates preserve energy.

Phrase: in which _____   Type: prepositional _____

Phrase: migrating to warm climates   Type: present participial ____

1. Generating sufficient profit is one measure of success for a new business.

   Phrase: _____ Type: _____

   Phrase: _____ Type: _____

   Phrase: _____ Type: _____

2. To preserve natural habitat is the main principle of many modern zoos.

   Phrase: _____ Type: _____

   Phrase: _____ Type: _____

3. Discuss methods of finding fossils in loamy soil.

   Phrase: _____ Type: _____

   Phrase: _____ Type: _____

4. Many birds displaying bright plumage are trying to attract a mate.

   Phrase: _____ Type: _____

   Phrase: _____ Type: _____

   Phrase: _____ Type: _____

5. Discuss the ways registering for college classes can be a frustrating experience for a student returning to school after a long absence.

   Phrase: _____ Type: _____

   Phrase: _____ Type: _____

   Phrase: _____ Type: _____

   Phrase: _____ Type: _____

   Phrase: _____ Type: _____

Uses of Phrases

The terms *participial, gerund, infinitive,* and *prepositional* help identify phrases, but the words alone don't tell how these phrases are used in a sentence. For that, you must examine what the phrase is <u>doing</u> in the sentence.

A phrase can be used in a sentence as a verb, a noun, or a modifier (adjective or adverb).

EXAMPLES:

Phrase as verb: American and Russian space explorers <u>had been working</u> separately for many years before they made joint missions in the 1990s.

Phrase as noun: <u>Gathering food for the winter</u> was one of the primary concerns of American homesteaders.

Phrase as modifier: <u>Revered by his troops,</u> George Washington was an effective leader.

In the first example above, the verb phrase is the group of words *had been working.* The phrase not only begins with a helping verb but also acts as a verb in the sentence. In the second example, the gerund phrase *Gathering food for the winter* is a noun that acts as the subject of the sentence because it answers the focusing question <u>*What* *was one of the primary concerns of American homesteaders?*</u> In the third example, the past participial phrase *Revered by his troops* describes *George Washington,* so it acts as an adjective. In each case, the group of words is a phrase acting as a single part of speech—a verb, a noun, or a modifier.

Remember that verb phrases are always used as verbs; participial phrases, present or past, are always used as adjectives; gerund phrases are always used as nouns; but infinitive phrases can be used as adjectives, adverbs, or nouns, and prepositional phrases can be used as adjectives or adverbs.

Exercise Seven **Identifying Phrases**

DIRECTIONS Find all the phrases in each of the following sentences, identify the type of each (verb, participial, gerund, infinitive, prepositional), and tell how each is being used (verb, noun, adjective, or adverb). Remember that verbs show action or condition; nouns name a person, place, or thing; adjectives describe nouns or pronouns; and adverbs describe verbs, adjectives, or other adverbs, and answer the questions *where?, when?, how?,* or *how much?* after the verb.

MODEL Wanting to possess all the great art in Europe, Nazi troopers were removing statues and paintings from the finest homes and museums as early as 1938.

Phrase: <u>Wanting to possess all the great art in Europe</u>

Type: <u>present participial</u>   Use: <u>adjective</u>

Phrase: *were removing* _____

Type: *verb* _____ Use: *verb* _____

Phrase: *from the finest homes and museums* _____

Type: *prepositional* _____ Use: *adverb* _____

1. Searching for birthparents is easier in some states than in others.

   Phrase: _____

   Type: _____ Use: _____

   Phrase: _____

   Type: _____ Use: _____

   Phrase: _____

   Type: _____ Use: _____

2. To be a contestant on a game show has become the goal of many trivia buffs.

   Phrase: _____

   Type: _____ Use: _____

   Phrase: _____

   Type: _____ Use: _____

   Phrase: _____

   Type: _____ Use: _____

   Phrase: _____

   Type: _____ Use: _____

3. Onion grass growing in livestock pastures in the spring can change the flavor of milk.

   Phrase: _____

   Type: _____ Use: _____

   Phrase: _____

   Type: _____ Use: _____

   Phrase: _____

   Type: _____ Use: _____

Phrase: _____

Type: _____   Use: _____

4. Driving cross-country can be an adventure or a struggle, depending on one's vehicle, experience, and preparation.

Phrase: _____

Type: _____   Use: _____

Phrase: _____

Type: _____   Use: _____

Phrase: _____

Type: _____   Use: _____

5. Giving in to public demand, Hilary Rodham Clinton cut back some of her official duties in the Clinton administration.

Phrase: _____

Type: _____   Use: _____

Phrase: _____

Type: _____   Use: _____

Phrase: _____

Type: _____   Use: _____

Phrase: _____

Type: _____   Use: _____

Topic Sentences

Now that you understand how groups of words behave in a sentence, you are ready to form the kind of sentence that introduces your response to an assignment. This sentence is called a **topic sentence.**

Like any other sentence, a topic sentence must have a subject and verb and express a complete thought. Topic sentences also have three parts: The subject of your topic sentence is the **topic** you get after you have narrowed down the subject of an assignment; the verb in your topic sentence expresses an action or condition that is appropriate for that topic; and the complete thought that your topic sentence expresses is based on your attitude, opinion, or claim about your topic. That attitude, opinion, or claim controls the rest of your paper because it tells your teacher and you what your paper must prove, so it is called the **controlling idea** of the topic sentence.

Consider the assignment *Describe one of your English teachers.* You might narrow the subject, *one of your English teachers,* to the topic *Mr. Ramirez.* Before you can go on, you need to narrow down your topic even further by deciding what attitude or opinion you want to express about Mr. Ramirez. As always, you narrow your focus by asking a focusing question. In this case, you could ask, <u>*What kind*</u> *of teacher was Mr. Ramirez?* You might answer that he was patient or stern or unreasonable or creative. Any one of these opinions can be the controlling idea of your topic sentence. If you put the topic together with an appropriate verb and a controlling idea, you might get a topic sentence like *My English teacher Mr. Ramirez was patient.* Now can you see what the rest of your paper will be about? Do you notice that the controlling idea not only tells your teacher what to expect in your paper but also reminds you what you are writing about every step of the way? In other words, a topic sentence makes a promise to the reader. Your job in writing the paper is to keep the promise you make in the topic sentence.

Assignments with Controlling Ideas

Sometimes your assignment will already have a controlling idea in it that you can use in your topic sentence. In the assignment *Tell about an experience that affected you powerfully,* you will have to narrow down the subject to a topic, but the controlling idea has been given to you in the modifier *that affected you powerfully.* To find the topic, you would ask a focusing question like <u>*Which*</u> *experience affected me powerfully?* You might answer, *Finishing the Boston Marathon.* The attitude about your topic that controls the rest of your paper is already expressed for you in the assignment, so your topic sentence could be *Finishing the Boston Marathon was an experience that affected me powerfully.*

Exercise Eight ## Topic Sentences

DIRECTIONS Write a topic sentence that responds to each of the following assignments. The subject of some assignments will need to be narrowed to a topic; however, the controlling idea is already given in each assignment.

1. Assignment: Tell about a time you behaved in a way you regret.

   Topic sentence: _____.

2. Assignment: Contrast two appliances you cannot live without.

   Topic sentence: _____.

3. Assignment: Tell how to perform a process you think everyone should know how to do.

   Topic sentence: _____.

4. Assignment: Tell why *Othello* is a tragic play.

   Topic sentence: _____.

5. Assignment: Examine why Chopin's music is pleasing to many people who do not ordinarily like classical music.

   Topic sentence: _____.

Assignments without Controlling Ideas

Sometimes your assignment will not have a controlling idea. When that happens, you will have to ask yourself focusing questions about your topic in order to discover how you think or feel about that topic. For instance, in the assignment *Describe prejudice,* your subject is already narrow enough to be a topic, but you still need a controlling idea to form a topic sentence. You will have to ask, <u>*What sort of thing do I think prejudice is?*</u> You might answer, *An unfair attitude toward a group of people,* so your topic sentence would be *Prejudice is an unfair attitude toward a group of people.* Can you see that the rest of your paper will show what you mean by *unfair attitude?*

Exercise Nine **More Topic Sentences**

DIRECTIONS For each of the following assignments, narrow the subject to a topic if necessary. Then ask a focusing question to find a controlling idea. Finally, write a topic sentence.

MODEL Assignment: Discuss an effect of gang violence on a neighborhood.

Topic: <u>an effect of gang violence on a neighborhood</u>

Focusing question: <u>What effect can gang violence have on a neighborhood?</u>

Controlling idea: <u>people become frightened</u>

Topic sentence: <u>One effect of gang violence on a neighborhood is to frighten people.</u>

1. Assignment: Describe the attitude of the typical college student.

   Topic: _____

   Focusing question: _____?

   Controlling idea: _____

   Topic sentence: _____.

2. Assignment: Describe how most reducing diets work.

   Topic: _____

   Focusing question: _____ ?

   Controlling idea: _____

   Topic sentence: _____ .

3. Assignment: Tell how layoffs in any city's main industry affect the local economy.

   Topic: _____

   Focusing question: _____ ?

   Controlling idea: _____

   Topic sentence: _____ .

4. Assignment: Describe the process of parallel parking.

   Topic: _____

   Focusing question: _____ ?

   Controlling idea: _____

   Topic sentence: _____ .

5. Assignment: Describe the motor skills of a two-year-old child.

   Topic: _____

   Focusing question: _____ ?

   Controlling idea: _____

   Topic sentence: _____ .

Assignments with Partial Controlling Ideas

Some assignments ask for causes for, reasons for, or effects of certain things; the ways things happen; or the steps by which they happen. The controlling idea for your topic sentence for this type of assignment will repeat the word *causes, reasons, effects, ways,* or *steps* from the assignment and then make the claim that there are *many* or *several* or even *a specific number* of them. For instance, for the assignment *Discuss the reasons for declining enrollment in community colleges,* your controlling idea would repeat the word *reasons* and add a number or numerical modifier like *some* or *many,* so your topic sentence might be *There are three reasons for declining enrollment in community colleges.*

Exercise Ten   **Even More Topic Sentences**

Directions   For each of the following assignments, identify the part of the controlling idea already given in the assignment, complete it, and write a topic sentence.

Model   Assignment: Discuss the reasons plagues spread.

Part given: reasons

Controlling idea: many reasons

Topic sentence: There are many reasons plagues spread.

1. Assignment: What are the effects of pesticides on the food chain?

   Part given: _____

   Controlling idea: _____

   Topic sentence: _____ .

2. Assignment: Give the reasons some societies change from farming to industry.

   Part given: _____

   Controlling idea: _____

   Topic sentence: _____ .

3. Assignment: What are the effects of multiple personality disorder on a patient's family?

   Part given: _____

   Controlling idea: _____

   Topic sentence: _____ .

4. Assignment: Examine the ways meat can be preserved.

   Part given: _____

   Controlling idea: _____

   Topic sentence: _____ .

5. Assignment: Describe the steps in fermentation.

   Part given: _____

   Controlling idea: _____

   Topic sentence: _____ .

Review Questions

Answer the following questions to help you review the material you have covered in this chapter.

1. What three things must a sentence have? (p. 67) _____

   _____   _____

2. What three things can a sentence express? (p. 67) _____

   _____   _____

3. Which two of those things end in a period? (p. 67)

   _____   _____

4. Which is usually the kind of sentence you write in response to your assignments? (p. 67)

   _____

5. What is the difference between the subject of an assignment and the subject of a sentence? (p. 68)

   _____

6. Where do you ask a focusing question to find the subject of a sentence? (p. 68)

   _____

7. What two parts of speech may be a subject in a sentence? (p. 68)

   _____   _____

8. What is the subject of all commands? (p. 68) _____

9. If a group of words has no verb, what else won't it have? (p. 68)

   _____   _____

10. What is a fragment? (p. 69) _____

11. What do a clause and a sentence have in common? (p. 70)

    _____   _____

12. What kind of clause can also be a sentence? (p. 70)

    _____

13. What kind of clause can't be a sentence? (p. 70)

    _____

14. Why not? (p. 70) _____

15. What is one kind of word that makes a clause dependent? (p. 71)

_____

16. What kind of dependent clause must <u>always</u> be joined to an independent clause to make a sentence? (p. 71) _____

17. If you don't join some dependent clauses to independent clauses, what is another way to make them sentences? (p. 71)

_____

18. Give an example of this kind of dependent clause. (p. 71)

_____

19. What is a phrase? (p. 73) _____

20. What are the five kinds of phrases called, based on the words they begin with? (p. 73) _____ _____

_____ _____ _____

21. How are phrases used in sentences? (p. 75) _____

_____ _____

22. What is a topic sentence? (p. 77) _____

23. What are the three parts of a topic sentence? (p. 77)

_____ _____ _____

24. What is another term for the attitude, opinion, or claim in the topic sentence? (p. 78)

_____

Writing Exercises

I. Writing a Paragraph with a Topic Sentence

Look at the paragraph you wrote for Writing Exercise I at the end of Chapter Four and write a topic sentence for it. If the assignment you were responding to already had a controlling idea, use the controlling idea given. If it did not, use focused brainstorming by asking focusing questions in order to come up with one. When you have your topic sentence, write the rest of the paragraph again, making sure all your sentences <u>support</u> the topic sentence. Finally, look at the two paragraphs, and tell why the new one is stronger.

II. Revising Paragraphs with Topic Sentences

Look back at the paragraphs you rewrote for Writing Exercise II in Chapter Four. Make sure your first sentence for each paragraph is a topic sentence that expresses a controlling idea about the topic. Then rewrite the rest of each paragraph to support the controlling idea in the topic sentence of each.

Looking Back and Looking Forward

In this chapter, you have learned how to begin your response to an assignment with a topic sentence that controls the rest of your paper by expressing an attitude, opinion, or claim. In the next chapter, you will learn how to express support for your controlling idea in order to keep the promise you make to the reader.

Chapter six

Agreement and Structure in Paragraphs

In the last chapter, you learned how to set up the topic of a paper in a sentence that expresses your opinion about that topic. In this chapter, you will learn to support that opinion or claim with proof in the form of primary details. Some primary details belong together, while others do not. Learning how to choose primary details that belong together and express them effectively is a matter of understanding how words agree in sentences.

Agreement in Grammar

In sentences that are grammatically correct, certain parts of speech agree with each other. There are several kinds of grammatical **agreement.**

Verb-Subject Agreement

As you recall from Chapter Five, verbs and subjects need each other. In order to work, a sentence must have **verb–subject agreement** in number. In other words, a singular verb needs a singular subject—one that refers to a single person, place, or thing—and a plural verb needs a plural subject—one that refers to more than one person, place, or thing. For instance, you should not write, *There is several reasons for joining the military.* Did you recognize *is* as the verb in the sentence? What is the subject? Do *is* and *reasons* go together? If you said that *is* is singular and *reasons* is plural, you know why they do not go together. How would you rewrite the sentence so that the verb and subject do agree? Very often, plural subjects end in *s,* and singular subjects do not, while plural verbs do not end in *s,* but singular verbs do. Consider the following example.

EXAMPLE: rabbit**s** nibble (plural)

a rabbit nibble**s** (singular)

Before you can see if a verb and subject agree, you must find them in the sentence. When finding verbs in a sentence, remember that verbals—gerunds, participles, and infinitives—are never used as verbs.

In many sentences that make a statement, the subject comes at the beginning of the sentence. However, in the flawed sentence *There is several reasons for joining the military,* the subject is not at the beginning. It may be harder to find the subject when it does not come at the beginning of a sentence, so it will help you to know the three kinds of sentences where this happens.

First, sentences beginning with *Here* or *There* reverse the usual order of subject and verb in the sentence. For instance, consider the assignment *There are several famous landmarks in Mexico City. Describe them.* In the first sentence of this assignment, the verb *are* comes before the subject *landmarks.*

Second, questions reverse the usual order of subject and verb in a sentence. For instance, consider the assignment *What is a whistleblower?* In this question, the verb *is* comes before the subject *whistleblower.*

Third, sentences beginning with a modifying phrase delay the subject until later in the sentence. For instance, consider the assignment *By a series of miscalculations, Christopher Columbus discovered the New World. Discuss the navigational errors that led to this discovery.* The first sentence of this assignment begins with the two prepositional phrases *By a series of miscalculations;* consequently, the subject *Christopher Columbus* does not occur until after the prepositional phrases. Remember that you learned in Chapter Five that phrases have neither verbs nor subjects. In addition to prepositional phrases, present and past participial phrases and infinitive phrases may occur at the beginning of a sentence before the subject.

Exercise One   **Finding Verbs and Subjects**

DIRECTIONS   In the following sentences, first find the complete verb. Then find the subject by asking *Who?* or *What?* before each verb. You will notice that sometimes a main verb and its helping verb can be separated from each other by other words. Finally, tell whether each verb and subject pair is singular or plural.

MODEL   Why do bridges collapse?

Verb: *do collapse*

Subject: *bridges*

Number: *plural*

1. Marsupials have an unusual child-rearing system.

   Verb: _____

   Subject: _____

   Number: _____

2. Discuss entropy.

   Verb: _____

   Subject: _____

   Number: _____

3. There are numerous UFO theories.

   Verb: _____

   Subject: _____

   Number: _____

4. How do comets form?

   Verb: _____

   Subject: _____

   Number: _____

5. Blinded by arrogance, General Custer made several fatal errors at the Battle of the Little Bighorn.

   Verb: _____

   Subject: _____

   Number: _____

Another thing that makes it difficult to find the subject in a sentence is a prepositional phrase <u>after</u> the subject. As you learned in Chapter Three, prepositional phrases begin with a preposition and end with a noun or pronoun. You also know that a subject is either a noun or pronoun, so you can see why it could be easy to mistake the noun or pronoun in a prepositional phrase for the subject of a sentence, especially when they are placed near each other. Consider the sentence *The causes of Russia's Bolshevik revolution were economic, psychological, and political.* What is the verb? When you ask *What <u>were</u> economic, psychological, and political?*, what do you get as the subject? If you say *causes,* you are right; if you say *revolution,* you are wrong. Do you

know why? It is because the subject of a sentence can never be found in a prepositional phrase, and the noun *revolution* is part of the prepositional phrase *of Russia's Bolshevik revolution*. In addition, in that sentence above, the verb does not agree with the
noun in the prepositional phrase. The verb *were* is plural, so the subject must be the
plural noun *causes,* not the singular noun *revolution*. When you are looking for verbs
and subjects, it will help if you <u>cross out all prepositional phrases</u> in the sentence first.

Exercise Two | **Finding More Verbs and Subjects**

DIRECTIONS | In the following sentences, first cross out all the prepositional phrases. Then find the
verb, and ask the appropriate question of it to find the subject. Finally, tell whether
the verb and subject pair is singular or plural.

MODEL | The preparation ~~for an embalming certificate~~ is nonmedical.

Verb: is

Subject: preparation

Number: singular

1. Training for Olympic athletes is a year-round process.

   Verb: _____

   Subject: _____

   Number: _____

2. Members of the International Whaling Commission have censored several nations for violating whaling bans.

   Verb: _____

   Subject: _____

   Number: _____

3. Earning an Associate's degree from a community college takes time and effort.

   Verb: _____

   Subject: _____

   Number: _____

4. Mining for copper is a different process from mining for gold.

   Verb: _____

   Subject: _____

   Number: _____

5. Ironically, fasting for health reasons can have serious negative effects on the body of an adolescent.

Verb: _____

Subject: _____

Number: _____

Exercise Three **Making Verbs and Subjects Agree**

DIRECTIONS   In each of the following sentences, find the verb and subject, and make sure they agree in number. If they do not, rewrite the sentence, changing either the verb or the subject to make them agree. Remember to cross out prepositional phrases first.

MODEL   Members ~~of the Warren Commission~~ still defends their controversial ruling ~~on the assassination of President John F. Kennedy.~~

Verb: _defends_____

Subject: _Members_____

Correction: _Members of the Warren Commission still __defend__ their controversial rul-_

ing on the assassination of President John F. Kennedy.

1. A variety of religious sects have joined forces recently to create larger denominations within the Protestant religion.

Verb: _____

Subject: _____

Correction: _____.

2. In preparation for the primary elections, Presidential candidates from all political parties begin campaigning almost two years before the national election.

Verb: _____

Subject: _____

Correction: _____.

3. A sampling of a wide variety of American art forms fill the homes of many private collectors.

Verb: _____

Subject: _____

Correction: _____.

4. Repeated applications of the medicinal herb Golden Seal often draws out infections.

   Verb: _____

   Subject: _____

   Correction: _____.

5. Graduates from culinary institutes are in great demand to host television cooking shows.

   Verb: _____

   Subject: _____

   Correction: _____.

Verb-Tense Agreement

Just as verbs and subjects must agree with each other in number, when a piece of writing discusses things that take place during the same time period, the verbs in that piece should agree with each other in time or tense. This kind of agreement is called **verb-tense agreement.** Consider the assignment *Leonardo da Vinci was a notable scientist as well as a great artist of the Renaissance. Discuss how his scientific knowledge influenced his art.* Can you find the verbs in the two sentences? Do you know how two of the verbs—*was* and *influenced*—agree with each other? If you think it is because both express a time that has passed, you are correct. These two verbs agree in tense, the past tense.

There are three basic types of verb tenses in the English language. The first type is the **simple verb tenses:** past, present, and future. The figure below shows the placement of these times on a line. Notice just as in real time, the future is ahead of the present, and the past is behind it.

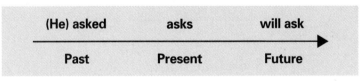

(He) asked	asks	will ask
Past	Present	Future

To help you identify simple verb tenses, keep in mind that many past tense verbs end in *ed* and that all future tense verbs have *will* or *shall* as a helping verb.

Identifying Simple Verb Tenses

DIRECTIONS   In each of the following sentences, identify the complete verb and its tense.

MODEL   Experiments in the desalinization of ocean water will influence future water use.

Verb: will influence

Tense: future

1. Musical historians collected songs from Finnish peasants in the nineteenth century to produce the folk epic *The Kalevala*.

   Verb: _____

   Tense: _____

2. The Sherpa guide, Tenzing Norgay, accompanied Edmund Hillary on the first successful ascent of Mt. Everest.

   Verb: _____

   Tense: _____

3. Due to industrial pollution, the canals of Venice, Italy, need constant maintenance.

   Verb: _____

   Tense: _____

4. Genetically-altered vegetables probably will fill the supermarkets in the twenty-first century.

   Verb: _____

   Tense: _____

5. All clothes designers plan their lines at least a year in advance.

   Verb: _____

   Tense: _____

In addition to the simple verb tenses, there are several other verb tenses which can be used in combination with the simple tenses; however, for now, you should be able to respond to your assignments by using the simple verb tenses covered in this chapter.

Pronoun-Antecedent Agreement

Just as verbs must agree with their subjects as well as with other verbs in a sentence, pronouns must also agree with other words in a sentence. Since the word a pronoun must agree with is called its *antecedent,* this form of grammatical agreement is called **pronoun-antecedent agreement.** An antecedent is the word that the pronoun replaces. That word may be in the same sentence, or it may be elsewhere in the paragraph. For instance, consider the sentence *The* President *is head of the executive branch of government, but* he *also plays several roles in both the judicial and legislative branches.* Which of the two underlined words is the pronoun? Which is the word it replaces? *President* is the antecedent of the pronoun *he* because it is the word *he* replaces. In the preceding sentence, the antecedent *President* comes before the pronoun *he.* In fact, the word *antecedent* comes from the Latin prefix *ante,* which means *before,* and the verb *cedere,* which means *to go,* so *antecedent* means something that goes before something else. In some cases, however, the antecedent follows the pronoun. Consider the sentence *Although* he *performs duties in all branches of government, the* President *is concerned mainly with the executive branch.*

Exercise Five	**Pronouns and Antecedents**

DIRECTIONS   In each of the following sentences, identify the pronoun and its antecedent. There may be more than one pronoun for the antecedent in some sentences.

MODEL   Though they helped to build America's early railroads, Chinese immigrants were discriminated against in many ways.

Pronoun: they _____

Antecedent: immigrants _____

1. Although most students do not expect math exams to have essays, in some classes they are included.

   Pronoun: _____

   Antecedent: _____

2. Free-verse poetry may seem to lack form, but if it is good, it follows some identifiable organizing principle.

   Pronoun: _____   Pronoun: _____

   Antecedent: _____

3. Because of recent medical advances in the treatment of infertility, many women who thought they would never bear children are now able to conceive.

Pronoun: _____ Pronoun: _____

Antecedent: _____

4. King Henry VIII of England caused the separation of church and state when he insisted on divorcing Catherine of Aragon in order to marry Anne Boleyn.

Pronoun: _____

Antecedent: _____

5. Nationalism is defined as fierce pride in a person's own country, but in some cases it can go too far.

Pronoun: _____

Antecedent: _____

Pronoun–Antecedent Agreement in Number

Pronouns must agree with their antecedents in several ways. First, like verbs and their subjects, they must agree in number. If the antecedent is singular, the pronoun that replaces it must also be singular; if the antecedent is plural, its pronoun replacement must be plural, too. For instance, you would not write *There are a number of things a homeowner can do in the yard before they call a professional landscaper.* Why not? If you say the pronoun *they* is plural, but its antecedent *homeowner* is singular, you are right.

Exercise Six

Pronoun–Antecedent Agreement in Number

Directions In each of the following sentences, identify the pronoun and its antecedent; identify the number of each; and correct the flawed sentences so that the pronoun and antecedent agree in number. Sometimes this means you will also have to change the verb or the noun so that they agree in number.

Model When a person cleans for a living, they must realize that different-sized jobs require different methods.

Pronoun: they   Number: plural

Antecedent: person   Number: singular

Correction: When people clean for a living, they must realize that different-sized jobs require different methods.

1. A woman approaching menopause is advised to engage in at least half an hour a day of weight-bearing exercise if they hope to minimize loss of bone density.

Pronoun: _____ Number: _____

Antecedent: _____ Number: _____

Correction: _____.

2. Even though proteins make up a necessary food group, most nutritionists say they are not as important to maintaining health as grains and legumes.

   Pronoun: _____ Number: _____

   Antecedent: _____ Number: _____

   Correction: _____.

3. Turlough O'Carolan, the blind sixteenth-century Irish harpist, never wrote out his music, but modern musicians still play them on the hammer dulcimer.

   Pronoun: _____ Number: _____

   Antecedent: _____ Number: _____

   Correction: _____.

4. Some educators believe that children taught in bilingual classrooms learn better, but other educators believe they do not.

   Pronoun: _____ Number: _____

   Antecedent: _____ Number: _____

   Correction: _____.

5. What many people think elevates a skill to an art is the ability to make things look easy when it is not.

   Pronoun: _____ Number: _____

   Antecedent: _____ Number: _____

   Correction: _____.

Pronouns must also agree with their antecedents in gender. Antecedents are feminine, masculine, or neutral. If an antecedent is feminine, it must have a feminine pronoun; if an antecedent is masculine, it must have a masculine pronoun; and if an antecedent is neutral, it must be replaced by a form of the neuter pronoun *it*. While gender errors are uncommon, they can occur when writers refer to ships, planes, colleges, and countries without realizing that traditionally these are all feminine. For instance, you should not write *While Howard Hughes' transport plane* The Spruce Goose *never flew commercially, it made one brief flight.* Why not? What is the antecedent, and what is its gender? What is the pronoun? How would you correct the sentence so that the antecedent and pronoun agree?

Finally, pronouns must agree with the nouns or pronouns they replace in case. In English there are three cases: the *subjective case,* the *objective case,* and the *possessive case.* Here are the three cases for each of the personal pronouns:

	Subjective	Objective	Possessive
Singular			
First person pronoun	I	me	my, mine
Second person pronoun	you	you	your, yours
Third person pronoun	he, she, it	him, her, it	his, her, hers, its
Plural			
First person pronoun	we	us	our, ours
Second person pronoun	you	you	your, yours
Third person pronoun	they	them	their, theirs

When a pronoun is used to replace the subject of a sentence, it must be in the **subjective case.** In the sentence *Isadora Duncan danced with the creative abandon of a child,* you can replace *Isadora Duncan* with the subjective pronoun *She* because both are subjects. When a pronoun is used to replace an object in a sentence, it must be in the **objective case.** Consider the assignment *Electrons are able to circle the nucleus in an atom in several ways. Describe the ways.* You can replace *the ways* in the second sentence with the objective pronoun *them.* When a pronoun is used to replace a noun that shows ownership, it must be in the **possessive case.** In the sentence *In Russia, Catherine the Great's seductive powers often made political allies out of ambassadors,* you can replace *Catherine the Great's* with the possessive pronoun *her.*

Exercise Seven Pronoun–Antecedent Agreement in Case

DIRECTIONS   Each of the following sentences has one or more underlined nouns. Identify the number of each noun as singular or plural and the case of each noun as subjective, objective, or possessive. Then rewrite each sentence, using a personal pronoun in the correct number and case for the underlined noun or pronoun.

MODEL   Throughout a brilliant career, <u>Marlon Brando</u> used an acting technique known as the Method.

Noun: <u>Marlon Brando</u>

Number: <u>singular</u>

Case: <u>subjective</u>

Rewritten sentence: <u>Throughout a brilliant career, he used an acting technique known as the Method.</u>

1. <u>American Sign Language</u> is one of many sign languages used around the world.

   Noun: _____

   Number: _____

   Case: _____

   Rewritten sentence: _____.

2. Compare and contrast the ways <u>Democrats and Republicans</u> attempt to balance the national budget.

   Noun: _____

   Number: _____

   Case: _____

   Rewritten sentence: _____.

3. Many authors have used <u>pseudonyms</u>, like Karen Blixen, who wrote under the pen name Isak Dinesen.

   Noun: _____

   Number: _____

   Case: _____

   Rewritten sentence: _____.

4. Satellite photographs taken from space have influenced <u>cartographers'</u> maps.

   Noun: _____

   Number: _____

   Case: _____

   Rewritten sentence: _____.

5. When <u>a student</u> takes an accounting course, a knowledge of computer spreadsheets is helpful.

   Noun: _____

   Number: _____

   Case: _____

   Rewritten sentence: _____.

Objective and Subjective Case Pronouns

You are used to seeing objects following action verbs. For instance, in the sentence *Instances of game-fixing have always plagued sports,* the direct object of the action verb *have plagued* is the noun *sports.* If you want to replace that noun with a pronoun, you will have to use a plural pronoun in the <u>objective</u> case, which is *them.* Sometimes, however, nouns or pronouns that follow verbs are not direct objects. When a noun or pronoun follows a condition verb, it means the same as the subject of the sentence and must therefore be in the <u>subjective</u> case. For instance, in the sentence *It was Shoeless Joe Jackson who was first implicated in the Chicago White Sox baseball scandal in 1919,* the personal pronoun in the subjective case you would use to replace *Shoeless Joe Jackson* is *he.* The rewritten sentence is *It was <u>he</u> who was first implicated in the Chicago White Sox baseball scandal in 1919.*

Exercise Eight

Using Objective and Subjective Case Pronouns

DIRECTIONS In each of the following sentences, pick a noun to replace and identify its number. Next, identify the verb that precedes or follows it, and tell whether it is an action or condition verb. Identify the case of the replacement pronoun. Finally, rewrite the sentence using the appropriate pronoun.

MODEL When Molly answers the phone, she says, "This is Molly speaking."

Word to be replaced: Molly _____ Number: singular _____

Verb: is _____ Type: condition _____

Pronoun case: subjective _____

Sentence: When Molly answers the phone, she says, "This is <u>she</u> speaking." _____

1. The best-known pointillist artist was Georges Seurat.

   Word to be replaced: _____ Number: _____

   Verb: _____ Type: _____

   Pronoun case: _____

   Sentence: _____.

2. Farmers often cover vegetables during cold snaps for protection.

   Word to be replaced: _____ Number: _____

   Verb: _____ Type: _____

   Pronoun case: _____

   Sentence: _____.

3. Doctors have mostly replaced the plaster of Paris cast with modern technologies.

   Word to be replaced: _____ Number: _____

   Verb: _____ Type: _____

   Pronoun case: _____

   Sentence: _____.

4. Diviners are people who search for water with forked sticks called divining rods.

   Word to be replaced: _____ Number: _____

   Verb: _____ Type: _____

   Pronoun case: _____

   Sentence: _____.

5. Some people blame poltergeists for unexplained noises and mayhem in their homes.

   Word to be replaced: _____ Number: _____

   Verb: _____ Type: _____

   Pronoun case: _____

   Sentence: _____.

Agreement in Structure

Just like a sentence has several grammatical elements that must agree, a paragraph has structural elements that must agree. Structural agreement is called **parallelism.** The structure of a paragraph begins with the topic sentence, which, as you learned in Chapter Five, expresses the topic and controlling idea of the paper. The rest of the structure is provided by at least two primary details, which support your topic.

When you learned in Chapter Four how to narrow the subject of an assignment to a particular topic, you also learned about wholes and parts. Now you can think of the topic sentence as a whole pie and primary details as parts or slices of that pie. Consider the following pie figures in response to the assignment *Describe a relative's most annoying habit.*

Can you see that the topic sentence—*Nagging is my mother's most annoying habit*—is like a whole pie, which is larger than the three slices in the figure next to it—*about my clothes, about my car, about my friends?* The three slices, on the other hand, are all equal in size to each other. In fact, when you put them together again,

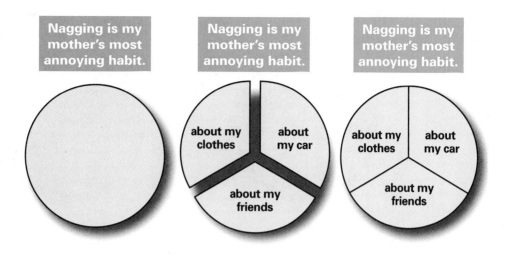

they form the whole pie. The relationship of the parts to the whole is that they are **subcategories** of the whole. The relationship of the parts to each other is that no matter how many parts you cut the pie into, they must all be the *same size* subcategory, smaller than the whole; they must all come from the *same kind* of pie, the one in the topic sentence; and they must all be expressed in *similar language*. Consider the following flawed examples:

EXAMPLE 1:

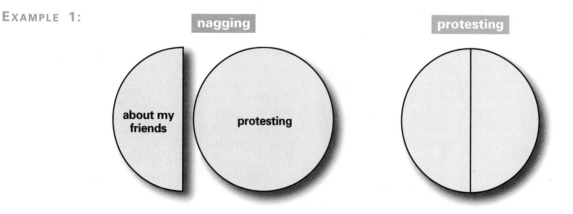

Explanation: *Nagging* is large enough to be the topic in the topic sentence *Nagging is my mother's most annoying habit.* The phrase *about my friends* is a smaller part of *nagging,* so it could be one of your primary details; however, *protesting* is the same size as the whole pie *nagging,* not the part *about my friends,* so it cannot be a primary detail. In fact, it would have to be another whole pie.

EXAMPLE 2:

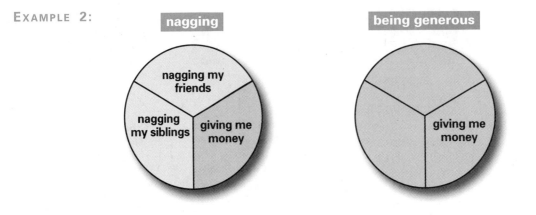

Explanation: Again, *nagging* is large enough to be the topic of the topic sentence *Nagging is my mother's most annoying habit.* All of the phrases—*nagging my friends, giving me money, nagging my siblings*—are small enough to be primary details, but they do not all come from the same pie. *Nagging my friends* and *nagging my siblings* come from the pie *nagging* because they both tell who is being nagged, but *giving me money* comes from a different pie, like *being generous,* which does not even respond to this assignment because it is not an <u>annoying</u> habit.

EXAMPLE 3:

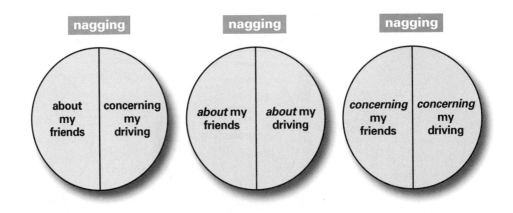

Explanation: About my friends and *concerning my driving* both come from the same pie expressed in the topic sentence *Nagging is my mother's most annoying habit* because they are both things my mother nags about; however, they are not expressed in the same language. Since each phrase satisfies the other two requirements of a primary detail, same size and same kind, we can use the language from either one for both. We could say *about my friends* and *about my driving,* or we could say *concerning my friends* and *concerning my driving.*

Exercise Nine

Building Structure From Wholes and Parts

DIRECTIONS Examine the following structural pies. Each should give only one whole topic above the figure of a whole pie that could be expressed in a topic sentence; in addition, there should be two equal parts or slices of it inside the whole. Correct those pies that do not express this relationship of parts to wholes, and explain your reason for correcting: wrong size, wrong kind, wrong language. Sometimes more than one thing in an item will need correcting.

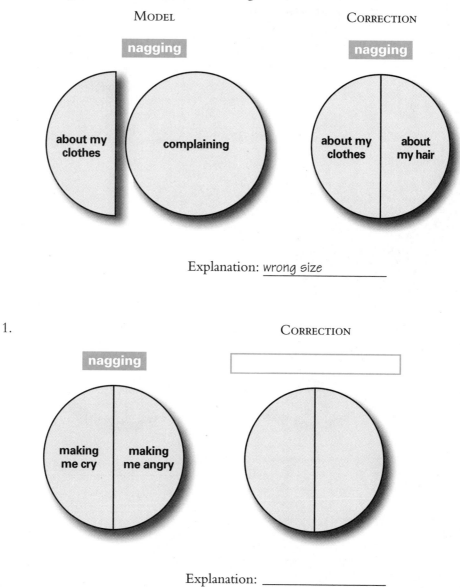

MODEL

CORRECTION

nagging

nagging

about my clothes

complaining

about my clothes

about my hair

Explanation: _wrong size_

1.

CORRECTION

nagging

making me cry

making me angry

Explanation: _____

2.   Correction

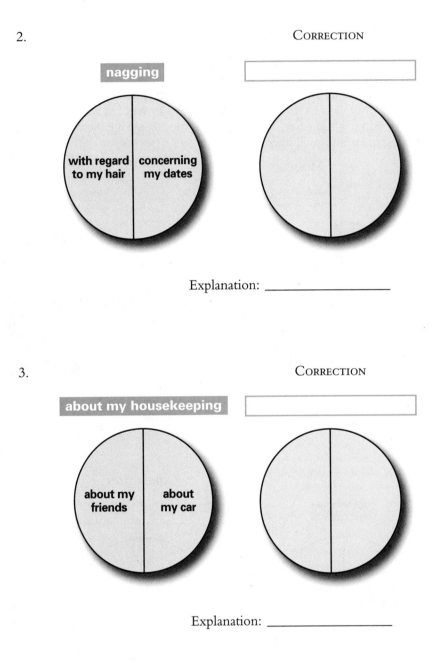

nagging

| with regard to my hair | concerning my dates |

Explanation: _____

3.   Correction

about my housekeeping

| about my friends | about my car |

Explanation: _____

4.

CORRECTION

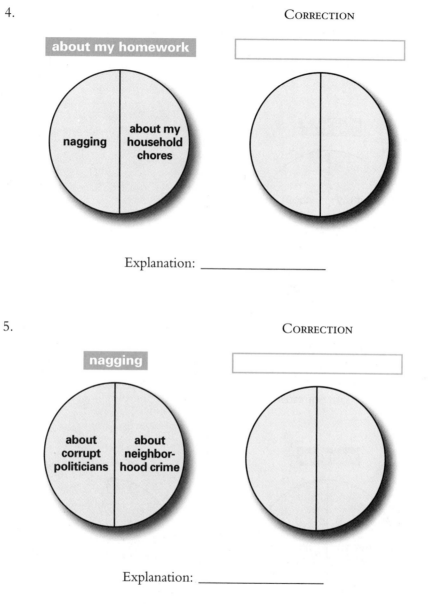

Explanation: _____

5.

CORRECTION

Explanation: _____

When the parts of a whole are expressed in the same language, this kind of grammatical agreement is also called parallelism. The way to divide a whole into parallel parts is to ask a focusing question of the whole and answer that same question for each part of the whole. For instance, look again at the first structural pie:

What focusing question do all the parts answer? If you say that they answer *What does my mother nag me about?*, you are right.

Do not be fooled by parts that are expressed in parallel language but do not answer the same question. Consider the following pie:

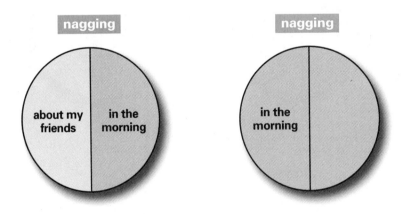

In this pie, both parts are expressed by prepositional phrases; however, they do not answer the same question. The first part answers the focusing question *What does my mother nag me about?* What question does the second part answer?

<u>Exercise Ten</u>   ## Correcting Structure

DIRECTIONS   For the following structural pies that respond to the assignment *Describe the rude behavior of some preschool children,* tell which focusing question each part answers. If any of the questions for a part is different, fix the part so that all parts of the pie answer the same focusing question.

MODEL

rude behavior

Focusing question 1: <u>How do they behave rudely?</u>

Focusing question 2: <u>How do they behave rudely?</u>

Focusing question 3: <u>When do they behave this way?</u>

Correction part 3: <u>   stalling at bedtime</u>

1.

rude behavior

Focusing question 1: _____

Focusing question 2: _____

Correction Part _____: _____

2.

rude behavior

1 at the beach
2 in the summer
3 in school

Focusing question 1: _____

Focusing question 2: _____

Focusing question 3: _____

Correction part _____: _____

3.

rude behavior

1 at naptime
2 because they're tired
3 because they're hungry

Focusing question 1: _____

Focusing question 2: _____

Focusing question 3: _____

Correction part _____: _____

4.

rude behavior

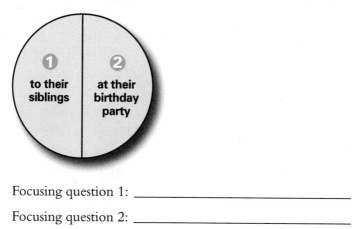

① swearing	**②** biting
③ because they're angry	**④** at lunch

Focusing question 1: _____

Focusing question 2: _____

Focusing question 3: _____

Focusing question 4: _____

Correction part _____: _____

Correction part _____: _____

5.

rude behavior

① to their siblings	**②** at their birthday party

Focusing question 1: _____

Focusing question 2: _____

Correction part _____: _____

From Parts to Primary Details

Now you see that in an effective paragraph, the whole and the parts of that whole will agree with each other in what they say and how they say it. In a paragraph where the whole is expressed as a topic sentence, the parts become **primary details.** To make primary details out of parts, you need to put the parts in whole sentences.

Consider the following corrected model for Exercise Ten. Remember that the model responds to the assignment *Describe the rude behavior of some preschool children:*

A topic sentence you could form from the assignment is *The behavior of some preschool children is rude.* The parts are not only subcategories of the topic but also prove or support the controlling idea of the topic sentence, which is *rude.* To make primary details out of these parts, you need to make complete sentences out of them. Here are several ways to do that, using the first part:

> Some preschool children spit.
> One kind of rude behavior of some preschool children is spitting.
> Spitting is one rude behavior of some preschool children.

Any of these sentences can be a primary detail for the first part. Just remember to use the <u>same</u> language or grammatical pattern for <u>each</u> primary detail because, as you recall, when primary details answer the same focusing question and are expressed in the same grammatical pattern, they are parallel.

Exercise Eleven

Turning Parts into Primary Details

DIRECTIONS For each of the following items, turn the parts that support the topic sentence into primary details by expressing them in complete sentences that are parallel to each other.

MODEL

Steven Spielberg's films show a fascination with childhood.

① supernatural elements **② children as heroes**

Primary detail 1: His films use supernatural elements.

Primary detail 2: His films use children as heroes.

1. **There are several ways to create hybrid plants.**

① grafting parts **② cross-fertilizing seeds**

Primary detail 1: _____.

Primary detail 2: _____.

2.

Psychologists teach us a number of ways to relieve stress.

1 biofeed-back
2 yoga
3 support groups
4 medi-tation

Primary detail 1: _____.

Primary detail 2: _____.

Primary detail 3: _____.

Primary detail 4: _____.

3.

Besides riding in planes, humans have developed many ways to satisfy their urge to fly.

1 hang-gliding
2 parasailing
3 hot-air ballooning

Primary detail 1: _____.

Primary detail 2: _____.

Primary detail 3: _____.

4.

Lawyers employ courtroom advisors to help them with several aspects of a trial.

❶ defendant's clothes

❷ jury selection

Primary detail 1: _____ .

Primary detail 2: _____ .

5.

Through the ages, people have used various instruments to measure time with varying degrees of accuracy.

❶ sundial

❷ hourglass

❸ atomic clock

Primary detail 1: _____ .

Primary detail 2: _____ .

Primary detail 3: _____ .

Review Questions

Answer the following questions to help you review the material you have learned in this chapter.

1. In what way must verbs and subjects agree? (p. 85) _____

2. What three kinds of sentences do not have subjects at the beginning? (p. 86)

    a) _____

    b) _____

    c) _____

3. Of these, which two reverse the usual order of subject and verb in a sentence? (p. 86) _____ and _____

4. When does the subject of a sentence occur in a prepositional phrase? (p. 88)

    _____

5. What must you cross out when looking for the verb and subject of a sentence? (p. 88) _____

6. Several verbs in the same sentence should agree in time or (p. 90) _____.

7. What are the three basic verb tenses? (p. 90) _____,

    _____, and _____

8. What is the word a pronoun agrees with called? (p. 92) _____

9. Where does it usually come in relation to the pronoun in a sentence? (p. 92)

    _____

10. What are three ways a pronoun agrees with its antecedent? (p. 93–95)

    _____, _____, and _____

11. What are two things that are unexpectedly female gender? (p. 94)

    _____ _____

12. What are the three pronoun cases? (p. 95) _____,

    _____, and _____

13. When a pronoun follows a condition verb, the pronoun must be in which case? (p. 97) _____

14. What must agree in a paragraph besides grammar? (p. 98) _____

15. What structural element of a paragraph did you learn about in this chapter, and how many of them do you need in a paragraph? (p. 98)

_____ and _____

16. The primary details, or parts of a whole, are like slices of a _____. (p. 98)

17. What three ways must the parts agree with each other? (p. 98)

_____ , _____ , and _____

18. Parts of a whole that are expressed in the same language demonstrate

_____. (p. 104)

19. What must all the parts, or primary details, answer? (p. 108) _____

20. How do you turn parts into primary details? (p. 108) _____

Writing Exercises

I. Writing Structural Paragraphs

For each of the following structural pies, construct a topic sentence and primary details in the present tense.

1.

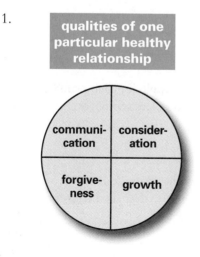

2.

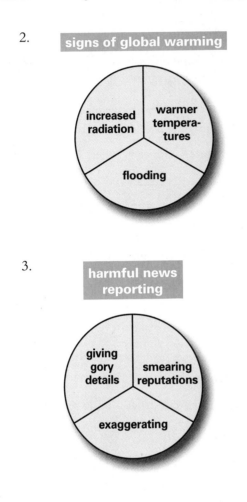

signs of global warming

increased radiation

warmer temperatures

flooding

3.

harmful news reporting

giving gory details

smearing reputations

exaggerating

II. Supporting the Parts

Choose one structural pie and add an example for each primary detail to explain it. Express that example in one or more complete sentences, using present tense. This is a skeletal paragraph.

III. Using Pronouns

Rewrite the skeletal paragraph in Writing Exercise II above, substituting pronouns for nouns wherever appropriate. Remember to make the pronouns agree with their antecedents in number, gender, and case.

IV. Revising Paragraphs for Structure

Look back at the paragraphs you rewrote for Writing Exercise II in Chapter Five. Use focused brainstorming, asking focusing questions of your topic sentence to come up with two or three primary details, which you should express in complete sentences. For each paragraph, insert the first of these primary details directly after the topic sentence. Then insert the other one or two primary details at places you think are appropriate, leaving room between the primary details for the support you will learn about in Chapter Eight.

Looking Back and Looking Forward

In this chapter, you have learned how parts of a sentence agree with each other and how the parts of a paragraph—the primary details—agree in what they say and how they say it. You have also seen how primary details support or prove the controlling idea in a topic sentence. In the next chapter, you will practice setting up this structure for paragraphs in response to specific assignments.

Completing the Skeletal Paragraph

I n Chapter Six, you learned how to support your topic sentence by dividing it into primary details that are parallel in language and structure. In this chapter, you will add a conclusion. These structural elements form a skeleton for your finished paragraph. This skeleton is a primary structure.

Conclusions

The purpose of a **conclusion** in a paragraph is to make the paragraph feel finished. It does this by returning to the main focus of the paragraph expressed in the topic sentence. As you learned in Chapter Six, the primary details support the claim that the topic sentence makes by <u>stating</u> it. However, the conclusion examines what the whole paragraph suggests by <u>implying</u> it. In other words, an effective conclusion does not just repeat the topic sentence; it arrives at a resolution. For instance, consider this figure from Chapter Six and the paragraph that could be written from it.

Paragraph:

> Nagging is my mother's most annoying habit. She nags me about my clothes. She nags me about my car. She nags me about my friends.

The topic sentence states that nagging is my mother's most annoying habit, but the topic sentence together with the primary details implies several possible conclusions:

1. If I want to live in peace with my mother, I have two choices: learn to live with her nagging or fix the things she nags about.

2. My mother's nagging makes her difficult to live with, so it may be time for me to get a place of my own.

3. While my mother's nagging about my clothes, car, and friends shows she is concerned about me, it still annoys me.

Any of these conclusions would be an appropriate finish for the above paragraph. Did you notice that Conclusion 3 does something that the others don't do? What does it do? Did you see that it repeats the three primary details before expressing what they imply?

Sometimes you know what you want to say to conclude your paragraph even before you finish writing it. Other times, however, you may need some help finding the implications of your paragraph. When this happens, look at your topic sentence and primary details, and then ask the conclusion question *So what?* For instance, Conclusion 2 above answers the question *So what?* by concluding that the three kinds of nagging are so annoying that it might be time to move.

Exercise One

Writing Conclusions

DIRECTIONS For each of the following paragraphs, examine the implications of the topic sentence and primary details, write a conclusion question that refers to them, and then write a conclusion that answers that question.

MODEL Paragraph:

> Migraine headaches can result from several conditions. They can result from food allergies. They can result from stress. They can result from hormonal changes.

Conclusion question: <u>If migraine headaches can result from all these conditions, so what?</u>

Conclusion: <u>Because migraine headaches can have different causes, they may also require different treatments.</u>

1. Paragraph:

   Literary analysis examines different aspects of a written work. It examines the characters. It examines the plot. It examines the setting. It examines the theme. It examines the tone and mood. It examines the symbols.

   Conclusion question: _____?

   Conclusion: _____.

2. Paragraph:

   For most pets, conscientious care requires attention to some of the same health concerns humans share. It requires dental care. It requires nail care. It requires vaccinations. It requires blood pressure monitoring.

   Conclusion question: _____?

   Conclusion: _____.

3. Paragraph:

   Our quest for new and different entertainment has resulted in many kinds of amusement areas. It has resulted in water parks. It has resulted in swap meets. It has resulted in street fairs. It has resulted in re-created historical villages.

   Conclusion question: _____?

   Conclusion: _____.

4. Paragraph:

   Despite modern scientific understanding of cause and effect, some human beings still cling to old superstitions. Some people cling to the superstition that breaking a mirror brings seven years of bad luck. Some people cling to the superstition that opening an umbrella indoors brings bad luck. Some people cling to the superstition that finding a four-leaf clover brings good luck.

   Conclusion question: _____?

   Conclusion: _____.

5. Paragraph:

   Although some people find mathematics difficult, it is useful in everyone's life. It is useful in balancing a checkbook. It is useful in buying a house. It is useful in cooking. It is useful in tailoring.

Conclusion question: _____?

Conclusion: _____.

Flawed Conclusions

Exercise One demonstrates that a variety of conclusions may be possible for a single paragraph; however, that does not mean that <u>any</u> conclusion is always appropriate. There are several reasons a conclusion might not be effective for a paragraph. Consider the following flawed conclusions for the paragraph written from the figure on page 99.

> Nagging is my mother's most annoying habit. She nags me about my clothes. She nags me about my car. She nags me about my friends.

Flawed conclusion 1: Although my mother nags me, she is still a great mother.

Even though this conclusion mentions nagging, its main point—*great mother*—has nothing to do with the focus of the paragraph, which is her annoying habit of nagging. It belongs to a different paragraph, one whose topic sentence might be *My mother supports me in many ways.* The error in this conclusion is an inappropriate **change of direction.**

Flawed conclusion 2: Nothing I do pleases my mother.

This conclusion is flawed because it is not proven by the paragraph, which deals with <u>only</u> three areas of the writer's life—clothes, car, and friends. The error in this conclusion is one of **exaggeration.**

Flawed conclusion 3: Nagging is definitely one of my mother's most annoying habits.

This conclusion is flawed because it simply repeats the topic sentence. In other words, the error in this conclusion is that it **does not answer the question** *So what?*

Exercise Two ## Correcting Flawed Conclusions

DIRECTIONS Read each of the following paragraphs. Tell which of the three reasons discussed in this chapter explains why each conclusion is flawed. Then rewrite the conclusion.

MODEL The British monarchy has always had its critics, but modern critics have been particularly vocal about the things they object to. They object to the financial burden of supporting the Royal Family. They object to the sexual escapades of the Royal Family. They object to the fact that the Royal Family is more decorative than functional. <u>Despite these objections, there will always be a Royal Family.</u>

Errors: *change of direction and doesn't answer So what?*

Rewritten conclusion: *If people continue to feel this way, in the future, Britain's monarchy may finally become a thing of the past.*

1. Paragraph: Despite their fierce image, sharks have had many beneficial uses for mankind. They have provided cartilage for cancer treatments. They have provided fins for soup. They have provided skin for sandpaper. Sharks could be the savior of mankind.

   Error: _____

   Rewritten conclusion: _____ .

2. Paragraph: People have demonstrated social protest in many ways. Some people have organized marches of social protest. Some people have written and sung songs of social protest. Some people have written plays and novels of social protest. Some people have painted pictures expressing social protest. Some people have protested social ills in a variety of ways.

   Error: _____

   Rewritten conclusion: _____ .

3. Paragraph: Mail order shopping can pose problems for shoppers. Shoppers may have to cope with unexpectedly difficult assembly of merchandise. Shoppers may receive merchandise of lesser quality than portrayed in the catalog. Shoppers may wait for merchandise a long time before learning that it is permanently out of stock. Shopping by catalog is clearly a bad idea.

   Error: _____

   Rewritten conclusion: _____ .

4. Paragraph: Children who train excessively in sports at an early age can damage their health. They can stunt bone growth. They can delay normal sexual development. They can develop addictive behavior. Obviously, parents are to blame for the problems of young athletes.

   Error: _____

   Rewritten conclusion: _____ .

5. Paragraph: **Several ways of decorating the human body involve painful procedures. Tattooing is painful. Decorative scarring is painful. Body-piercing is painful. Body-decorating can be painful.**

Error: _____

Rewritten conclusion: _____ .

Exercise Three

Correcting Exercise One

DIRECTIONS

Now that you have a better idea of how to write an appropriate conclusion, review the conclusions you wrote for Exercise One. Rewrite the conclusions that make any of the three errors you identified for Exercise Two.

Review Questions

Answer the following questions to help you review the material you have learned in this chapter.

1. What is the purpose of a conclusion? (p. 116) _____

2. How does a conclusion accomplish its purpose? (p. 116) _____

3. While the topic sentence states the main idea of a paragraph, what do the topic sentence and primary details together do? (p. 117) _____

4. What question should your conclusion answer? (p. 117) _____

5. What are three reasons a conclusion might not be effective for a paragraph? (p. 119) _____   _____   _____

Writing Exercises

I. Writing Paragraphs with Structure

The following exercise will help you review what you have learned so far. For each assignment, set up the structure of a paragraph. If necessary, narrow the subject of the assignment to a topic and add a controlling idea. Now form a topic sentence. Ask an appropriate focusing question three times of the topic sentence to come up with primary details. Then ask the conclusion question *So what?* Finally, put all of your answers together in a skeletal paragraph, using complete sentences. (To check your structure, you can put your topic sentence and primary details into the structural pie you learned about in the figure on page 99 in Chapter Six.)

MODEL   Assignment: Describe your funniest relative.

Focusing question: Who is my funniest relative? _____

Topic: Uncle Benny _____

Topic sentence: Uncle Benny is my funniest relative. _____

Focusing question: How is Uncle Benny funny? _____

Primary details: He makes silly faces. _____

He does animal impressions. _____

He pulls party gags. _____

Conclusion question: If Uncle Benny does funny things, so what? _____

Conclusion: Because he makes me laugh, Uncle Benny is the relative I call when I

need cheering up. _____

Paragraph: Uncle Benny is my funniest relative. He makes silly faces. He does animal impressions. He pulls party gags. Because he makes me laugh, Uncle Benny is the relative I call when I need cheering up.

1. Assignment: Describe the effects of an eating disorder.

Focusing question: _____?

Topic: _____

Controlling idea: _____

Topic sentence: _____ .

Focusing question: _____?

Primary details: _____

_____

_____

Conclusion question: _____?

Conclusion: _____ .

Paragraph: _____

_____

_____

2. Assignment: Describe a person who makes you uncomfortable.

Focusing question: _____?

Topic: _____

Controlling idea: _____

Topic sentence: _____.

Focusing question: _____?

Primary details: _____

_____

_____

_____

Conclusion question: _____?

Conclusion: _____.

Paragraph: _____

_____

_____

3. Assignment: Describe how to play a game that requires strategy.

Focusing question: _____?

Topic: _____

Controlling idea: _____

Topic sentence: _____.

Focusing question: _____?

Primary details: _____

_____

_____

Conclusion question: _____?

Conclusion: _____.

Paragraph: _____

_____

_____

II. Revising with Structure

Look back at the paragraphs you rewrote for Writing Exercise IV in Chapter Six. Paying particular attention to the topic sentences and primary details for each, examine the last sentence in each to see that it is an appropriate conclusion. If it is not, rewrite it.

Looking Back and Looking Forward

In this chapter, you have learned to conclude the structure of a paragraph, which is like a skeleton. In the next chapter, you will learn how to put flesh on the bones of this skeleton.

Chapter eight

Developing
Support

In Chapter Seven, you learned how to write the skeletal paragraph. Keep in mind that this paragraph needs development to put flesh on its bones. Development in the form of secondary details explains the primary details and makes them clearer. In this chapter, you will learn how to add this kind of development to your skeletal paragraph.

Secondary Details

As you recall from Chapter Four, every time you break a whole into smaller parts, you are going from one level of generality to another that is narrower or more specific. For example, a primary detail is more specific than a topic sentence, and a secondary detail is more specific than a primary detail. In fact, a **secondary detail** is the most specific part of your paragraph. When a secondary detail is fully developed, it will be longer than the primary detail it supports and may even require several sentences.

You can think of a secondary detail as an *example* of the primary detail it supports. When you write an effective example, you make the primary detail real to the reader by directing his senses. In other words, you make your reader *see* the same picture, *hear* the same sound, *taste* the same flavor, *feel* the same texture, and *smell* the same scent as you see, hear, taste, feel, and smell. Consider the following examples.

EXAMPLE 1:

Topic sentence: My friend is a slob.

Primary detail: She makes a mess of her clothes.

Secondary detail: She often drops food on her clothes.

Even though this secondary detail is an example of the primary detail because it goes from *makes a mess* to *drops food,* it is not as specific as it should be. What questions does it still leave you with? Did you notice that you can't see how the friend makes a mess because you don't know what kind of food she drops or what clothes she drops it on. You will find the following example more effective because it answers those questions.

EXAMPLE 2:

Topic sentence: My friend is a slob.

Primary detail: She makes a mess of her clothes.

Secondary detail: Whenever we go out for Italian food, she dribbles so much chunky spaghetti sauce onto her white silk blouse that it tumbles down her chest like loose gravel rolls down a hillside.

The secondary detail in Example 2 is better than the secondary detail in Example 1 because it answers all the questions and lets the reader see the primary detail.

Can you tell how the secondary detail in Example 2 makes a picture clear to you? By practicing a few techniques, you can write secondary details that answer all the questions a reader may have about how your primary detail looks, sounds, tastes, feels, and smells.

Techniques for Writing Secondary Details

Four techniques help you write effective secondary details:

1. use strong verbs

2. use specific nouns

3. use modifiers when necessary

4. use comparisons

Use Strong Verbs

One way you can develop effective secondary details is to choose **strong verbs** instead of weak ones. The secondary detail in Example 2 replaces the weak verb *drops* from Example 1 with the strong verb *dribbles,* which lets you see the action more vividly.

Exercise One

DIRECTIONS

Replacing Weak Verbs

For each of the following sentences, replace the weak verb with a strong one. You may want to use a thesaurus to help you find strong verbs that mean the same as the underlined words.

MODEL   Jackie <u>threw</u> the softball.

Revision: <u>*Jackie hurled the softball.*</u>

1. The actor <u>complained</u> about his small part.

   Revision: _____.

2. She <u>thought</u> about the handsome new student in class.

   Revision: _____.

3. Fido <u>ran</u> after the stick.

   Revision: _____.

4. The teacher <u>looked</u> at the tardy student as he <u>walked</u> into class.

   Revision: _____.

5. The boxer <u>hit</u> his opponent.

   Revision: _____.

Don't be fooled by weak verbs that have adverbs to describe them. If the verb is weak, even a modifier won't help it. For instance, if you add the adverb *slowly* to the weak verb *drops,* you can see that *drops slowly* still does not create as specific a picture as the strong verb *dribbles.* A strong verb can replace not only a weak verb but also a weak verb-adverb combination.

Remember from Chapter One that some verbs have a word that follows them which is part of the verb. For instance, consider the sentence *Sheila* <u>picked at</u> *her parsnips.* In this sentence, *at* is part of the main verb *picked.* Don't confuse weak verb-adverb combinations with strong verbs made up of two words. For instance, *Sheila* <u>fussily ate</u> *her parsnips* uses a weak verb-adverb combination that can be replaced effectively by the strong two-word verb *picked at.*

Exercise Two   **Replacing Weak Verb-Adverb Combinations**

DIRECTIONS   Replace each of the following weak verb-adverb pairs with one or more strong verbs that mean the same.

1. The mayor <u>walked angrily</u> into her office.

   Revision: _____.

2. When unexpected guests arrived, Keith <u>quickly put</u> his dirty underwear in the clothes hamper.

   Revision: _____.

3. The new recruit <u>moved slowly</u> to formation after reveille.

   Revision: _____.

4. Sylvia <u>ate</u> her peanut butter sandwich <u>quickly</u> on her fifteen-minute break.

   Revision: _____.

5. The commuter <u>watched angrily</u> as the train left the station without him.

   Revision: _____.

Use Specific Nouns

Another way you can develop effective secondary details is to choose **specific nouns.** The secondary detail in Example 2 replaces the general noun *clothes* with the specific noun *blouse,* which lets you see what kind of clothes the friend is making a mess of.

Exercise Three
Replacing General Nouns

DIRECTIONS   Replace the general nouns below with nouns that are more specific.

MODEL   Ling was able to identify a rare <u>bird</u> with her binoculars.

   Revision: <u>Ling was able to identify a rare Blue-Footed Booby with her binoculars.</u>

1. For his final exam in Auto Mechanics II, Michael fixed the transmission on a <u>car.</u>

   Revision: _____.

2. The archeology students discovered <u>parts</u> of an <u>animal</u> when they excavated the dig site.

   Revision: _____.

3. In meteorology class today, we learned about the origin of <u>storms.</u>

   Revision: _____.

4. The students' favorite module in Home Economics was making <u>desserts.</u>

   Revision: _____.

5. The use of miniatures to create the <u>monster</u> in <u>the movie</u> is a technique not often used anymore by filmmakers.

   Revision: _____.

Use Modifiers When Necessary

Another way you can develop secondary details is to use modifiers when necessary. As you recall from Chapter Three, modifiers are <u>adjectives</u>, which describe nouns and pronouns, and <u>adverbs</u>, which describe verbs, adjectives, and other adverbs. Don't forget that modifiers do not have to be single words; they can be phrases or clauses. For instance, you could say *the dented Honda,* or *the Honda with a dent,* or *the Honda that has a dent.*

A **necessary modifier** fine-tunes a secondary detail by adding something new, relevant, or important to it. Consider the following items that contain both necessary and unnecessary modifiers. Can you pick which one is necessary in each case?

Item 1:   The <u>blond</u> pianist struggled through the <u>difficult</u> arpeggios.

Which of the two modifiers is necessary? Can you tell why *blond* is not necessary? It is because the hair color of the pianist is <u>irrelevant</u> to his playing the piano. On the other hand, *difficult* is necessary because it answers why he was struggling with the arpeggios.

Item 2:   The <u>long, shiny, sleek, black</u> limousine took the teenagers <u>in their tuxedos and sequined gowns</u> to their prom.

Which of the modifiers is necessary? How many modifiers are there for the noun *limousine?* Can you see that four modifiers for one noun are too many? Any one or two of the modifiers would give the reader a clear picture of the limousine. For instance, you could say a *long, sleek limousine* or a *shiny, black limousine.* However, using all four together is <u>excessive</u>; it gives the reader too much information to keep in his head at one time. On the other hand, *in their tuxedos and sequined gowns,* which is a prepositional phrase describing the noun *teenagers,* is a <u>single</u> modifier even though it gives two details, *tuxedos* and *sequined gowns.* Therefore, this modifier is not excessive.

Item 3:   Monica screamed <u>loudly</u> as her Saint Bernard bounded <u>unexpectedly</u> from behind the door.

Which of the two modifiers is necessary? Can you tell why the adverb *loudly* is not necessary? Since the verb *screamed* means having made a loud noise, the modifier is <u>redundant</u> or repetitive. On the other hand, bounding is a type of action that can be expected or unexpected. In fact, it was the unexpectedness of the bounding that made Monica scream.

Item 4:   Details of the <u>unappetizing</u> pizza and the <u>vinegary</u> saki filled Sybil's review of Uncle Vito's Pizza Emporium and Sushi Bar.

Which of the two modifiers is necessary? Can you see that the adjective *unappetizing* is not necessary because it does not tell us what is wrong with the pizza? It does not add any information to this secondary detail because it is <u>not specific</u>. On the other hand, the adjective *vinegary* tells us what is wrong with the saki, so it helps us understand why Sybil wrote a negative review of the restaurant.

Exercise Four ## Identifying Unnecessary Modifiers

DIRECTIONS   In each of the following sentences, identify the unnecessary modifier and tell whether it is irrelevant, excessive, redundant, or not specific.

MODEL   The <u>weary</u> firemen fought the <u>raging</u> inferno.

Unnecessary modifier: <u>raging</u>

Reason: <u>redundant</u>

1. The <u>soft</u>, <u>fluffy</u>, <u>furry</u> kitten peeked from the rim of <u>Ellen's</u> <u>Christmas</u> stocking.

   Unnecessary modifiers: _____

   Reason: _____

2. Toby was aware of the <u>spoiled</u> milk because it smelled <u>bad.</u>

   Unnecessary modifier: _____

   Reason: _____

3. The <u>tall</u> carpenter used a <u>claw</u> hammer to remove the nails from the flooring.

   Unnecessary modifier: _____

   Reason: _____

4. The technician separated the <u>circular</u> disks with a <u>circular</u> saw.

   Unnecessary modifier: _____

   Reason: _____

5. Lee investigated the <u>disturbing</u> sounds coming from the <u>root</u> cellar.

   Unnecessary modifier: _____

   Reason: _____

Exercise Five	**Correcting Unnecessary Modifiers**

DIRECTIONS   In each of the following sentences, find the unnecessary modifier and replace it with a specific verb, a specific noun, or a necessary modifier, or remove it if it is redundant or irrelevant.

MODEL   Cumulus clouds appear dense, white, puffy, and billowy.

Revision: <u>Cumulus clouds appear dense and white</u> (or any two of the above adjectives).

1. Beautiful flowers line the walkway to the horticulture institute.

   Revision: _____.

2. The abandoned puppy cried weakly from the Dumpster.

   Revision: _____.

3. The essential requirement of a freshman composition class is a research paper.

   Revision: _____.

4. Once a month, the Norwegian nurse practitioner visited homebound patients who could not get to the clinic.

   Revision: _____.

5. After her knee operation, Anne began a program of mild exercise.

   Revision: _____.

Exercise Six	**Adding Necessary Modifiers**

DIRECTIONS   In each of the following sentences, add necessary modifiers where indicated. Remember that necessary modifiers add something that is new, relevant, or important and that they can be phrases or clauses, as well as single words.

MODEL   In order to get his sick rabbit to the veterinary hospital, Cory swerved <u>maniacally</u> through traffic.

1. The _____ spokesperson for the cereal company was fired for incompetence.

2. Rachel was so distraught at the news that she fled the room _____.

3. The _____ cocker spaniel bit the man who wanted to adopt him.

4. The _____ watered rose bush turned yellow and died.

5. Joe's doctor advised him to drink a glass of _____ milk before bed to help his insomnia.

Use Comparisons

A final way you can develop secondary details is to make **comparisons.** A comparison shows similarity between two apparently unlike things. For instance, consider the secondary detail for Example 2 at the beginning of the chapter:

> Whenever we go out for Italian food, she dribbles so much chunky spaghetti sauce onto her white silk blouse that it tumbles down her chest like loose gravel rolls down a hillside.

Notice that the chunky spaghetti sauce is being compared to loose gravel. While the spaghetti sauce and loose gravel are different substances, they are alike in the way they tumble. Also, they are alike in size and shape since both are small and chunky. Finally, the context or situation in which the two occur is similar because both the chest and a hillside slope down. Now can you see that the two apparently different things that are being compared are really similar in many ways?

Consider the following comparison:

EXAMPLE 3: Joan wore so much rouge on her cheeks that she looked like a marionette.

Notice that Joan is being compared to a marionette, a type of puppet that usually has exaggerated make-up painted on it. In this case, the verb is not important because Joan and the marionette are not doing anything; they just look alike.

Together these examples show that you can compare the way things act or look. When you compare the way things act, pay attention to verbs. Example 2 about spaghetti sauce tells you that the sauce tumbles *down her chest.* In order to complete the comparison, *like loose gravel rolls down a hillside,* the writer has asked himself, *What else tumbles down something?* When you compare the way things look, pay attention to nouns and modifiers. Example 3 about Joan uses the noun *rouge* and the modifier *on her cheeks.* In order to complete the comparison, *like a marionette,* the writer has asked himself, *What else looks like Joan?*

A good comparison avoids cliches. A **cliche** has tired, overused language that is no longer effective in making the reader see, hear, taste, feel, or smell something because he has heard it too often. If you have heard a comparison before, don't use it. Which of these cliches have you heard before?

red as a rose	white as the snow
shaking like a leaf	quiet as a mouse
bright as the sun	tough as an old boot
black as midnight	strong as an ox
tall as a tree	light as a feather

Exercise Seven # Replacing Cliches in Comparisons

DIRECTIONS In each of the following sentences, replace the cliche with a fresh comparison that you think up yourself.

MODEL Aunt Cecilia's buttermilk biscuits were light as a feather.

Revision: Aunt Cecilia's buttermilk biscuits were light as meringue on a lemon pie.

1. The saleslady described the angora sweater as being soft as a baby's bottom.

   Revision: _____.

2. Marco thought his geography instructor was as crazy as a loon when she spun the globe on the tip of her finger.

   Revision: _____.

3. The coach ordered an extra large pizza with five toppings because his quarterback was hungry as a horse.

   Revision: _____.

4. Psychologists tell parents to beware when a two-year-old is sweet as sugar.

   Revision: _____.

5. The rookie policeman could not believe that he missed the target when it was as big as a house.

   Revision: _____.

Exercise Eight # Developing Secondary Details

DIRECTIONS Replace all undeveloped parts of the following secondary details with specific details, using any or all of the methods you learned in this chapter. Remember you may use as many sentences as you need for a well-developed secondary detail.

1. The botany students take care of plants in the greenhouse as part of their course requirements.

   Revision:

2. The place where Bree kept her shoes looked like a tornado had hit it.

   Revision:

3. The Broadway understudy was panned by the critics for making exaggerated body movements.

Revision:

4. Sally's husband was upset because she burned the roast on an important occasion.

Revision:

5. The small animal was trained to help the injured person.

Revision:

When you write a fully developed paragraph, each primary detail should be supported by at least two secondary details. With at least two secondary details for each primary, you have a better chance of making the reader see, hear, taste, feel, and smell what you have expressed in your primary details than you do if you use only one secondary detail.

Review Questions

Answer the following questions to help you review the material you have learned in this chapter.

1. What is the most specific part of your paragraph? (p. 125) _____

2. What is the relationship of a secondary detail to a primary detail? (p. 125)

_____

3. How do you make a primary detail real to a reader? (p. 125) _____

4. How long can a secondary detail be? (p. 125) _____

5. Two ways you can develop effective secondary details are by using strong

_____ and specific _____. (p. 126)

6. In addition to weak verbs, what else can a strong verb replace? (p. 127)

_____

7. When necessary, what else can you use to develop secondary details? (p. 129)

_____

8. What do they add if they are really necessary? (p. 129)

_____ _____ _____

9. What four ways are modifiers unnecessary? (p. 129) _____

_____ _____ _____

10. What does a comparison show? (p. 132)_____

11. Comparisons concentrate on how things _____ or

_____. (p. 132)

12. If you compare what things do, what part of speech do you pay attention to? (p. 132) _____

13. If you compare how things look, what parts of speech do you pay attention to? (p. 132) _____ and _____

14. What should a good comparison avoid? (p. 132)_____

15. Why? (p. 132)_____

16. How many secondary details should you use to support each primary detail? (p. 134) _____

17. Why? (p. 134) _____

Writing Exercises

I. Writing Secondary Details for Support

For each of the following topic sentence and primary detail pairs, write two fully developed secondary details, using all the techniques you learned in this chapter. Remember, you may use as many sentences as you need to develop a secondary detail.

1. Topic sentence: Reading can add to our knowledge.

   Primary detail: It can provide useful knowledge about the jury selection process.

   Secondary detail 1: _____.

   Secondary detail 2: _____.

2. Topic sentence: People can show nervousness in several ways.

   Primary detail: They can show nervousness with their hands.

   Secondary detail 1: _____.

   Secondary detail 2: _____.

3. Topic sentence: Some animals are threatened with extinction because of the things human beings do.

   Primary detail: Human beings destroy animal habitat.

   Secondary detail 1: _____.

   Secondary detail 2: _____.

4. Topic sentence: People can be attracted to people who may not be good for them.

   Primary detail: Some people are attracted to people who seem dangerous.

   Secondary detail 1: _____.

   Secondary detail 2: _____.

5. Topic sentence: Interior design students learn a number of ways to decorate inexpensively.

   Primary detail: They learn to use brightly-patterned sheets and pillowcases creatively.

   Secondary detail 1: _____.

   Secondary detail 2: _____.

II. Revising Secondary Details for Support

Look back at the three paragraphs you rewrote for Writing Exercise II in Chapter Seven. Pay particular attention to what you wrote after each of the primary details. Is it specific? Do you have at least two examples to support each primary detail? If not, revise your paragraph until you have two fully developed secondary details for each primary detail.

Looking Back and Looking Forward

In this chapter, you have learned to develop supporting details. Now you are ready to add the final ingredient of a finished paragraph. In the next chapter, you will learn to join the parts of your paragraph with transitions.

Transitions

I n Chapter Eight, you learned how to develop secondary details to support your structure. In this chapter, you will learn how to use transitions to tie your paragraph together.

Relating Ideas with Transitions

The word **transition** means *change* or *passage*. It comes from the Latin word *transire*, which means *to go across*, like a bridge. In fact, transitions act as bridges between ideas expressed in sentences and paragraphs. Transitions do this by showing the relationship between ideas. Consider the following paragraph:

> California orange growers have several worries. They worry about bad weather. Temperatures that dip below thirty-two degrees Fahrenheit bring frost that burns the fruit, drying it out. Smog and fog that block out the sunlight often cause mildew. They worry about competition from distant growers. Growers in Central America with more temperate winter weather can produce high yields more consistently. Growers in Florida produce new varieties before they are tried in California, like the sweet Honeybell Tangelo, a cross between a navel orange and a tangerine. To deal with fluctuations in the weather and competition from other markets, California orange growers have to be resourceful.

Did you have trouble following the ideas expressed in the primary details and the examples in the secondary details? Could you easily tell the difference between the two? Did the paragraph seem choppy? Now read the same paragraph aloud with transitions added:

> California orange growers have several worries. <u>First of all</u>, they worry about bad weather. <u>For example</u>, temperatures that dip below

thirty-two degrees Fahrenheit bring frost that burns the fruit, drying it out. <u>In addition</u>, smog and fog that block out the sunlight often cause mildew. <u>Second</u>, they worry about competition from distant growers. Growers in Central America, <u>for instance</u>, with more temperate winter weather can produce high yields more consistently. <u>Also</u>, growers in Florida produce new varieties before they are tried in California, like the sweet Honeybell Tangelo, a cross between a navel orange and a tangerine. <u>Consequently</u>, to deal with fluctuations in the weather and competition from other markets, California orange growers have to be resourceful.

The transitions used in the revised paragraph act as bridges between separate ideas and levels of generality, showing their relationships and connecting them. In other words, they help to make the paragraph cohesive. Notice that the <u>first primary detail</u> begins with the transition *First of all.* The <u>first secondary detail</u>, which supports it by giving an example, begins appropriately with the transition *For example.* The <u>second secondary detail</u>, which is on the same level of generality as the example before it, begins with the transition *In addition.* The <u>second primary detail</u> is introduced with the transition *Second,* which logically follows the first primary detail's transition *First of all.* The <u>first secondary detail</u> for the second primary includes the transition *for instance* to show that it is an example of that primary. The <u>second secondary detail</u> for the second primary begins with the transition *Also.* The <u>conclusion</u> of this paragraph looks at the consequence of the primary and secondary details, so it uses the appropriate transition *Consequently* to introduce it. Now do you see how transitions announce the relationship of ideas to each other?

Did you notice that a transition also does not have to come at the beginning of a sentence? Which of the transitions in the paragraph above does not come at the beginning of a sentence? In fact, there is no set rule for where transitions occur in a paragraph. In general, a transition may be placed at the beginning, in the middle, or at the end of a sentence, depending on where it fits smoothly. When a transition comes at the beginning of a sentence and is two or more words long, it is followed by a comma; when a transition comes in the middle of a sentence, it has a comma before it and a comma after it; and when a transition comes at the end of a sentence, it has a comma before it.

In addition to the transitions in the revised paragraph, what other transitions do you know? What relationships do they express? Some of the relationships that transitions can express are equality, contradiction, order or time, reinforcement, development, and consequence.

Some transitions that express **equality** of one idea to another are

also	in addition	furthermore
and	next	another
moreover	first of all	second
third	finally	last of all

Some transitions that express the **contradiction** of a previous statement are

but	on the other hand	in contrast
however	on the contrary	yet
still	otherwise	nevertheless

Some transitions that express a logical **order** or **time sequence** of ideas are

first	next	finally
then	while	after
before	during	as
after all	subsequently	at the end
when	once this is done	

Some transitions that express the **reinforcement** of an idea are

it is valuable to note	as a matter of fact
special attention should be paid to	remember that
most important	principally
keep in mind	it is especially significant that
the biggest advantage/disadvantage/ cause/effect	in other words
a primary part	in fact
the best thing/the worst thing	clearly
most of all/least of all	it is apparent that

Some transitions that express the **development** of a statement are

for instance	for example	to illustrate
as an illustration	such as	like
this means	in addition	moreover
furthermore	not only . . . but also	

Some transitions that express the **consequence** of an idea are

finally	last of all	thus
then	as a result	therefore
in summary	to conclude	consequently
in fact	clearly	this means that
it is obvious	because of this	

Did you notice that some transitions can be used in more than one way? For instance, *then* can show order or time as well as consequence. What other transitions can be used in more than one way?

Exercise One | **Identifying Transitions**

DIRECTIONS | For each of the following sentences, identify the transition. Remember that transitions may occur anywhere in a sentence.

MODEL | Clearly Mary Shelley's novel *Frankenstein* is an underrated classic.

Transition: <u>Clearly</u>

1. Most people in the United States pay state as well as federal income tax; however, residents of several states, such as New Hampshire and Wyoming, pay only federal.

   Transition: _____

2. Among elected officials in Congress, the Speaker of the House is, as a matter of fact, the most powerful.

   Transition: _____

3. Artist Robert Mapplethorpe received federal funding for an art exhibit that many people found objectionable; the National Endowment for the Arts has never recovered from the criticism, consequently.

   Transition: _____

4. While wolves have a reputation for ferocity, it is especially significant that there has never been a documented case of a wolf attacking a human being in the United States.

   Transition: _____

5. Anyone starting an exercise program should begin with a visit to his doctor; once this is done, he can choose exercises that are physically challenging but do not raise his heart rate to dangerous levels.

   Transition: _____

Moving Transitions

DIRECTIONS Rewrite each of the sentences from Exercise One, moving the transition somewhere else in the sentence. Make sure the rewritten sentence reads smoothly.

1. Most people in the United States pay state as well as federal income tax; however,
   residents of several states, such as New Hampshire and Wyoming, pay only federal.

   Revision: _____ .

2. Among elected officials in Congress, the Speaker of the House is, as a matter of
   fact, the most powerful.

   Revision: _____ .

3. Artist Robert Mapplethorpe received federal funding for an art exhibit that
   many people found objectionable; the National Endowment for the Arts has
   never recovered from the criticism, consequently.

   Revision: _____ .

4. While wolves have a reputation for ferocity, it is especially significant that there
   has never been a documented case of a wolf attacking a human being in the
   United States.

   Revision: _____ .

5. Anyone starting an exercise program should begin with a visit to his doctor; once
   this is done, he can choose exercises that are physically challenging but do not
   raise his heart rate to dangerous levels.

   Revision: _____ .

Replacing Transitions

DIRECTIONS This time, replace each of the transitions in the following sentences with a different
transition that mean the same thing. You may use transitions from the previous lists
or come up with your own.

1. Most people in the United States pay state as well as federal income tax; however,
   residents of several states, such as New Hampshire and Wyoming, pay only federal.

   Revision: _____ .

2. Among elected officials in Congress, the Speaker of the House is, as a matter of
   fact, the most powerful.

   Revision: _____ .

3. Artist Robert Mapplethorpe received federal funding for an art exhibit that many people found objectionable; the National Endowment for the Arts has never recovered from the criticism, consequently.

   Revision: _____.

4. While wolves have a reputation for ferocity, it is especially significant that there has never been a documented case of a wolf attacking a human being in the United States.

   Revision: _____.

5. Anyone starting an exercise program should begin with a visit to his doctor; once this is done, he can choose exercises that are physically challenging but do not raise his heart rate to dangerous levels.

   Revision: _____.

Review Questions

Answer the following questions to help you review the material you have learned in this chapter.

1. What does the word *transition* mean? (p. 137) _____

2. What do transitions show? (p. 137) _____

3. Transitions make a paragraph _____. (p. 138)

4. Where do transitions occur in a sentence? (p. 138) _____

5. Where do you put a comma if the transition comes at the beginning of a sentence? (p. 138) _____

6. Where do you put commas if the transition comes in the middle of a sentence? (p. 138) _____

7. Where do you put a comma if the transition comes at the end of a sentence? (p. 138) _____

8. What are six relationships transitions can express? (p. 138)

   _____   _____   _____

   _____   _____   _____

9. Give two transitions that express equality. (p. 139)

   _____ _____

10. Give two transitions that express contradiction. (p. 139)

   _____ _____

11. Give two transitions that express time. (p. 139)

   _____ _____

12. Give two transitions that express reinforcement. (p. 139)

   _____ _____

13. Give two transitions that express development. (p. 139)

   _____ _____

14. Give two transitions that express consequence. (p. 140)

   _____ _____

Writing Exercises

I. Adding Transitions

Read the following paragraph. It has a topic sentence, three primary details, two secondary details for each primary detail, and a conclusion; however, the paragraph lacks cohesiveness because there are no transitions. Rewrite the paragraph, supplying appropriate transitions to connect the parts of the paragraph.

Some children can be very enterprising when it comes to earning money. Some sell homemade goodies. They add crushed strawberries and raspberries to giant pitchers of lemonade and sell frosty cups of it on scorching days to neighbors whose throats are as dry as old cornstalks. They get their parents to help them bake cookies that ooze melted chocolate and gingerbread men that crunch like autumn leaves underfoot, which they sell to other children at school. Some children do chores to earn money. In winter, they offer to shovel their neighbors' walks and dig out their snow-laden cars after a blizzard. In summer, they offer to water parched lawns and cut back flower gardens whose rhododendrons and petunias are being choked by weeds. Some children put on entertainment for money. They produce fairy tales like Jack-in-the-Beanstalk, sewing peasant costumes out of old bedspreads and adding songs for Jack, the Giant, and even the

Golden Goose to sing. They learn magic tricks to perform at birthday parties, like tearing up the Sunday edition of *The New York Times,* stuffing the pieces into a top hat, and pulling out a whole paper, to the astonishment of their audience. Children who are enterprising when it comes to earning money often grow into adults who are just as creative about earning a living.

Revision:

II. Revising Transitions

Read the following paragraph. It has a topic sentence, three primary details, two secondary details for each primary detail, and a conclusion; however, the transitions between ideas are not appropriate because they do not express the correct relationships between those ideas. Rewrite the paragraph, substituting appropriate transitions.

College can be less stressful if you use good learning skills. Finally, you should choose a place where it is easy to study. Also be sure you have a large enough table or desk on which to spread out all your books and notes. For example, the place you study should be free of distracting noises, like a television blaring the half-time show at the Super Bowl. It is especially important to be an active reader. Furthermore you can take part in your reading by making notes in the margins of your book as you read, summarizing main points, like the principal causes of the Wars of the Roses in fifteenth-century England, and defining difficult terms, such as *primogeniture,* which means the right of the eldest child to inherit. Nevertheless you can note questions you have about material you don't understand, such as "Why shouldn't I look at magnesium when it burns?" Least of all, good test-taking skills are important. Thus when you get the test, read the directions carefully so that you do not squander your time trying to answer all three essay questions when the directions tell you to choose only one and answer it fully. As a result, you should budget your time for each portion of the test so that you will have time at the end to review your answers for sense, correct spelling errors, supply missing words, and explain vague terms. Good learning skills, in other words, are skills that carry you from the classroom to the boardroom.

Revision:

III. Revising Paragraphs for Transitions

Look back at the three paragraphs you rewrote for Writing Exercise II in Chapter Eight. Pay particular attention to how you made your ideas flow from sentence to sentence. If you did not use appropriate transitional words and phrases at the beginning, the middle, or the end of your sentences, revise or insert them now.

IV. Writing a Complete Paragraph

Choose one of the following assignments and write a complete paragraph in response, using all of the steps you have learned so far. When you are finished, pay special attention to how your ideas and sentences flow. Add tranisitions where necessary.

1. Tell how the step-by-step process you are learning in this class makes it easier for you to write papers.

2. Describe the best way to make your opinion on a campus policy known to a large number of people.

3. Describe a favorite time in your life.

Looking Back and Looking Forward

In Chapters Four through Nine, you have learned to respond to assignments by narrowing an assignment to a topic and then developing that topic into a paragraph with primary and secondary details, a conclusion, and transitions. Now you are ready to refine your paragraph. In the next section, you will learn about style, which refers to <u>how</u> you express your ideas.

Section two review   *Responding to Assignments*

Remember what you have learned in Chapters Four through Nine about the structure and development of a paragraph. Choose at least two of the following five assignments, and follow these steps to produce a fully developed paragraph for each:

- Notice that each assignment has been narrowed by a controlling idea, so you can form a topic sentence by adding a specific topic.

- Ask a focusing question to come up with three primary details. Make sure all are parallel.

- Ask *So what?* of your topic sentence and primary details to come up with a conclusion.

- Use the four techniques—strong verbs, specific nouns, necessary modifiers, and comparisons—to develop two secondary details for each primary detail.

- Add transitions to show relationships between ideas and to make the paragraph flow.

Assignments

1. Describe a friend or relative who is fussy.

2. Describe a recent event that was frightening.

3. Give reasons why a particular practice in college is fair/unfair.

4. Tell about a time in history when a person or group of people was treated badly.

5. Describe a friend your family disapproves of.

Word Choices

In the second section, you learned how to respond to assignments by writing paragraphs. In this section, you will learn how to choose appropriate words and sentence patterns that make those paragraphs convincing to your reader.

Tone

The language you use should be appropriate for your assignment or subject. For instance, for the assignment *Describe your funniest relative,* which of these two topic sentences sounds more appropriate?

1. My Uncle Benjamin is my most humorous family member.

2. Uncle Benny is my funniest relative.

Which topic sentence sounds too formal for the assignment? Why? Did you notice how stiff *humorous family member* sounds in comparison to *funniest relative?* After all, the assignment itself uses informal language; therefore, the response to the assignment should also use informal language.

On the other hand, for the assignment *Describe the most positive characteristic of a controversial politician,* which of the next two topic sentences sounds more appropriate?

1. Professor Anderson is unfailingly diplomatic.

2. Professor Anderson never hurts people's feelings.

Which topic sentence sounds too informal for the assignment? Why? Did you notice that the assignment uses formal words like *characteristic, controversial,* and *politician?* Therefore, the response should use formal words like *unfailingly diplomatic* instead of the informal phrase *never hurts people's feelings.*

The way language *sounds* to the reader is called **tone.** Just as people can speak in different tones of voice, writers can express different tones also. One way of doing this is by choosing either **formal** or **informal language.**

Identifying Formal Language and Informal Language

DIRECTIONS   For each pair of the following assignments, identify which uses formal language and which uses informal language.

MODEL   a. Indicate the sequence of events precipitating the American Revolution.

Language: formal

b. Trace what led up to the American Revolution.

Language: informal

1a. Contrast a permanent care facility with a supervised living facility.

Language: _____

b. What are the differences between a nursing home and a retirement home?

Language: _____

2a. Describe a time when you had a change of heart about someone you know.

Language: _____

b. Describe a time when circumstances led you to alter your initial opinion of an acquaintance.

Language: _____

3a. Explain why half of all new restaurants go under in their first year of business.

Language: _____

b. Explain the causes for the high failure rate of new food service businesses during their first year of operation.

Language: _____

4a. Tell how to protect yourself outdoors during a thunder and lightning storm.

Language: _____

b. Discuss safe outdoor behavior during an electrical storm.

Language: _____

5a. Is lethal injection "cruel and unusual" punishment? Why or why not?

Language: _____

5b. Does lethal injection violate the Constitutional injunction against "cruel and unusual" punishment? Discuss.

Language: _____

Parallelism and Tone

In Chapter Six, you learned about parallelism when you made sure your primary details agreed in content and grammar. Now you are using parallelism in language when you make the tone of your paragraph agree with the tone of the assignment. In other words, parallelism in language can mean using formal language for an assignment that uses formal language and using informal language for an assignment that uses informal language. You will find that most academic assignments use formal language because the subject of those assignments is objective rather than personal. That is why it requires language that is different from the way you speak. As you remember from Chapter Five, when writing a topic sentence in response to your assignment, you may repeat some of the language from that assignment. When that happens, notice how the repetition of language from the assignment helps you set a tone for your response.

Exercise Two | **Writing Topic Sentences to Reflect Tone**

DIRECTIONS | For each of the following assignments, identify the tone of the language as formal or informal. Then write a topic sentence for that assignment that uses the same tone by repeating important language from the assignment.

MODEL | Assignment: Tell how to break bad news to someone.

Tone: <u>informal</u>

Topic sentence: <u>A person should always break bad news to someone gently.</u>

1. Assignment: Describe the interior of your automobile.

   Tone: _____

   Topic sentence: _____ .

2. Assignment: Examine the differences between two methods of transportation.

   Tone: _____

   Topic sentence: _____ .

3. Assignment: Tell about a narrow escape.

   Tone: _____

   Topic sentence: _____ .

4. Assignment: Discuss the most appropriate way of responding to a traffic citation for a moving violation.

Tone: _____

Topic sentence: _____ .

5. Assignment: Tell what a "mooch" does.

Tone: _____

Topic sentence: _____ .

Excessively Formal Language or "Collegese"

Although most college writing is formal, sometimes when you use formal language, you might get carried away and put too much of it together. Language like this sounds <u>unnaturally</u> formal and is called **collegese** because college students sometimes think they have to use many big words to impress their teachers. Remember that more is not always better. Which of the following sentences is written in "collegese"?

1. Roger perambulated back and forth at his place of creative endeavor.

2. Roger paced at work.

If you think the first sentence sounds ridiculously formal, you are right. "Collegese" pushes meaning away. The reader has to translate it like a foreign language because there are too many unfamiliar words together or because the words are not specific. Remember, you have more power as a writer when you use language that you and your reader completely understand. Formal writing does not mean that every word must be a big word.

Exercise Three | **Replacing "Collegese"**

DIRECTIONS | Rewrite each of the following sentences, replacing the "collegese" with more effective language. Remember that some of the formal language may remain in your revision.

MODEL | The suspect effected his egress from the edifice.

Revision: <u>The suspect left the building</u>.

1. The deficiencies in his attendance record were rationalized by the student in order to preclude his untimely excision from the class roster.

Revision: _____

_____ .

2. Andrew's nostrum container admonished against usage when operating a motor vehicle.

   Revision: _____

   _____ .

3. At the portals of those homo sapiens they favor, felines deposit small wildlife they have dispatched.

   Revision: _____

   _____ .

4. Dwellings and vehicles should be habitually safeguarded with anti-theft devices by the denizens of metropolitan areas.

   Revision: _____

   _____ .

5. Giselle was instructed by her physician to masticate edibles thirty-two times before swallowing in order to prevent distress from excessive gastric enzyme action.

   Revision: _____

   _____ .

Did you find that your revisions in the preceding exercise were not only clearer but also shorter than the originals in "collegese"? That is because using too much formal language in one sentence usually results in **wordiness,** which is using too many words to express an idea that could have been expressed more simply.

Another time "collegese" is wordy is when it uses passive voice. **Voice** refers to whether the subject in a sentence performs an action or receives an action. In most sentences that make a statement, the subject comes first and performs the action expressed by the verb. For instance, consider the sentence *Hortensia picked up José at the daycare center.* In this sentence, *Hortensia* is the subject, and she performs the action of picking up José. When the subject of the sentence performs the action, the sentence is in **active voice,** as in the preceding sentence.

On the other hand, consider the sentence *José was picked up by Hortensia at the daycare center.* In this sentence, *José* is the subject, but he performs no action; in fact, he <u>receives</u> the action in this sentence because it is done <u>to</u> him. When the subject of the sentence receives the action rather than performs it, the subject is passive; therefore, the sentence is in the **passive voice.**

Now look at both sentences together:

1. Hortensia <u>picked up</u> José at the daycare center.

2. José <u>was picked up by</u> Hortensia at the daycare center.

Did you notice that when the subject receives the action of the verb, the verb itself changes form? In fact, the active or passive voice of a sentence is expressed by the verb. When you look at the sentences, can you see which is wordier? The reason Sentence 2 is wordier is that it uses two more words than Sentence 1 uses—*was* and *by*. That may not seem like a lot of extra words, but they do make a difference. Usually sentences using active voice are shorter than sentences using passive voice.

Exercise Four

Reviewing Exercise Three for Passive Voice

DIRECTIONS

Some of the sentences in Exercise Three use the passive voice. Copy your original revisions below, and then correct any revisions in which you kept or used the passive voice.

1. Revision 1: _____

   _____.

   Revision 2: _____

   _____.

2. Revision 1: _____

   _____.

   Revision 2: _____

   _____.

3. Revision 1: _____

   _____.

   Revision 2: _____

   _____.

4. Revision 1: _____

   _____.

   Revision 2: _____

   _____.

5. Revision 1: _____

   _____.

Revision 2: _____

_____.

Changing Passive Voice to Active Voice Verbs

For each of the following sentences, change the voice from passive to active.

Passive: The captive-bred condors were released by park officials into the wild.

Active: <u>Park officials released the captive-bred condors into the wild.</u>

1. Passive: The Mozart sonatina was played by Yousef.

   Active: _____.

2. Passive: Many common herbs are used by naturopaths to treat human illness.

   Active: _____.

3. Passive: The graphs were plotted in error by the algebra students during their exam.

   Active: _____.

4. Passive: The journalism students were warned by their advisor against sensation-alism.

   Active: _____.

5. Passive: The fraternity members were put on suspension by the Dean of Students after they were caught by him with open beer cans on campus.

   Active: _____.

Excessively Informal or Conversational Language

The opposite of "collegese" is **conversational language,** which is the kind of language you use when you speak with your friends. There are several ways you can make *conversational* errors in your writing.

Interjections

First of all, when you speak, you often buy a little extra time to gather your thoughts by starting with a word like *Well, Gosh, Oh,* or *No!* These *fillers* or words that express mild emotion are called **interjections** and are sometimes followed by exclamation marks when written. For instance, if a friend asks what you thought of a recent concert, you might say, *Well, it was dull* or *Gosh! It was dull!* In academic writing, the emotional words are removed, and the sentence should read, *The concert was dull.*

You

There is also another word you do not use in college writing because it is conversational. This is the second person personal pronoun **you** or any form of it, which implies you are <u>speaking</u> directly to your reader. You can replace the second person pronoun with any number of third person or indefinite pronouns like *he, she, it, one, anyone, someone, a person, everyone, people,* or even a person's proper name. For instance, the conversational sentence <u>*You* should floss *your* teeth every day</u> can be rewritten as <u>*A person*</u> should floss <u>*his*</u> teeth every day or <u>*People*</u> should floss <u>*their*</u> teeth every day.

Slang

Another form of informal language you should avoid in academic writing is **slang.** Slang is a kind of jargon that is usually popularized by young people. Slang can be hard to understand because it sounds like a code. For instance, not everyone knows that *Hey, dude, your clothes are the bomb* means *Hey, friend, I like your clothes.* Not only is slang informal, but also it does not last because it is constantly being replaced by new slang. In fact, by the time you read this, the example about "the bomb" will be out of fashion.

Contractions

A final kind of informal language you should try to avoid in academic writing is **contractions.** A contraction is a combination of two or more words in which an apostrophe replaces missing letters. For instance, *don't* is a contraction of *do not.* Notice that an apostrophe replaces the *o* missing from *not.* Similarly, *should've* is a contraction of *should have.* Here, the apostrophe replaces *ha* in *have.* To avoid using contractions, you can rewrite the conversational sentence *My aunt and uncle <u>couldn't</u> have children of their own, and they <u>weren't</u> able to adopt* as *My aunt and uncle <u>could not</u> have children of their own, and they <u>were not</u> able to adopt.*

<table>
<tr><td>Exercise Six</td><td>**Replacing Conversational Language**</td></tr>
<tr><td>DIRECTIONS</td><td>In each of the following sentences, replace the four types of conversational language presented in this chapter with more formal language.</td></tr>
<tr><td>MODEL</td><td>You can't keep live lobsters in fresh water.</td></tr>
</table>

Revision: <u>*One cannot keep live lobsters in fresh water.*</u>

1. It's never too late to learn to write well.

    Revision: _____.

2. If you're thinking about careers, well, you should consider your natural talents.

   Revision: _____.

3. Many successful television shows didn't find their audiences until they'd been on the air more than a year.

   Revision: _____.

4. You know, gorillas are really cool; they're primarily vegetarians.

   Revision: _____.

5. Some people get so uptight at work that for health reasons they need to find ways to chill.

   Revision: _____.

Word Errors

Even if the tone of your writing is not excessively formal or excessively informal, you may still make several kinds of word choice errors in an attempt to find a balance between the two. First, students may make several kinds of **context** errors. The context of a word is the setting or situation in which the word is placed. One kind of context error results from misunderstanding the definition of a word. In an effort to impress their teachers with formal words, students sometimes use a word they have looked up in a thesaurus or dictionary without understanding the proper context of the definition. For instance, if you look up the word *bitter* in a thesaurus, you will find one word that means the same is *acrimonious*. Which of the following sentences uses *acrimonious* in the proper context?

1. I had an acrimonious cup of coffee.

2. I had an acrimonious argument.

Sentence 1 is wrong because the proper context for *acrimonious* is in reference to words, not food. A thesaurus, however, will not tell you that.

There are several ways to learn how to use new words in their proper context. First, read widely. When you read, unfamiliar words appear already in their proper context. Second, ask your teacher or librarian to refer you to a good vocabulary builder. These books often include Latin roots, prefixes, and suffixes that help you figure out the meanings of unfamiliar words and then give you sentences with the proper context for their use. For instance, if you know that the Latin root *cred* means *believe,* you can figure out that the word *credibility* probably means *believability.* Then you might find a sentence like this in the vocabulary builder to help you with the word's context: *Cory's credibility was called into question when he said he saw Elvis ride through his backyard on a moose.* Finally, you can ask a <u>qualified person</u>, like a teacher or librarian, to tell you if you are using an unfamiliar word correctly.

Exercise Seven
Understanding Definitions and Choosing the Correct Context

DIRECTIONS Each of the following items gives a word and definition, followed by two sentences using that word. Identify which sentence uses the word in the correct context and write in the appropriate letter.

MODEL Word: <u>cryptic</u>   Definition: <u>hidden</u>

a. Charles left a cryptic message on Sara's phone.

b. On Easter, many children hunt for cryptic eggs.

Correct context: *a*

1. Word: <u>banal</u>   Definition: <u>empty</u>

   a. The cookie jar is banal.

   b. The two acquaintances had a banal conversation at the barber shop.

   Correct context: _____

2. Word: <u>obtuse</u>   Definition: <u>blunt; not sharp</u>

   a. Gene's father called him obtuse when Gene failed to understand that he was grounded for a week.

   b Jenny attempted to slice the bread with an obtuse knife.

   Correct context: _____

3. Word: <u>precocious</u>   Definition: <u>ripened or matured earlier than usual</u>

   a. Growers harvested the precocious avocados in January, rather than in April.

   b. Keisha's precocious daughter was reading at the age of two.

   Correct context: _____

4. Word: <u>binary</u>   Definition: <u>double or a whole composed of two</u>

   a. Until Henrietta's glasses were adjusted, she had binary vision.

   b. The astronomer discovered a binary star system in a distant galaxy.

   Correct context: _____

5. Word: <u>lucid</u>   Definition: <u>clear</u>

   a. Jeff delivered the most lucid campaign speech at the rally.

b. After the rain cleared away the fog, the day was perfectly lucid.

Correct context: _____

Another kind of context error students may make results from not recognizing that two words used in a similar context actually have different definitions. For instance, the words *bring* and *take* are both used in the context of carrying or moving something. However, their definitions are different. Consider the two sentences below:

1. If you love me, <u>bring</u> chocolates to me on St. Valentine's Day.

2. If you love me, <u>take</u> those chocolates away from me.

Can you see the difference between the definitions of *bring* and *take?* In this case, the clue is in the prepositions *to* and *from.* Did you guess that *bring* means to carry <u>to</u> or <u>toward</u> someone, while *take* means to carry <u>away from</u> someone? Here are some more pairs of words that are confused because they are used in similar contexts:

---

because of   as a result of (used in neutral or positive circumstances)
     e.g., <u>Because of</u> her English teacher's recommendation, Jitan received a full scholarship to graduate school.

due to   as a result of (used in negative circumstances)
     e.g., <u>Due to</u> rain, the football game was canceled.

can   to know how to or to be able to
     e.g., Gladys <u>can</u> be very persuasive when she wants to be.

may   to have permission or to be possible
     e.g., Stephan <u>may</u> spend spring semester in London if his loans are approved.

fewer   a smaller number than
     e.g., A bowl of cherries has <u>fewer</u> calories than a cherry pie.

less   a smaller amount than
     e.g., There is <u>less</u> room in my refrigerator since I discovered that Sara Lee makes cheesecakes.

(continued)

good   having positive qualities
      e.g., David did a <u>good</u> job on his biology project.

well   skillfully or proficiently
      e.g., Richard played the piano quite <u>well</u> after only a few lessons.

imply   to hint or suggest; to put meaning into
      e.g., Carole did not mean to <u>imply</u> that she disliked Bill by refusing
         a date with him.

infer   to conclude; to take meaning out of
      e.g., Bill was wrong to <u>infer</u> that Carole disliked him when she re-
         fused a date with him because she was already busy.

raise   to lift something
      e.g., <u>Raise</u> your hand when you know the answer.

rise   to go up or to get up
      e.g., Everyone was asked to <u>rise</u> when the judge entered the court-
         room.

set   to put something in a specified place
      e.g., Bruno <u>set</u> his French book on the table.

sit   to rest, as on a chair
      e.g., Vassiley had to <u>sit</u> on a cushion to do his homework because
         the chair was not high enough.

Exercise Eight

Understanding Definitions and Choosing the Correct Word

DIRECTIONS   For each of the following sentences, fill in the blank with the correct word choice, based on the definitions in the preceding box.

MODEL   The pastry chef *set* _____ (sit, set) the coconut cream pies on the racks to cool.

1. The instructor did not mean to _____ (imply, infer) the students were

    lazy when she said they needed to spend more time on their essays.

2. The journalist wanted to _____ (raise, rise) the issue of animal rights

    in his story about factory farming.

3. _____ (Due to, Because of) his strong pitching arm, Gary won the game for his college team.

4. Several sections of Art History I were canceled this semester because _____ (fewer, less) students registered for these classes than last semester.

5. I know the actor _____ (can, may) give a _____ (good, well) reading of Hamlet's soliloquy on suicide tonight because he did it _____ (good, well) last night.

In addition to context errors, students may make other word choice errors because some words sound and/or look alike. Here are the meanings of more commonly confused words.

---

accept   to receive willingly
     e.g., The teacher will <u>accept</u> all the students' late papers.

except   leaving out
     e.g., The teacher will not accept any late papers <u>except</u> from those students who asked for extensions before the paper was due.

advice   an opinion about what to do
     e.g., Academic counselors give students <u>advice</u> on what courses to take to fill transfer requirements.

advise   to offer an opinion about what to do
     e.g., Sometimes students <u>advise</u> each other on which teachers to take.

affect   to influence
     e.g., The D- for his trigonometry class will <u>affect</u> Ray's G.P.A.

effect   the result
     e.g., The <u>effect</u> of Ray's D- in trigonometry on his G.P.A. was drastic.

all ready   completely ready or prepared
     e.g., By the time dinner was <u>all ready</u>, the guests had eaten the rolls.

(continued)

already   by that time
> e.g., By the time dinner was all ready, the guests had <u>already</u> eaten the rolls.

allusion   a reference to a person, place, or event in history, literature, or religion
> e.g., Clarise made an <u>allusion</u> to Harry Houdini's escape tricks.

illusion   a mistaken perception of reality
> e.g., Clarise made an allusion to the magician's <u>illusion</u> of sawing a woman in half.

are   a condition verb
> e.g., Inline skates <u>are</u> replacing skateboards in popularity.

our   of or belonging to or done by us
> e.g., <u>Our</u> mistake was to pack all light clothes for a trip to Southern California in winter.

brake   to slow down
> e.g., My favorite bumper sticker says, "I <u>brake</u> for whales."

break   to split, crack, or smash into pieces; an interruption
> e.g., A chemistry student may <u>break</u> a test tube during an experiment; then he must take a <u>break</u> to find a replacement.

choose   to select
> e.g., Students sometimes ask their friends' advice before they <u>choose</u> an instructor.

chose   past tense of *choose*
> e.g., Batya <u>chose</u> to take Dr. Berman's French class after asking a friend's advice.

coarse   rough; vulgar
> e.g., Lupe ground the corn into <u>coarse</u> meal.
> e.g., The driver used <u>coarse</u> language when the policeman stopped him on the freeway.

(continued)

course   a direction or a way to proceed; part of a meal; part of a pro-
            gram of study
            e.g., The waiter's <u>course</u> of action was to serve the main <u>course</u> of
            a meal fifteen minutes after the salad.
            e.g., Phillipe's <u>course</u> in hotel management was challenging.

complement to complete or go with
            e.g., Tia bought a burgundy scarf to <u>complement</u> her new suit.

compliment something said in praise
            e.g., Tia's boss paid her a <u>compliment</u> on her burgundy scarf.

desert   a dry, barren, sandy region
            e.g., Many people feel the <u>desert</u> has a healthy climate.

dessert   the final course of a meal, typically something sweet
            e.g., Grandpa always leaves his spinach untouched and asks for two
            helpings of <u>dessert</u> instead.

discreet   careful about what one does or says
            e.g., Because their high school frowned on public displays of affec-
            tion, Antoine and Patricia kept their behavior <u>discreet</u>.

discrete   separate and distinct
            e.g., The words *discreet* and *discrete* may look and sound alike, but
            their meanings are really quite <u>discrete</u>.

elicit   to draw forth or evoke a response
            e.g., Emeka posed a controversial theory to <u>elicit</u> a spirited response
            from his students.

illicit   unlawful or improper
            e.g., The Border Patrol often stops cars to check for <u>illicit</u> drugs.

evoke   to call forth or elicit
            e.g., Manuel was desperate to <u>evoke</u> some sort of response from his
            uncommunicative wife.

(continued)

invoke   to call on or in the name of for blessing or help
> e.g., Elisabeth is always tempted to <u>invoke</u> the name of the muse of writing whenever she has to produce an essay for her journalism class.

flaunt   to show off proudly or defiantly
> e.g., After winning the Lottery, Errol lost his friends when he began to <u>flaunt</u> his wealth.

flout   to mock or scorn
> e.g., Rock stars often <u>flout</u> convention by wearing outrageous clothing.

grate   to grind; a frame of metal bars
> e.g., Sylvia had to <u>grate</u> the peel of an orange into the cake frosting.
> e.g., The student teacher was so nervous, she dropped her keys through the sewer <u>grate</u>.

great   fine, excellent, or important
> e.g., Stephen Hawking is a <u>great</u> astrophysicist.

have   to hold, own, or possess
> e.g., The Lehto brothers would <u>have</u> accepted the logging contract if it had been offered.

of   about, from, belonging to
> e.g., If the fortune-teller had told Natasha she would have lots <u>of</u> suitors, she would have waited instead of accepting the first man who proposed.

its   possessive pronoun meaning *belonging to it*
> e.g., The house lost <u>its</u> roof in the hurricane.

it's   a contraction meaning *it is* or *it has*
> e.g., <u>It's</u> true that everyone who has seen the play thinks <u>it's</u> been running too long.

lead   direct or go before; a metal
> e.g., The first violinist must <u>lead</u> the orchestra in tuning up.
> e.g., The <u>lead</u> content in paint makes it dangerous for children to eat.

(continued)

led   past tense of verb *to lead*
     e.g., The first violinist <u>led</u> the orchestra in tuning up.

loose   not tight
     e.g., When Aunt Lina was pregnant, she wore <u>loose</u> clothing be-
        cause it was comfortable.

lose   to experience the loss of
     e.g., After Aunt Lina had her baby, she went to a gym to <u>lose</u> the
        extra pounds she had gained.

moral   involving right or wrong
     e.g., Cheating on an examination is a <u>moral</u> issue.

morale   strong sense of enthusiasm
     e.g., The <u>morale</u> of the women's soccer team was low after their
        third straight loss.

passed   went, moved forward, or went through successfully
     e.g., As Cassandra <u>passed</u> Roger in the hall, she told him she had
        <u>passed</u> her calculus exam.

past   indicating a time gone by
     e.g., At their twentieth reunion, Cassandra and Roger talked about
        <u>past</u> times.

personal   private
     e.g., Indira's music teacher never answers <u>personal</u> questions about
        her family.

personnel   persons employed in any work; a department for hiring
        employees
     e.g., Maria is the head of the <u>personnel</u> department and the person
        to whom all <u>personnel</u> go with work-related problems.

prescribed   ordered or directed
     e.g., Mila's doctor <u>prescribed</u> a mild sleeping pill for her.

proscribed   outlawed, banished, forbidden
     e.g., Running near the municipal pool is <u>proscribed</u> behavior.

(continued)

pretend   to make believe
      e.g., Some days we all like to <u>pretend</u> we are someone else.

portend   to be an omen of
      e.g., Those black clouds <u>portend</u> a fierce thunderstorm.

principal   first in rank or importance; the head of a school; the amount
          of a debt minus the interest
      e.g., The <u>principal</u> thing to remember about <u>Principal</u> Smith is that
          he paid back the <u>principal</u> on his house loan within five years.

principle   a fundamental truth or law
      e.g., A universal <u>principle</u> for human behavior is the Golden Rule:
          Treat people as you would like people to treat you.

prostate   a male gland at the base of the bladder
      e.g., <u>Prostate</u> cancer is a common concern as men age.

prostrate   lying face downward
      e.g., Celeste found herself <u>prostrate</u> on the sidewalk after tripping
          over a tree root.

quiet   hushed, not noisy, silent
      e.g., Ruien needed a <u>quiet</u> room to write his term paper.

quite   completely, really
      e.g., When Ruien got his term paper back, he was <u>quite</u> pleased
          with his grade.

than   a word used as part of a comparison
      e.g., Emilio is taller <u>than</u> his brother Francisco.

then   at that time or next in time
      e.g., As Bob and Signe discussed their days in junior high, it was
          <u>then</u> that Bob confessed he had had a crush on her; <u>then</u> Signe
          confessed to a similar crush.

their   of or belonging to or done by them
      e.g., The students gave <u>their</u> teacher a standing ovation at the end
          of the semester.

(continued)

there   at or in a particular place
> e.g., The wedding was held at the church, and the reception was held <u>there</u>, also.

threw   past tense of *throw*
> e.g., Cedric <u>threw</u> the shotput for a new school record.

through   all around; finished
> e.g., The dance troupe traveled <u>through</u> Europe before their tour was <u>through</u>.

to   toward
> e.g., Li walks <u>to</u> work each day.

too   also or very
> e.g., Felix is bossy, and he is <u>too</u> arrogant, <u>too</u>.

two   one more than one
> e.g., Many pizza restaurants offer <u>two</u> pizzas for the price of one.

weather   condition of the atmosphere involving temperature and moisture
> e.g., New Englanders say, "If you don't like the <u>weather</u>, wait a minute, and it will change."

whether   if it be the case that
> e.g., <u>Whether</u> or not a student does well in college is his own choice.

were   past tense of *are*
> e.g., Last Christmas, the lights in our town <u>were</u> spectacular.

where   at or in a particular place
> e.g., The administration has not yet decided <u>where</u> to hold the graduation ceremony.

who's   contraction of *who is* or *who has*
> e.g., The custodian wants to know <u>who's</u> responsible for the broken window.
> e.g., He asked, "<u>Who's</u> got that information?"

(continued)

> whose   of or belonging to or done by whom
>   e.g., <u>Whose</u> gym shorts are these?
>
> you're   contraction of *you are*
>   e.g., <u>You're</u> taking too much time in the shower.
>
> your   of or belonging to or done by you
>   e.g., <u>Your</u> class participation will affect your semester grade.

Exercise Nine

Choosing the Correct Word

DIRECTIONS   In each of the following sentences, fill in the blanks with the correct word choice.

MODEL   When Monica was called to the <u>personnel</u> (personal, personnel) office, she was under the <u>illusion</u> (allusion, illusion) she was going to be promoted.

1. The _____ (principal, principle) characters in the steamy soap opera tried to keep their _____ (elicit, illicit) affair _____ (discreet, discrete) so that _____ (their, there) neighbors would not find out.

2. The ambassador's guests gave a _____ (complement, compliment) to his chef on the elegant _____ (desert, dessert).

3. When Jim sued his ex-wife for custody of their child, his lawyer's _____ (advice, advise) was to avoid all _____ (prescribed, proscribed) behavior.

4. The _____ (affect, effect) of the violent _____ (weather, whether) patterns this winter was to flood all low-lying areas in the Mississippi Delta _____ (accept, except) those protected by levees.

5. Rather than leaving the details to his relatives after his death, Malcolm _____ (chose, choose) to have the details of his funeral _____ (already, all ready) planned.

6. Alicia could _____ (have, of) _____ (lead, led) _____ (are, our) drill team in the Founders' Day parade, but she came down with the flu.

7. _____ (It's, Its) too bad the deadline for the short story contest has _____ (passed, past) because it was a _____ (grate, great) opportunity for Dennis to _____ (flaunt, flout) his talent.

8. In the journalism _____ (coarse, course), we _____ (were, where) told that a good reporter needs to anticipate _____ (were, where) the action is in order to _____ (brake, break) a major story.

9. In order to get _____ (threw, through) medical school these days, one must be _____ (quiet, quite) determined.

10. If you _____ (loose, lose) _____ (your, you're) _____ (moral, morale) convictions, _____ (your, you're) no better off _____ (than, then) an animal, according _____ (to, too, two) some philosophers.

Review Questions

Directions: Answer the following questions to help you review the material you have covered in this chapter.

1. Tone is determined by the _____ or _____. (p. 149)

2. What is tone? (p. 149) _____.

3. What are two kinds of tone? (p. 150) _____ and _____

4. Making the tone of a paragraph agree with the tone of an assignment is using _____. (p. 151)

5. Is formal or informal writing usually more appropriate for college assignments? (p. 151) _____

6. Excessively formal language is called _____. (p. 152)

7. What are the two reasons that "collegese" must be translated? (p. 152)

   _____ and _____

8. What are the characteristics of a sentence that uses active voice? (p. 153)

   _____ _____

9. What are the characteristics of a sentence that uses passive voice? (p. 153)

   _____ _____ _____

10. What part of speech expresses the voice in a sentence? (p. 153) _____

    _____

11. What is excessively informal language called? (p. 155) _____

12. What are four errors of excessively informal language? (p. 155–156)

    _____ _____

    _____ _____

13. What does *context* mean? (p. 157) _____

14. What are two kinds of context errors? (p. 157–159) _____ and

    _____

15. What are two good ways to learn the correct context for new vocabulary

    words? (p. 157) _____ and _____

16. Other word choice errors result because some words _____

    and/or _____ alike. (p. 161)

Writing Exercises

I. Constructing Sentences with Vocabulary Words

Look up each of the following words in a college dictionary. Then write a sentence
for each word. Be sure the sentence illustrates the meaning of the word.

MODEL   Word: uncanny

Definition: inexplicable

Sentence: Humberto had an <u>uncanny</u> ability to foretell the future.

1. Word: fleeting

   Definition: _____

   Sentence: _____ .

2. Word: definitive

   Definition: _____

   Sentence: _____ .

3. Word: prospective

   Definition: _____

   Sentence: _____ .

4. Word: contingent (on)

   Definition: _____

   Sentence: _____ .

5. Word: heinous

   Definition: _____

   Sentence: _____ .

II. Writing Paragraphs Using New Words

Choose one of the following topics, and write a paragraph on it, using the required vocabulary words. Be sure you understand the definition and context of each word. You may use any form of the word; for example, if the word is *convince,* you may use *convinced* or *convincing,* as well as *convince.* Also make sure your paragraph is correctly structured and fully developed with a topic sentence, three primary details (each with two secondary details for support), a conclusion, and appropriate transitions.

1. Describe a violent movie or television show you have seen.

   Vocabulary: traumatic   desensitize   villain   gory

2. Describe three student services on your campus.

   Vocabulary: buttress   intervention   advocate   opportune

3. Discuss three methods of changing bad behavior in children.

   Vocabulary: provoke   intractable   hyperactive   exemplify

III. Revising for Word Choice

Look back at the three paragraphs you rewrote for Writing Exercise III in Chapter Nine. Pay particular attention to your word choices. Revise your paragraphs to eliminate slang, contractions, collegese, the pronoun *you,* wordiness, passive voice, and interjections. Also, replace incorrectly used words.

Looking Back and Looking Forward

In this chapter, you have learned how word choice helps establish the tone of your paragraph. In the next chapter, you will learn how to vary your sentence structure for interest, emphasis, and clarity.

Chapter Eleven

Choosing Sentence Patterns

In Chapter Ten, you learned how to make appropriate language choices in response to an assignment. In this chapter, you will learn how to combine sentences in a variety of patterns to keep your reader interested in your response. In order to combine sentences effectively, you must first review the characteristics of a complete sentence and learn to avoid the most common sentence-combining error, the run-on.

As you recall from Chapter Five, the characteristics of a sentence are a verb, a subject, and a complete thought. You also learned that a group of words that is missing any of these things cannot be called a sentence. If this group of words is presented as a sentence—beginning with a capital letter and ending with a period—it is an error called a **fragment.** In other words, a fragment has <u>too little</u> of what it takes to be a sentence. On the other hand, a group of words that has <u>too much</u> of what it takes to be a sentence is called a *run-on.*

Run-ons

A **run-on sentence** has more than one verb, more than one subject, and more than one complete thought, joined incorrectly. Consider the following group of words.

> In the middle of the parking lot, surrounded by her adoring fans, the film star, dressed in a sequined gown and bedecked with diamonds that twinkled in the sunlight, signed autographs before disappearing into a pink limousine, which swept her away to the Academy Awards ceremony at the Dorothy Chandler Pavilion.

Now consider this group of words.

> We sat and we talked.

Which of these two groups of words in the examples is a run-on sentence? If you said the first group of words is a run-on sentence because it goes on and on, you have made a common error. The length of a sentence is not what makes it a run-on. In the first sentence, there is only one independent clause:

The film star signed autographs.

The remaining words belong to phrases and dependent clauses that add more information. If you need to review phrases and clauses, see Chapter Five.

Most effective writers go beyond the basic sentence of verb, subject, and complete thought; they add information that gives their sentences variety and interest. The long sentence about the film star provides many examples. Which phrases add information about where the film star is? Which phrases add information about the film star's appearance? Which phrase adds information about when the film star signed autographs? Which clause adds information about the star's limousine? Finally, which phrase adds information about where the Academy Awards ceremony is held?

Even though this long sentence about the film star is not a run-on, it is still not an effective sentence in terms of style. It presents too much information in one sentence for a reader to focus on. While an effective sentence will probably contain more than just a verb and subject and complete thought, too much additional information is as ineffective as too little.

On the other hand, the second group of words does not contain too much information, but it is ineffective grammatically because it is a run-on sentence. It contains two independent clauses: *We sat* and *we talked.* These clauses have been linked with the joining word *and,* which is <u>not</u> a correct way of joining two independent clauses; therefore, this group of words is a run-on.

Now look at the same independent clauses linked another way:

We sat, we talked.

This time, the two independent clauses have been linked by a comma, which is also <u>not</u> a correct way of joining two independent clauses; therefore, this group of words is a kind of run-on sentence called a **comma splice** because it attempts to splice the two independent clauses by means of a comma, the way a film editor splices two pieces of film with tape.

Finally, look at the same independent clauses written this way:

We sat we talked.

This time, the two independent clauses have been run together with no joining word and no punctuation, which is also <u>not</u> a correct way of joining two independent clauses; therefore, this group of words is a run-on sentence, too.

There are several ways to correct a run-on sentence. Consider the following corrections:

1. We sat. We talked.
2. We sat; we talked.
3. We sat, and we talked.
4. While we sat, we talked.
5. We sat, talking.

While the first two corrections separate the two independent clauses with a period and a semicolon respectively, the result is a choppy rhythm. In other words, they are not as stylistically effective as the remaining corrections. There is more to an effective paper than correct grammar: **Style** is also important. Good style is a matter of choosing effective words and sentence patterns when you add bits of information to a sentence. Information can be added by using the same three methods used in Corrections 3, 4, and 5, methods that also help you avoid run-ons: coordination, subordination, and modification.

Coordination

Coordination is bringing together information of <u>equal</u> importance in a sentence with the correct punctuation. One way to coordinate information of equal importance is to bring the information together with joining words called **coordinating conjunctions**. For instance, consider the sentence *Cinderella wanted to go to the ball, yet she had nothing suitable to wear.* Notice that the two bits of information that are joined in this sentence are

1. Cinderella wanted to go to the ball.
2. She had nothing suitable to wear.

These independent clauses express two things about Cinderella that are equally important, so they can be joined by a coordinating conjunction like *yet* and the correct punctuation.

Punctuation for Coordination

Did you notice what punctuation goes with the coordinating conjunction when it joins two independent clauses? A comma must come <u>before</u> any coordinating conjunction that joins two independent clauses.

There are seven coordinating conjunctions, one for each letter in the acronym **FANBOYS**. Although all coordinating conjunctions are used to bring together things of equal importance in a sentence, not all express the same relationship between those equal things.

for	=	because
		The gardener threw out the potting soil, <u>for</u> it contained whitefly eggs.
and	=	also
		Darryl was coughing, <u>and</u> he was sniffling.
nor	=	also not this
		Pamela did not want to sing, <u>nor</u> did she want to dance in the show.
but	=	yet
		Waverly enrolled in Home Economics I, <u>but</u> she did not finish out the term.
or	=	if not one, then the other
		Andrew might transfer to Cornell, <u>or</u> he might transfer to UCLA.
yet	=	however
		I don't agree with you, <u>yet</u> I see your point.
so	=	therefore
		Norma was caught cheating on her chemistry exam, <u>so</u> she was expelled from school.

Coordination

Exercise One

DIRECTIONS   Combine each of the following pairs of sentences, using the appropriate coordinating conjunction. Do not forget to use a comma before the coordinating conjunction. Also, in some cases, more than one coordinating conjunction might be appropriate, but you may need to reverse the order of the two sentences when you combine them so that the coordinating conjunction you choose makes sense.

MODEL   a. Annie took a course in exotic animal care.

b. Annie has always wanted to work with orangutans.

Combination: <u>Annie has always wanted to work with orangutans, so she took a</u> <u>course in exotic animal care.</u>

1a. Celia stopped taking saxophone lessons.

  b. Celia's neighbors complained about the noise from her apartment.

Combination:

_____.

2a. Creed wanted to keep the stray kitten he had found.

  b. Creed's landlord did not allow tenants to have pets.

Combination:

_____.

3a. Kenny did not want to spend his summer working in a salmon cannery in Sitka.

  b. Kenny did not want to spend his summer mending fishing nets on Prince Edward Island.

Combination:

_____.

4a. The Little League pitcher got a division award for sportsmanship.

  b. She also got a division award for Most Valuable Player.

Combination:

_____.

5a. Moravian spice cookies can be made with real butter.

  b. Moravian spice cookies can be made with margarine.

Combination:

_____.

Sometimes the things of equal importance you want to bring together do not have to remain in independent clauses. If the subject and the verb are the same in each sentence, there is no need to repeat them. The additional information can be expressed as single words joined with a coordinating conjunction. In this case, there is no comma. Consider these sentences:

1. He likes avocados.

2. He likes persimmons.

Combination: He likes avocados <u>and</u> persimmons.

In addition, the things of equal importance can be expressed as phrases joined with a coordinating conjunction. There is no comma in this case, as well. Consider these sentences:

1. We knew Jim might be in the house.

2. We knew Jim might be in the barn.

Combination: We knew Jim might be in the house <u>or</u> in the barn.

Finally, the things of equal importance can be expressed as dependent clauses joined with a coordinating conjunction. Again, there is no comma. Consider these sentences:

1. Caramia has a good time when she prepares the motions for a case.

2. Caramia has a good time when she argues a case before a jury.

Combination: Caramia has a good time when she prepares the motions for a case <u>and</u> when she argues a case before a jury.

Remember that although you use a comma before the coordinating conjunction to join independent clauses, when you combine two bits of information in single words, phrases, and dependent clauses with a coordinating conjunction, you do not use a comma before the conjunction.

However, items in a series are different. A series is <u>three</u> or more words, phrases, dependent clauses, or independent clauses in a row. Consider the following series:

1. This semester Jamshid is taking <u>chemistry</u>, <u>physics</u>, and <u>Shakespeare</u>. (single words)

2. Leigh cheered himself up after getting a D in Statistics 101 <u>by eating a banana split</u>, <u>goint to a jazz concert</u>, <u>playing a fast game of racquetball</u>, and <u>buying himself a Brooks Brothers shirt.</u> (phrases)

3. Brad cleans his room only <u>when his mother threatens to visit</u>, <u>when his girlfriend threatens to leave him</u>, and <u>when his roommate threatens to throw him out.</u> (dependent clauses)

4. In order to have her short stories critiqued, <u>Katie can join a writers' group</u>, <u>she can ask her friends to read her work</u>, or <u>she can send her manuscripts to an agent.</u> (independent clauses)

Did you notice that a comma comes between each item in a series, even between the last two items which are joined by a coordinating conjunction?

<table>
<tr><td>Exercise Two</td><td colspan="2">**Coordinating Conjunctions and Punctuation**</td></tr>
<tr><td>DIRECTIONS</td><td colspan="2">For each set of sentences, decide which bits of information need to be combined. You may join independent clauses, single words, phrases, or items in a series. Be sure to use commas and coordinating conjunctions appropriately.</td></tr>
<tr><td>MODEL</td><td>a.</td><td>In spring, birds migrate north.</td></tr>
<tr><td></td><td>b.</td><td>In spring, birds build nests.</td></tr>
<tr><td></td><td>c.</td><td>In spring, birds incubate their eggs.</td></tr>
</table>

Combination: <u>In spring, birds migrate north, build nests, and incubate their eggs.</u>

1a. Some actors do research to prepare for a role.

  b. Other actors do not do research to prepare for a role.

Combination: _____.

2a. Clancy dug up the petunias.

  b. Clancy chased the cat into traffic.

  c. Clancy chewed the new sofa pillows.

  d. Clancy raided the garbage pail.

Combination: _____.

3a. The new tenants created problems when they let their children swim in the pool unsupervised.

  b. The new tenants created problems when they threw a lot of loud parties.

Combination: _____.

4a. Athena went to Neiman Marcus to register her china pattern.

  b. Athena went to Neiman Marcus to register her silver pattern.

Combination: _____.

5a. Tracy caught the trout.

 b. Tracy cleaned the trout.

 c. Robin cooked the trout.

Combination: _____ .

Sometimes the items in a series may be complicated by a comma within each item. When that happens, your sentence will be easier to understand if you use a semicolon <u>after</u> each item instead of a comma. Consider the following model:

> Several distinguished scientists attended the conference: Dr. William Riley, a physicist from Boston; Dr. Manuel Gomez, a biologist from Denver; Dr. Nigel Cuthbertson, an astronomer from Leeds, England; and Dr. Yetty Vanderhoek, a chemist from Edam, The Netherlands.

Did you notice that a comma follows each scientist's name and some commas separate the name of a city from the name of a country? Can you see how the semicolons between items make it easier to see where each item ends in these cases?

Another way to coordinate independent clauses is to express the equal relationship between the bits of information with **adverbial conjunctions.** Consider the sentence *Cinderella wanted to go to the ball; however, she had nothing suitable to wear.* In this sentence, the adverbial conjunction *however* means the same as the coordinating conjunctions *yet* and *but*. In fact, many of the coordinating conjunctions have equivalent adverbial conjunctions:

for	=	(no equivalent)
and	=	moreover, furthermore Ed was afraid of the Space Mountain ride at Disneyland; <u>moreover,</u> he was not keen about the Twister at Knott's Berry Farm.
nor	=	(no equivalent)
but	=	however, on the other hand, nevertheless Charlene's academic credentials were impressive; <u>nevertheless,</u> she lacked the practical experience required for the job.

(continued)

> **or** = on the other hand
> Delilah made a comment that might have been intentionally sarcastic<u>; on the other hand,</u> her comment might have been quite innocent.
>
> **yet** = however
> We had made dinner reservations for seven o'clock<u>; however,</u> we still waited an hour for our table.
>
> **so** = therefore, consequently, thus, as a result
> The actor's first feature film brought him instant success<u>; thus,</u> he gave up his day job as a waiter.

Did you notice that several adverbial conjunctions are more than one word, like *on the other hand* and *as a result*?

Now compare how these sentences are punctuated when they use a coordinating conjunction and when they use an adverbial conjunction:

1. Cinderella wanted to go to the ball, yet she had nothing suitable to wear.

2. Cinderella wanted to go to the ball; however, she had nothing suitable to wear.

While the coordinating conjunction is preceded by a comma, adverbial conjunctions are preceded by a semicolon and followed by a comma. You can think of a semicolon as a weak period. It comes between two independent clauses that do not want to be fully separated because they have a strong relationship; consequently, the independent clause after the semicolon begins with a small letter (unless it is a proper noun or the pronoun *I,* which are always capitalized). Did you notice that the sentence you just read is a good example?

Exercise Three   **Adverbial Conjunctions and Punctuation**

DIRECTIONS   Combine each of the following pairs of sentences, using an appropriate adverbial conjunction. Do not forget to use a semicolon before the adverbial conjunction and a comma after it.

MODEL   a. Tristan positively identified the suspect in a line-up.

b. The suspect was released from custody anyway.

Combination: <u>Tristan positively identified the suspect in a line-up; however, the suspect was released from custody anyway.</u>

1a. Lynette heckled the controversial speaker at the campus rally.

b. Lynette threw two rotten tomatoes and a soggy eggplant at the speaker.

Combination: _____.

2a. Ginger and sassafras root are both digestive aids.

b. Too much ginger and sassafras root can upset the stomach.

Combination: _____.

3a. The heat in Phoenix reached 120 degrees in May.

b. Even though he did not like air conditioning, Mr. Velasquez was happy he had bought a new cooling unit in April.

Combination: _____.

4a. Hope could take a day job and work on her novel at night.

b. Hope could take a night job and work on her novel during the day.

Combination: _____.

5a. The only time Jerzy could schedule an appointment with his dermatologist was 9 A.M. on Wednesday.

b. Jerzy had to get his boss's permission to arrive late to work Wednesday morning.

Combination: _____.

Another way of combining sentences that avoids run-ons involves subordination.

Subordination

Subordination is bringing together information in a sentence by making some information less important than other information. One way to subordinate information is to introduce it with a dependent word called a **subordinating conjunction**. A subordinating conjunction makes some information a dependent clause. For instance, consider the sentence *When Cinderella left the ball, she lost one of her glass slippers.* Can you see that Cinderella's leaving the ball and her losing one of her glass slippers are both actions that could have been expressed as two independent clauses joined by a coordinating conjunction and a comma?

Cinderella left the ball, and she lost one of her glass slippers.

However, we have emphasized one action as more important by putting it in an independent clause and the other action as less important by putting it in a dependent clause beginning with the subordinating conjunction *When*. When you wish to make one clause more important than another clause, you should join them with subordination, rather than coordination. To choose which clause you should make more important, you will have to use your critical thinking skills.

Identifying Important Information

DIRECTIONS   For each of the following sets of sentences, choose which sentence you think contains the more or most important information.

MODEL   a. Sven hated cold weather.

b. Sven moved to Costa del Sol.

c. Sven hated gray skies.

Most important information: <u>Sven moved to Costa del Sol.</u>

1a. The water commission found harmful microorganisms in the municipal water supply.

b. The water commission ordered chlorine to be added to the municipal water supply.

More important information: _____.

2a. Annette's paper on abnormal psychology represented a wide variety of sources.

b. Annette included on-line interviews with experts in the field.

c. Annette included data from recent articles in professional psychology journals.

d. Annette included case studies of patients with psychological disorders.

Most important information: _____.

3a. Jack hopes to keep his grade point average high and his golf score low.

b. Jack can win a John Evans golf scholarship to Northwestern University.

More important information: _____.

4a. All the neighborhood children went to Freddy's birthday party.

b. A clown made balloon animals at Freddy's party.

c. Freddy's mother grilled hot dogs and hamburgers at Freddy's party.

Most important information: _____.

5a. Sophia played a rented clarinet in the spring concert.

b. Sophia's own clarinet was being repaired.

More important information: _____.

Here are the most common subordinating conjunctions that make a clause dependent. They are arranged in categories that might help you remember them.

Time

after	during	since	when
as	now that	till	whenever
as long as	once	until	while
before			

Cause and Effect   *Contradiction*

because	although	though
in order (that)	even if	unless
so that	even though	whereas
	except (that)	

Comparison   *Condition*

as	like	if	in case
as if	than	if only	provided that
as though	the way that		

Place

where
wherever

Punctuation and Placement for Subordination

Have you noticed that you can put an independent clause before or after a dependent clause? However, the punctuation differs in each case. If the dependent clause comes <u>after</u> the independent clause, there is usually no comma between the two clauses, but if the dependent clause comes <u>before</u> the independent clause, the dependent clause is followed by a comma. In fact, any long introduction before an independent clause is followed by a comma. Consider the following sentences:

(dependent clause)   ,   (independent clause)

1. When the clock struck twelve, Cinderella fled from the ball.

(independent clause)   (dependent clause)

2. Cinderella fled from the ball when the clock struck twelve.

Exercise Five

Subordination

DIRECTIONS   For each set of sentences, identify which presents the more or most important information. Then use subordination to combine the sentences, choosing the appropriate subordinating conjunction to introduce the less important information. Do not forget to put a comma between the clauses if the dependent clause comes before the independent clause.

MODEL   a. Dwight's car lasted 150,000 miles.

b. Dwight changed his car's oil every 3,000 miles.

c. Dwight tuned his car's engine every 15,000 miles.

Most important information: Dwight's car lasted 150,000 miles.

Combination: Because Dwight changed his car's oil every 3,000 miles and tuned his car's engine every 15,000 miles, his car lasted 150,000 miles.

1a. Violet had a root canal after her tooth abscessed.

b. Violet's tooth continued to ache even after her root canal.

More important information: _____ .

Combination: _____

_____ .

2a. Sunny wants to attend the Stanley Cup playoffs this year.

b. First, she must find a friend to go with her.

More important information: _____ .

Combination: _____

_____ .

3a. The most famous site of the opera *Aida* was the Baths of Caracalla outside Rome.

  b. Real elephants and horses could be used on this outdoor stage.

More important information: _____.

Combination: _____

_____.

4a. Walking through the Fun House at Salisbury Beach made Allan shiver.

  b. Leaves shiver in the wind.

More important information: _____.

Combination: _____

_____.

5a. Mikhail proposed to Minerva on the promenade deck.

  b. Mikhail and Minerva met on a cruise.

More important information: _____.

Combination: _____

_____.

A final way of combining sentences that avoids run-ons involves modification.

Modification

Modification is adding information to a sentence that describes the information in that sentence in more detail. Modification is a form of subordination because it does not contain the important parts of the sentence, the subject and verb. Even though modifiers are not essential, they add detail and make sentences more interesting. That is why sentence combining with modification improves your writing style.

Just like coordination and subordination, modification can involve *single words, phrases,* and *clauses.*

Single-Word Modifiers

As you recall from Chapter Three, single words that describe other information are called *adjectives* and *adverbs*. Adjectives describe nouns and pronouns. Adverbs describe verbs, adjectives, and other adverbs. Consider these sentences:

1. The valedictorian rubbed her eyes.

2. The valedictorian was <u>Gwendolyn</u>.

3. She rubbed her eyes <u>gently</u>.

4. Her eyes were <u>bloodshot</u>.

5. Her eyes were <u>itchy</u>.

6. She was <u>weary</u>.

7. She was <u>discouraged</u>.

Combination: The weary and discouraged valedictorian, Gwendolyn, gently rubbed her itchy, bloodshot eyes.

In the preceding example, the first sentence is the basic sentence because it contains the verb, the subject, and a complete thought, but no modifiers. Each of the sentences that follows the basic sentence repeats information from that basic sentence and adds a modifier which can be absorbed by the basic sentence in a combination.

Placement and Punctuation for Single-Word Adjectives

What are the adjectives in the sentence combination about the valedictorian who rubbed her eyes? Did you notice the punctuation that comes between two adjectives that modify the same noun? When two adjectives describe the same noun, they are called **coordinate adjectives,** and they are separated from each other with a comma, for example, *itchy, bloodshot eyes.* However, when coordinate adjectives have an *and* between them, there is no comma, such as *weary and discouraged valedictorian.*

Did you notice where the adjectives are placed in relation to the nouns they describe? If you said that the adjectives *weary* and *discouraged* come <u>before</u> the noun *valedictorian* and that the adjectives *itchy* and *bloodshot* come <u>before</u> the noun *eyes,* then you can see that most adjectives come before the words they describe. However, you may vary your style to make it more interesting by occasionally changing the usual order of adjectives and the nouns they modify. For instance, if you have coordinate adjectives, you can join them with *and* and put them <u>after</u> the noun with commas before and after them:

The valedictorian, Gwendolyn, <u>weary and discouraged,</u> gently rubbed her itchy, bloodshot eyes.

Not all adjectives that appear side by side are coordinate adjectives. True coordinate adjectives can be separated by the word *and.* Consider the phrase *a frosty winter morning.* Can you put *and* between *frosty* and *winter?* Does *frosty and winter morning* sound right? When you want to test for coordinate adjectives, simply place *and* between them and determine if they sound right. If they do, you may choose to leave the *and* or separate the adjectives with a comma. If they do not sound right, you must leave them alone without punctuation between them.

Exercise Six

Modification with Coordinate and Non-Coordinate Adjectives

DIRECTIONS   Each of the following sentences is followed by three adjectives. Two of them are co-ordinate adjectives, while one is not. Write each sentence three ways, using coordinate adjectives before the noun, non-coordinate adjectives before the noun (leaving out one coordinate adjective), and coordinate adjectives after the noun. Punctuate all modifiers correctly.

MODEL   The gate would not open. (rusty, old, wire)

a. The rusty, old gate would not open.

(coordinates before noun)

b. The wire gate would not open.

(non-coordinate before noun)

c. The wire gate, old and rusty, would not open.

(coordinates after noun and non-coordinate before noun)

1. The scrolls were authenticated by Biblical scholars. (Dead Sea, fragile, decaying)

a. _____.

(coordinates before noun)

b. _____.

(non-coordinate before noun)

c. _____.

(coordinates after noun and non-coordinate before noun)

2. The drama club put on a French farce for their spring production. (Restoration, hilarious, bawdy)

a. _____.

(coordinates before noun)

b. _____.

(non-coordinate before noun)

c. _____.

(coordinates after noun and non-coordinate before noun)

3. The chemistry lab was contaminated when the student spilled chemicals. (caustic, several, toxic)

   a. _____.

   (coordinates before noun)

   b. _____.

   (non-coordinate before noun)

   c. _____.

   (coordinates after noun and non-coordinate before noun)

4. The library held a sale every spring to sell their books. (excess, outdated, paperback)

   a. _____.

   (coordinates before noun)

   b. _____.

   (non-coordinate before noun)

   c. _____.

   (coordinates after noun and non-coordinate before noun)

5. Miriam's home economics class experimented with a recipe for cookies. (granola, low fat, crispy)

   a. _____.

   (coordinates before noun)

   b. _____.

   (non-coordinate before noun)

   c. _____.

   (coordinates after noun and non-coordinate before noun)

Placement for Single-Word Nouns

If you go back to the original sentence about the weary and discouraged valedictorian, you will notice that one of the modifiers was a noun. Which one? Can you see that the proper noun *Gwendolyn* describes the noun *valedictorian* because it gives us more information about who the valedictorian is? When a noun comes right after another noun or pronoun it describes, it is called an **appositive.** Like coordinate adjectives that follow a noun, an appositive has commas before and after it.

Modification with Appositives

DIRECTIONS   One sentence of each of the following pairs contains a noun that can be used as an appositive in a sentence combination with the other sentence. Remember to punctuate the appositive correctly.

MODEL   a. The new chef overcooked the noodles for his stroganoff.

b. The chef was Ulric.

Combination: <u>The new chef, Ulric, overcooked the noodles for his stroganoff.</u>

1a. Rochelle's dentist is Dr. Watanabe.

b. Rochelle's dentist performed a root canal on her damaged tooth.

Combination: _____

_____.

2a. The archeology dig site was unbearably hot during the day.

b. The archeology dig site was Olduvai Gorge.

Combination: _____

_____.

3a. Kevin's new furniture is Shaker style.

b. The style of Kevin's new furniture has simple, unadorned lines.

Combination: _____

_____.

4a. The two major American political parties differ in their views on government spending.

b. The two parties are the Democratic Party and the Republican Party.

Combination: _____

_____.

5a. The Baltic States are Latvia, Lithuania, and Estonia.

b. The Baltic States used to be part of the Soviet Union.

Combination: _____

_____.

Placement for Single-Word Adverbs

Now identify the adverb in the sentence *The weary and discouraged student gently rubbed her itchy, bloodshot eyes.* What word does *gently* describe? Where does the adverb *gently* occur in relation to that word? Is the placement of the adverb as important as the placement of adjectives? Do you agree that most adverbs can come anywhere in a sentence? Consider these variations in which the adverb can move within the sentence:

Gently the weary and discouraged student rubbed her itchy, bloodshot eyes.

The weary and discouraged student gently rubbed her itchy, bloodshot eyes.

The weary and discouraged student rubbed gently her itchy, bloodshot eyes.

The weary and discouraged student rubbed her itchy, bloodshot eyes gently.

Do you see that even though the adverb comes in a different place in each sentence, the meaning remains the same in all the sentences? However, several adverbs are exceptions. Adverbs that limit the words they describe in *time, distance,* and *amount* must be placed right before those words. These adverbs include *almost, nearly, only, hardly, very, barely,* and *just.* Observe the placement of the adverbs in the following sentences.

1. Just Carlos wanted to sell the family business. (Carlos was the only family member who wanted to sell.)

2. Carlos just wanted to sell the family business. (Carlos didn't sell the family business, but he wanted to.)

3. Carlos wanted just to sell the family business. (Carlos didn't want to lease it, or go out of business, or do anything else with the business except sell it.)

4. Carlos wanted to sell just the family business. (Carlos didn't want to sell anything else.)

Can you see how the meaning of the sentence changes every time the adverb *just* is moved? That is because this kind of adverb describes only the thing it comes before. Did you also notice that single-word adverbs do not require punctuation no matter where you put them in a sentence?

Exercise Eight

Modification with Adverbs

DIRECTIONS For the following sentences, place the accompanying adverb(s) appropriately. Remember that while some adverbs can be placed almost anywhere in a sentence, other adverbs require specific placement.

MODEL By the midnight deadline, the election votes were all counted.
(barely)
Modified sentence: By midnight, the election votes were barely all counted.

1. In the desert, many cacti bloom.

   (seasonally)

   _____ .

2. The agriculture students must milk the dairy herd.

   (regularly)

   _____ .

3. Renaldo is so compulsive that he gets anxious when there are 250 shopping days until Christmas.

   (only)

   _____ .

4. Queen bees leave their hives to recolonize or die.

   (reluctantly, just)

   _____ .

5. The skinny-dippers were caught with no clothes on by the patrolman and reprimanded by the judge.

   (nearly, severely)

   _____ .

Exercise Nine

Sentence Combining with Single-Word Modifiers

DIRECTIONS   First, determine which sentence in each of the following sets is the basic sentence. Then add the modifiers from the rest of the sentences to form a sentence combination. Remember how to punctuate coordinate and non-coordinate adjectives. Remember also that some adverbs require specific placement in a sentence.

MODEL   a. Junior accepted the prize proudly.

b. The competition was at the state level.

c. Junior accepted first prize in the photography competition.

d. It was a still life photography competition.

Basic sentence: Junior accepted first prize in the photography competition.

Combination: Junior proudly accepted first prize in the state still life photography

competition.

1a. The meeting of the administrators was crucial.

  b. There were three administrators.

  c. The administrators had their meeting in a classroom.

  d. The classroom in which they met was empty.

  e. They met privately.

  f. The three administrators were top administrators.

Basic sentence: _____ .

Combination: _____

_____ .

2a. Beverly liked the way her professor taught.

  b. Her professor taught chemistry.

  c. Her professor was old.

  d. She thought he taught very clearly.

  e. He was cranky.

  f. Her professor was Bill Dahlgren.

Basic sentence: _____ .

Combination: _____

_____ .

3a. Arthur's headband was Day-Glo.

  b. His chess set was incomplete.

  c. Arthur held a yard sale.

  d. He wanted to sell his chess set.

  e. He wanted to sell his albums.

  f. His albums were by Lawrence Welk.

  g. The albums were warped.

  h. He wanted to sell his headband.

  i. His lava lamp was broken.

  j. He wanted to sell his lava lamp.

k. He held the sale enthusiastically.

Basic sentence: _____ .

Combination: _____

_____ .

4a. The cases involved violence.

b. The nuisance was public.

c. The cases were DUI.

d. The violence was domestic.

e. The morning was busy.

f. The cases involved nuisance.

g. The judge spent a morning hearing cases.

Basic sentence: _____ .

Combination: _____

_____ .

5a. One skill is delegating tasks.

b. D'Andre's job requires skill.

c. The job is office manager.

d. The delegating must be appropriate.

e. One skill is solving problems.

f. The problems involve personnel.

g. The problem-solving must be done quickly.

h. The problem-solving must be done effectively.

Basic sentence: _____ .

Combination: _____

_____ .

Phrase Modifiers

As you recall from Chapter Five, a phrase is a group of words that does not contain a verb, a subject, or a complete thought, but it acts as a single part of speech. Phrases that can act as modifiers include infinitive phrases, participial phrases, and prepositional phrases. Remember that a phrase is identified by the kind of word it begins with. For example, the infinitive phrase *to impress a date* begins with the infinitive *to impress.*

Do you remember the two kinds of participial phrases? What is the ending for a present participle? What are the endings for a past participle? If you do not remember, you should review Chapter Five.

Do you remember what modifiers a prepositional phrase can be? Do you remember what modifier a participial phrase is? What modifiers can an infinitive phrase be? Again, you can review this information. You will find prepositional phrases in Chapter Three and verbal phrases (participial and infinitive) in Chapter Five.

Punctuation and Placement for Phrase Modifiers

When phrase modifiers are added to a basic sentence, they are frequently set off by commas. First, if the phrase modifier comes <u>before</u> the basic sentence, it is <u>followed</u> by a comma:

> <u>Rowing frantically,</u> the second-place crew overtook the lead scull to win the Henley Regatta.   (present participial phrase)

> <u>In the Henley Regatta,</u> the second-place crew rowed frantically and overtook the lead scull to win.   (prepositional phrase)

> <u>To win the Henley Regatta,</u> the second-place crew rowed frantically and overtook the lead scull.   (infinitive phrase)

Notice that each phrase is followed by a comma. You can think of these phrases as introductions to the basic sentence, and, as you recall, long introductions to an independent clause are followed by a comma.

Some phrase modifiers that come at the end of a basic sentence are preceded by a comma, and some are not:

> The lead scull was overtaken by the second-place crew<u>, rowing frantically</u>.

What kind of phrase modifier comes at the end of this sentence? Now consider the following sentences:

> The lead scull was overtaken by the second-place crew <u>in the Henley Regatta</u>.

The second-place crew in the Henley Regatta rowed frantically <u>to overtake the lead scull</u>.

What two kinds of phrase modifiers come at the ends of these two sentences? A participial phrase that comes at the end of a sentence is preceded by a comma, but a prepositional phrase and an infinitive phrase usually are not.

If the phrase modifier comes in the middle of the basic sentence, commas come before and after the phrase:

The second-place crew<u>, rowing frantically,</u> overtook the lead scull in the Henley Regatta.

Now consider this sentence:

The second-place crew<u>, the rowers from Oxford,</u> overtook the lead scull in the Henley Regatta.

What kind of phrase modifier occurs in the middle of the first sentence? What kind occurs in the middle of the second sentence? Do you recall from the earlier section on single-word modifiers what a noun is called when it is put in the middle of a sentence to describe the word it follows? In this case, the whole noun phrase *the rowers from Oxford* describes the noun it follows, *crew*, so it is an <u>appositive</u> phrase. Notice that both this present participial phrase and the appositive phrase have commas before and after them because they occur in the middle of the sentence instead of before the noun they modify.

Whether a phrase modifier occurs at the beginning, at the end, or in the middle of a sentence, it must be placed <u>beside</u> the person, place, or thing it describes. Consider the following sentences:

1. <u>Ignoring his teacher's advice,</u> Robert did not reread his paper before handing it in.

2. Hans bought a cocker spaniel <u>with Parvo virus</u> from a breeder.

3. When he went to the Sundance Film Festival, Felix saw a biographical film <u>considered a future Oscar contender</u>.

What kind of phrase modifier begins the first sentence? What word does *Ignoring his teacher's advice* describe? Where does that word come in relation to the phrase modifier? What kind of phrase modifier comes in the middle of the second sentence? What word does *with a virus* describe? Where does that word come in relation to the phrase modifier? What kind of phrase modifier comes at the end of the third sentence? What word does *considered a future Oscar contender* describe? Where does that word come in relation to the phrase modifier?

Now consider the same sentences when the modifiers have been moved away from the words they modify:

1. Robert did not reread his paper, <u>ignoring his teacher's advice</u> before handing it in.

Even though this sentence may sound correct, it is not right because the phrase modifier *ignoring his teacher's advice* is closer to the word *paper* than it is to *Robert,* which implies that the paper was ignoring the teacher's advice; however, it was really Robert who ignored the teacher's advice.

2. Hans bought a cocker spaniel from a breeder <u>with Parvo virus.</u>

In this sentence, the phrase modifier *with Parvo virus* is closer to the word *breeder* than it is to *cocker spaniel,* which implies that the breeder has a virus only dogs can get.

3. <u>Considered a future Oscar contender,</u> Felix saw a biographical film when he went to the Sundance Film Festival.

In this sentence, the phrase modifier *Considered a future Oscar contender* is closer to the word *Felix* than it is to *film,* which incorrectly implies that Felix, not the film, may get an Oscar. When a phrase modifier is placed nearer a word it does not describe than to the word it does describe, the error is called a **misplaced modifier.**

Exercise Ten **Correcting Misplaced Modifiers**

DIRECTIONS In each sentence, find the phrase modifier that is misplaced and rewrite the sentence correctly.

MODEL Suzannah fed the sandwich to the begging bears with the moldy bread.

Misplaced phrase: <u>with the moldy bread</u>

Revision: <u>Suzannah fed the sandwich with the moldy bread to the begging bears.</u>

1. Based on her test results, we made a decision to let Nedra skip a grade.

    Misplaced phrase: _____

    Revision: _____.

2. The waitress cheerfully served her customers, hoping for a large tip.

    Misplaced phrase: _____

    Revision: _____.

3. Stolen from a rich merchant ship, the pirates hid their treasure in a trunk.

   Misplaced phrase: _____

   Revision: _____ .

4. Cleopatra stuck her hand in a basket of poisonous snakes, avoiding political sub-jugation.

   Misplaced phrase: _____

   Revision: _____ .

5. To treat others as one would like to be treated, Lindsay tried to live by the Golden Rule.

   Misplaced phrase: _____

   Revision: _____ .

Another modification error occurs when the person, place, or thing being described by the phrase modifier does not actually appear in the sentence. Sometimes a word in the sentence that is closely related to the absent word is mistaken for the absent word. When a phrase modifier has nothing to modify in a sentence, the error is called a **dangling modifier.** Consider this sentence:

Hitting a high note in *Rigoletto,* the opera singer's tights split up the middle.

What is the phrase modifier at the beginning of the sentence? Does the person it is supposed to modify appear in the sentence? If you said yes, you have confused the opera singer's tights with the opera singer. In other words, the possessive form of the noun, *opera singer's,* is not the same as the noun itself, *opera singer.* The noun *opera singer* does not appear in the sentence, so the phrase modifier *hitting a high note in Rigoletto* is left dangling, with nothing to modify.

There are several ways to correct a dangling modifier. One changes the phrase; the other changes the clause.

1. Turn the phrase modifier into a dependent clause by adding a subordinating con-junction. You will also have to add the missing noun or pronoun and sometimes a helping verb.

   As the opera singer was hitting a high note in *Rigoletto,* his tights split up the middle.

2. Add the noun or pronoun that is missing, which will change the independent clause in some way.

   Hitting a high note in *Rigoletto,* the opera singer split his tights up the middle.

Correcting Dangling Modifiers

DIRECTIONS In each sentence, find the dangling modifier and correct it using one of the methods in the preceding model.

1. Eating a tofu burger, Sally's stomach rebelled noisily.

   Correction: _____ .

2. Wanting to seem nonchalant, his arm draped casually on the back of his date's chair.

   Correction: _____ .

3. With no hope of finishing this exercise, the student's attitude turned sullen.

   Correction: _____ .

4. With only a faulty compass for a guide, the hikers' evening was cold and wet.

   Correction: _____ .

5. Barbara's yard sale was a failure, offering only her broken appliances.

   Correction: _____ .

Sentence Combining with Phrases

DIRECTIONS First, determine which sentence in each of the following sets is the basic sentence. Then add phrase modifiers from the rest of the sentences to form a sentence combination. Be sure to place phrase modifiers near the words they modify, either at the beginning, middle, or end of sentences to avoid misplaced modifiers. Also avoid dangling modifiers. Finally remember to punctuate phrase modifiers correctly.

MODEL a. The burglar broke into the house and stole a necklace.

b. The necklace was a choker.

c. The necklace was of solid gold.

d. The necklace had five diamonds.

Sentence combination: The burglar broke into the house and stole a necklace, a solid gold choker with five diamonds.

1a. Reiko's mother rejected her excuse.

b. The excuse was for denting the family car.

c. Reiko's mother scowled fiercely.

d. Reiko's mother is a suspicious woman.

Sentence combination: _____

_____ .

2a. Elsie's uniform has a blue blazer.

  b. The blazer has a Happy Hot Dog emblem.

  c. The emblem is on the pocket.

  d. Elsie must wear a uniform at work.

Sentence combination: _____

_____ .

3a. Cherie's brother had a broken leg.

  b. Cherie drove her brother to the hospital.

  c. She drove him in a minivan.

  d. The hospital was on the other side of town.

  e. Cherie is a nurse.

Sentence combination: _____

_____ .

4a. Khalifa was overdrawn at the bank.

  b. Khalifa took his guitar to the pawnbroker.

  c. The guitar was a gift from Khalifa's father.

  d. The pawnbroker had been recommended by a member of Khalifa's band.

  e. The band was called Hummus.

Sentence combination: _____

_____ .

5a. They provided packing boxes.

  b. The packing boxes had sturdy lids.

  c. They wrapped all furniture.

  d. The furniture wrapping was made of quilted fabric.

  e. The moving company was very thorough in their preparations.

Sentence combination: _____

_____ .

Clause Modifiers

As you recall from Chapter Five, a clause is a group of words that contains a verb and a subject and expresses a complete thought. Of the two kinds of clauses you learned about in that chapter—independent and dependent—*only the dependent clause can act as a modifier.* Just as a phrase is identified by the kind of word it begins with, a clause modifier is identified by the kind of word it begins with. A clause modifier begins with the relative pronouns *who, whom, that,* or *which,* or the subordinating conjunctions *where* or *when.* Generally, clause modifiers act as adjectives.

Punctuation and Placement for Clauses Modifiers

Clauses modifiers never occur at the beginning of a sentence. The reason for this is that they must follow the noun or pronoun they describe. Consider these two sentences:

1. The computer <u>which processes campus payroll</u> is already obsolete.

2. My son's computer, <u>which we bought last year,</u> is already obsolete.

Both of the underlined clauses modify the word *computer,* but they are punctuated differently. Do you know why? Unlike single-word modifiers and phrase modifiers, which provide additional information that is not essential for the rest of the sentence to make sense, some clause modifiers are essential to the meaning of a sentence. Which of the two sentences about a computer contains a clause modifier that is necessary for the sentence to express a complete idea? If you said the first sentence, you are right. There may be many computers on campus in addition to the payroll computer, but it is the payroll computer that is obsolete; therefore, the clause modifier *which processes campus payroll* is necessary to identify the subject. In other words, if we remove the clause modifier, the resulting sentence *The computer is obsolete* means something completely different. In this case, the sentence implies that any machine that is a computer is obsolete.

On the other hand, the subject in the second sentence has already been identified by the modifiers *My son's;* therefore, the clause modifier *which we bought last year* provides additional information about the subject that is not essential for the sentence to make sense. In other words, if we remove the clause modifier, the resulting sentence *My son's computer is obsolete* means exactly the same as it did with the clause modifier.

When the clause modifier would change the meaning of the sentence if it were removed, do not use commas to set it off from the rest of the sentence; however, when the clause modifier would <u>not</u> change the meaning of the sentence if it were removed, you must use commas to set it off from the rest of the sentence. You may think of commas around this kind of modifier as handles on the side of a basket containing the unnecessary information. Those comma handles tell you that you can lift the information out of the sentence without hurting the sentence.

Exercise Thirteen **Identifying and Punctuating Necessary and Unnecessary Clause Modifiers**

DIRECTIONS   Each of the following sentences contains a clause modifier. For each pair, decide which sentence contains the unnecessary clause modifier and add commas where appropriate.

MODEL   a. The logic professor gave a pop quiz on syllogisms which the class found difficult.

   b. Dr. Jones is the only professor who accepts late papers.

   Punctuated sentence: The logic professor gave a pop quiz on syllogisms, which the class found difficult.

1.a. The Two Old Coots Microbrewery which was started by a pair of retired mailmen grossed a million dollars in sales this year.

   b. The English ivy that is hanging in front of the window desperately needs water.

   Punctuated sentence: _____.

2a. The cat which I thought was pregnant was not.

   b. Marie had her wedding in the campus chapel where the chaplain officiated.

   Punctuated sentence: _____.

3a. The whale that played Willy in the movie *Free Willy* has been moved to Iceland in preparation for being released back into the wild.

   b. Keiko who played Willy in the movie *Free Willy* has been moved to Iceland in preparation for being released back into the wild.

   Punctuated sentence: _____.

4a. Blended eyeglasses which are more expensive than regular bifocals are often easier to get used to.

   b. Eyeglass frames that are small are preferred for thick lenses.

   Punctuated sentence: _____.

5a. Esophageal reflux syndrome which can affect the vocal cords causes stomach acid to rise into the esophagus.

b. The doctor whom I consulted about my esophageal reflux syndrome was a gastroenterologist.

Punctuated sentence: _____.

Exercise Fourteen Sentence Combining with Clauses

DIRECTIONS First determine which sentence in each of the following sets is the basic sentence. Then use the correct dependent word to make a clause modifier from the other sentence or sentences. Form a sentence combination by placing the clause modifier or clause modifiers near the middle or at the end of the basic sentence. Be sure to punctuate correctly.

MODEL a. Charles Dickens wrote about the problems of a highly-industrialized society.

b. The society Dickens wrote about was nineteenth-century London.

Sentence combination: Charles Dickens wrote about the problems of a highly-industrialized society, which was nineteenth-century London.

1a. For some people, marshmallows, jelly beans, and licorice are guiltless candies.

b. Those people have a sweet tooth.

c. Those candies are low in fat.

Sentence combination: _____.

2a. Florence Nightingale is often called *The Lady with the Lamp.*

b. Florence Nightingale is remembered as a tireless nurse from Crimean War battlefields.

c. On the battlefields she often roamed through the tents of the wounded at night with her lamp to look after those in pain.

Sentence combination: _____.

3a. Writers bring their experience of the writing process to students.

b. Those students would not otherwise get this firsthand perspective.

c. These writers speak on college campuses.

Sentence combination: _____.

4a. Some elderly people should not live in cold climates.

b. These elderly people are prone to osteoporosis.

c. In cold climates the old people must walk on dangerously icy surfaces in winter.

d. Osteoporosis is loss of bone density.

Sentence combination: _____.

5a. The movie *King of Hearts* is about the folly of war.

b. *King of Hearts* played continuously for five years when first released.

Sentence combination: _____.

<table>
<tr><td>Exercise Fifteen</td><td></td></tr>
</table>

Exercise Fifteen

Putting It All Together

DIRECTIONS   Combine the information in each of the following sets of sentences to form a single sentence using single-word modifiers, phrase modifiers and clause modifiers. Place and punctuate all modifiers correctly.

MODEL   a. The Oracle prophesied Oedipus would kill his own father.

b. The Oracle prophesied Oedipus would marry his mother.

c. Oedipus was the King of Thebes.

d. King Laius and Queen Jocasta feared the Oracle's prophecy.

e. King Laius and Queen Jocasta tried to have Oedipus killed in infancy.

f. Oedipus was the son of King Laius and Queen Jocasta.

Sentence combination: Oedipus, King of Thebes, was the son of King Laius and Queen Jocasta, who tried to have him killed in infancy because they feared the Oracle's prophecy that Oedipus would kill his own father and marry his mother.

1a. Folk music often deals with social problems.

b. Folk music was popularized by groups like the Chad Mitchell Trio.

c. Folk music was popularized by groups like the Kingston Trio.

d. Folk music was popularized in the 1960s.

e. Folk music often deals with children's fantasies.

f. Folk music was popularized by groups like Pete Seeger and the Weavers.

g. Folk music was popularized by groups like Peter, Paul, and Mary.

Sentence combination: _____

_____.

2a. Collagen injections fill in pitted areas of scarring.

b. Some scars can be treated in several ways.

c. These scars are facial.

d. The treatments include laser surgery.

e. The treatments include dermabrasion.

f. Laser surgery burns away the scars.

g. The treatments include collagen injections.

h. Dermabrasion scrapes away the scars.

i. Some scars used to be disfiguring.

j. This disfiguring was permanent.

Sentence combination: _____

_____.

3a. Fire has been a foe to humans.

b. Fire has cooked their food.

c. Fire has forged their tools.

d. Fire has burned their cities.

e. Fire has been a friend to humans.

f. Fire has burned their heretics.

g. Fire has warmed humans in cold weather.

h. Fire has burned their homes.

i. Fire has done these things all through history.

Sentence combination: _____

_____.

4a. Fireflies glow in the dark.

b. Fireflies produce a catalyst.

c. The catalyst is called *luciferase*.

d. Fireflies get their "lamp" from a catalyst.

e. *Luciferon* is another substance used by fireflies.

f. *Luciferase* helps *luciferon* consume oxygen.

Sentence combination: _____

_____.

5a. Sharks have skin.

  b. Sharks' skin does not have scales.

  c. Sharks are mammals.

  d. Sharks belong to a group of fish.

  e. Sharks' skin is rough.

  f. The group of fish sharks belong to has skeletons.

  g. Sharks have mottled skin.

  h. Sharks' skeletons are made of cartilage.

  Sentence combination: _____

  _____.

Did you notice that some sentence combinations involve only punctuation, others involve rearranging the whole sentences or parts of them, still others involve changing the form of some words, and others add or leave out words? In other words, you have choices. You may combine the same bits of information in sentences by presenting that information in single words, phrases, or clauses, and you may join the information to your sentences using coordination, subordination, or modification. The point is that all these methods create variety in your writing, and variety is at the heart of your style.

Review Questions

Answer the following questions to help you review the material you have covered in this chapter.

  1. What is a run-on sentence? (p. 173) _____

  2. Is there a relationship between the length of a sentence and a run-on? (p. 174)

  _____

  3. Why do effective sentences add information to the basic sentence containing a

  verb, subject, and complete thought? (p. 174) _____

  4. What happens when a sentence contains too much additional information?

  (p. 174) _____

5. Give three ways of incorrectly joining two independent clauses. (pp. 174)

   a. _____

   b. _____

   c. _____

6. What are five ways of correcting a run-on sentence? (p. 175)

   a. _____

   b. _____

   c. _____

   d. _____

   e. _____

7. What is good style? (p. 175) _____

8. What are the three methods of adding information to a basic sentence? (p. 175)

   _____ _____ _____

9. What is coordination? (p. 175) _____

10. What are the joining words used in coordination called? (p. 175)

    _____

11. What punctuation must go with these joining words when they join two independent clauses? (p. 175) _____

12. What is the acronym that helps you remember these joining words? (p. 176)

    _____

13. What are the seven joining words? (p. 176) _____ _____

    _____ _____ _____ _____ _____

14. Give an example of two independent clauses combined with coordination.

    _____.

15. Besides independent clauses, what can joining words add to a basic sentence? (p. 177) _____ _____ _____

16. How does the punctuation for joining two independent clauses differ from the punctuation for joining single words, phrases, or dependent clauses? (p. 178)

_____

17. What is a series? (p. 178) _____

18. How is a series punctuated? (p. 179) _____

19. Write a sentence with a series. _____ .

20. When items in a series are complicated by commas within the series items, what punctuation replaces the comma at the end of each item? (p. 180)

_____

21. Besides coordinating conjunctions and commas, what is another way to relate independent clauses? (p. 180) _____

22. How does the punctuation differ for adverbial conjunctions from coordinating conjunctions? (p. 181) _____

23. Give three adverbial conjunctions. (p. 180–181) _____

_____   _____

24. What is subordination? (p. 182) _____

25. What does a subordinating conjunction do to the information it joins to an independent clause? (p. 182) _____

26. What helps you remember the subordinating conjunctions? (p. 184) _____

_____

27. Give three subordinating conjunctions that show time. (p. 184)

_____   _____   _____

28. Give three subordinating conjunctions that show cause and effect. (p. 184)

_____   _____   _____

29. Give three subordinating conjunctions that show contradiction. (p. 184)

_____   _____   _____

30. Give three subordinating conjunctions that show comparison. (p. 184)

_____   _____   _____

31. Give three subordinating conjunctions that show condition. (p. 184)

    _____   _____   _____

32. Give two subordinating conjunctions that show place. (p. 184)

    _____   _____

33. Where can the dependent clause go in a sentence? (p. 184)

    _____

34. Why is there a comma after a dependent clause at the beginning of a sentence?
    (p. 185) _____

35. What is modification? (p. 186) _____

36. What forms of information does modification add to a basic sentence? (p. 186)

    _____   _____   _____

37. What are coordinate adjectives? (p. 187) _____

38. How are coordinate adjectives punctuated? (p. 187) _____

39. How can you tell if two adjectives are coordinate? (p. 187) _____

40. Where are most adjectives placed in a sentence? (p. 187) _____

41. What is an appositive? (p. 189) _____

42. How is an appositive punctuated? (p. 189) _____

43. What three parts of speech can be single-word modifiers? (p. 189)

    _____   _____   _____

44. Where are most adverbs found in a sentence? (p. 191) _____

45. What are three of the adverbs that must be placed <u>right</u> before the words they
    describe? (p. 191) _____   _____

    _____

46. How do those adverbs limit the words they describe? (p. 191)

    _____   _____   _____

47. When a phrase is used as a modifier at the beginning of a sentence, what punc-
    tuation follows it? (p. 195) _____

48. What kind of phrase at the end of a sentence is usually preceded by a comma? (p. 196) _____

49. What two kinds of phrases at the end of a sentence are usually not preceded by a comma? (p. 196) _____ _____

50. How do you punctuate a phrase modifier in the middle of a sentence? (p. 196)

_____

51. What do you call a phrase modifier that is incorrect because it is not beside the person, place, or thing it describes? (p. 197) _____

52. What do you call a phrase modifier that is incorrect because it has nothing in the sentence to describe? (p. 198) _____

53. What are the six words a clause modifier can begin with? (p. 201)

_____ _____ _____

_____ _____ _____

54. Where are these clause modifiers placed in a sentence? (p. 201)

_____ _____

55. When does a clause modifier need commas to set it off from the rest of the sentence? (p. 201) _____

56. When does a clause modifier <u>not</u> need commas to set it off from the rest of the sentence? (p. 201) _____

57. What do all of the sentence combining methods create in your writing? (p. 206) _____

Writing Exercises

I. Combining Sentences

Combine the information in each of the following sets of sentences three times, once using coordination, once using subordination, and once using modification.

1a. The swimming counselor was exasperated.

b. The swimming counselor yelled at the campers.

Coordination: _____.

Subordination: _____.

Modification: _____.

2a. The College Resource Center is located in the Student Services Building.

b. The College Resource Center provides computers for typing papers.

Coordination: _____.

Subordination: _____.

Modification: _____.

3a. Student writers have deadlines.

b. Student writers are like professional writers.

Coordination: _____.

Subordination: _____.

Modification: _____.

II. Rewriting a Paragraph with Coordination, Subordination, and Modification

Read the following sentences about pioneer dwellings and rewrite them, using all the sentence combination techniques you have learned in this chapter.

Sod dwellings were common on the American prairie in the nineteenth century. They were the first homes for many Western pioneers. They were common for several reasons. The dwellings were easy to build. The dwellings were dug into the sides of hills. These dwellings were called *soddies.* So were the people who lived in these dwellings. Sod dwellings had several advantages. They were insulated from extreme temperatures. Their earthen walls and roofs insulated them. They also protected their inhabitants from dust storms. The soddies were exposed to dust on only one side. Soddies considered their temporary homes practical. Other people looked down on them. These people thought the homes and the people who lived in them were poor. They also thought the homes were an eyesore.

III. Revising for Coordination, Subordination, and Modification

Look back at the three paragraphs you rewrote for Writing Exercise III in Chapter Ten. Pay particular attention to short, choppy sentences that need to be combined. Combine these sentences appropriately, using coordination, subordination, and modification.

IV. Writing with Coordination, Subordination, and Modification

Choose two of the following topics and write a paragraph on each. Using focused brainstorming, write a topic sentence and primary details; develop secondary details using strong verbs, comparisons, and specific details; choose an appropriate conclusion and transitions; make sure your word choices are appropriate; and finally, combine your sentences effectively wherever possible, using coordination, subordination, and modification.

1. Describe some ways to economize.

2. Describe the characteristics of your favorite kind of music.

3. Give reasons why you think an activity should be made an Olympic sport. The activity you choose can be athletic, non-athletic, humorous, or serious.

4. Choose a well-publicized crime and describe how the media treated it.

5. Describe ways to prevent hate crimes.

Looking Back and Looking Forward

In these chapters, you have learned how your word choices and sentence combination patterns give your writing style. In the next section, you will use critical thinking to edit your paragraphs, correcting errors in structure and development before you write your final draft.

Section three review   *Refining Style*

I. Rewriting for Style

Remember what you learned in Chapters Ten and Eleven about word choice and sentence combinations which help establish style. Then read the following paragraph on lemons and rewrite it, correcting these errors. The number in front of each error tells you the number of times that error occurs in the paragraph.

(1) collegese/wordiness
(3) slang
(3) passive voice
(3) the pronoun "you"
(2) sentence combinations
    that make no sense

(5) contractions
(5) commonly confused words
(2) run-ons
(1) misplaced modifier

  A *lemon* is a product that fails to perform as promised. A lemon can be a defective vehicle, for example, a lemon can be a 4-wheel drive Bronco that's supposed to take you effortlessly along old, muddy logging roads but instead it gets stuck in the wet grass while it's being backed out of your driveway and refuses to budge until a tow truck pulls it out. It is also an economical Yugo that costs double it's purchase price because the whole shebang from the transmission to the tailpipe croaks the first year. Likewise, a lemon can be an appliance. A lemon is a new fridge that promises to keep one's Haagen-Dazs desert bars frozen but instead lets them melt into a chocolate lake across the bottom of the freezer that flows. It can also be a toaster oven that turns a perfectly soft and chewy onion bagel into a charcoal briquette. Finally, a lemon can be found in a piece of electronic equipment. It's a VCR programmed to record *Monday Night Football* that turns itself to "Stop" in the last five minutes of the forth quarter with a score at 21–20, rewinds to the beginning of the tape, or then starts up again on "Record" just in time to catch the 3 a.m. cubic zirconia sellathon on *Home Shopping Club*. It's also a CD that begins to digest your favorite John Denver disc right in the middle of the second chorus to *Country Roads*. The affect leaves poor John warbling like a Rocky Mountain goat. Of course, most products do exactly what they're designed to do; consequently, once in a while, we are forced to admit something hovering between the colors of burnt umber and ochre that is acrid in taste makes an appearance in there place.

II. Writing with Style

Choose one or more of the following assignments and write a paragraph on it. Remember all of the structural elements of a paragraph—topic sentence, primary details, transitions, and conclusion. Also remember to develop your secondary details. Finally, pay attention to word choice and sentence combinations. You will notice that these choices reflect a variety of college assignments across the curriculum.

1. Describe the different kinds of percussion instruments in an orchestra.

2. Trace the stages of language development in children.

3. Discuss all of the factors that contributed to the overwhelming loss of life in the Titanic disaster.

4. Describe the characersitics of horror films.

5. Trace the shifting of the earth's land masses from one great continent to the present seven.

6. Choose a main character from a short story and tell how that character grows and changes from the beginning of the story to the end.

7. Choose a vocational field, such as auto mechanics, drafting, cosmetology, refrigeration and air conditioning, electrical wiring, or plumbing. Then show how several specific courses in that field will help you achieve a career goal.

8. Explain why an ancient civilization died out.

9. Discuss the causes you think are contributing to the possible extinction of human life on Earth.

10. Describe the treatments for one of the most common kinds of sports injuries.

11. Discuss some reasons people become criminals.

12. Describe how what you have learned about the writing process has influenced how you write.

13. Describe some major differences betwen spoken language and written language.

III. Editing for Style

Review the two paragraphs you wrote in response to Section Two Review for accurate word choices and effective sentence combinations. Find and correct any errors in style.

Editing

Chapter twelve

Errors in Structure

In the third section, you learned to choose words and sentence patterns that helped you create an effective tone and style. In this section, you will learn how to recognize and correct errors in the focus, primary details, and conclusion that form the structure of your paragraph, as well as in the secondary details that develop that paragraph. Correcting your errors is called **editing.** Editing can occur at any time in the writing process, but it is especially important to do a final editing when you finish writing your paper. Editing structure means correcting errors in topic sentences, primary details, and conclusions.

Editing Topic Sentences

As you recall from Chapter Four, focusing your response to an assignment means narrowing the subject of your assignment to a topic you can write about. Your topic sentence reflects that focus by stating an attitude or opinion about your topic that you support or prove in the rest of your paper. In this way, the attitude you express in your topic sentence controls what you say in the rest of your paragraph. When you finish that topic sentence, your mind should be overflowing with ideas for support. If you had a difficult time finding things to write about in the paragraphs you wrote for the Writing Exercises in Chapters One through Eleven, there may be something wrong with the topic sentences you wrote. You may have made one or more of the following errors focusing your topic or your controlling idea:

1. unfocused topic

2. split focus

3. unsupportable focus

4. overly subjective focus

5. overly complicated focus

At this point you need to edit your structure.

Editing Unfocused Topics

A topic sentence with an unfocused topic gives the writer a subject that is too broad for one paragraph. As you learned in Chapter Four, you must narrow a broad subject to a topic by asking focusing questions before you can write about it. Consider the following topic sentence:

The history of civilization is marked by aggression.

What is the topic? Common sense should tell you that it is not possible to write about the history of civilization in a single paragraph. In order to find a topic in this broad subject, you should ask several focusing questions such as *What period of the history of civilization?* and/or *What event within that period of the history of civilization?* Consider this edited topic sentence:

The settling of the American West was marked by aggression.

Is this a topic you can write about in a single paragraph? Even this topic may be too broad. You may write a very general summary, or you may continue asking focusing questions until you get to a topic sentence like the following:

The settling of Kansas was marked by violence between farmers and ranchers.

<table>
<tr><td>Exercise One</td><td colspan="2">**Editing Unfocused Topics**</td></tr>
<tr><td>DIRECTIONS</td><td colspan="2">In each of the following topic sentences, identify the unfocused topic and correct it by asking focusing questions.</td></tr>
<tr><td>MODEL</td><td colspan="2">Topic sentence: Some educators exert pressure on individuals who do not conform.

Unfocused topic: <u>some educators</u>

Focusing question: <u>Which educators?</u>

Focused topic sentence: <u>Some kindergarten teachers exert pressure on individuals who do not conform.</u></td></tr>
</table>

1. Topic sentence: Some films give people dangerous ideas.

   Unfocused topic: _____

Focusing question: _____?

Focused topic sentence: _____.

2. Topic sentence: The judicial process can be lengthy.

Unfocused topic: _____

Focusing question: _____?

Focused topic sentence: _____.

3. Topic sentence: Many mishaps are the result of human error.

Unfocused topic: _____

Focusing question: _____?

Focused topic sentence: _____.

4. Topic sentence: Performers are often shy.

Unfocused topic: _____

Focusing question: _____?

Focused topic sentence: _____.

5. Topic sentence: Some modern practices can be physically harmful.

Unfocused topic: _____

Focusing question: _____?

Focused topic sentence: _____.

Editing Split Focuses

A topic sentence that introduces two or more controlling ideas has a split focus. Consider the following topic sentence:

Leprosy is an emotionally devastating and physically debilitating disease.

How many opinions are being expressed about leprosy? What are they? Can you see that this topic sentence really sets up two paragraphs, one about how leprosy is emotionally devastating and one about how leprosy is physically debilitating? Any time you have two attitudes joined by the coordinating conjunctions *and, or,* or *but,* you have a split focus. A split focus can also be expressed by two coordinate modifiers separated by a comma. Consider this topic sentence:

Leprosy is an emotionally devastating, physically debilitating disease.

Even without the *and* between the controlling ideas, can you see that this topic sentence also has a split focus? Why? Now consider the following:

Leprosy is a disease that is both disabling and debilitating.

The *and* between the controlling ideas *disabling* and *debilitating* gives this topic sentence the appearance of a split focus. In reality, it has one focus expressed twice. What is the meaning of *disabling?* What is the meaning of *debilitating?* If you said that both *disabling* and *debilitating* mean *weakening,* then you know that this topic sentence repeats the same controlling idea. Some students repeat the same controlling idea using different words because they think a topic sentence must be long to be impressive, but this repetition is unnecessary, and it may make the reader expect two different ideas when there is really only one.

To correct a split focus, whether it is redundant or not, simply eliminate one of the two controlling ideas. The one you should keep is the one that provides you with more ideas for support.

Exercise Two | **Editing Split Focuses**

DIRECTIONS | In each of the following topic sentences, identify the split focus and correct it by choosing one of the two controlling ideas.

MODEL | Topic sentence: Jazz can be both tonal and atonal.

Split focus: tonal and atonal

Correction: Jazz can be atonal.

1. Topic sentence: High-rise construction is a risky, dangerous profession.

   Split focus: _____

   Correction: _____ .

2. Topic sentence: On American highways in the 1950s, Burma Shave jingles broke up the monotony of highway driving and provided income for farmers who leased their land for the signs.

   Split focus: _____

   Correction: _____ .

3. Topic sentence: As one ages, certain conditions, like asthma, can reverse themselves or disappear entirely.

   Split focus: _____

   Correction: _____ .

4. Topic sentence: The Flying Karamazov Brothers are funny, multitalented performers.

   Split focus: _____

   Correction: _____ .

5. Topic sentence: El Niño is a predictable but destructive weather pattern.

   Split focus: _____

   Correction: _____ .

Editing Unsupportable Focuses

There are several kinds of unsupportable focuses. One is a <u>statement of fact</u> rather than a sentence that has an attitude or opinion. Consider the following topic sentence:

Halogen lamps burn hot.

What is the controlling idea expressed in this topic sentence? How would you support *hot?* Do you see that once you tell your reader exactly how hot the lamps burn, there is not much else you can say? In other words, your focus is too narrow to provide you with enough supporting detail for a fully developed paragraph.

To fix some statements of fact you may add a modifier. Consider this edited version of the topic sentence above:

Halogen lamps burn <u>dangerously</u> hot.

Now what is the controlling idea? Do you have more ideas of how to support *dangerously hot?* Can you see you are really supporting what makes the heat dangerous, not how hot the lamp is?

Another kind of unsupportable focus is a topic sentence that <u>leads to a list</u> rather than true development. Consider the following:

King Midas turned everything he touched to gold.

What is the controlling idea? How can you support *turned everything he touched to gold?* Can you see that if you just name the things he turned to gold, you are giving the reader a list, not a fully developed paragraph? In this case, there is no modifier you could add that would fix the controlling idea. Instead, you must change the whole controlling idea to an opinion. Consider this revision:

King Midas was cursed by the gift of turning everything he touched to gold.

Now your controlling idea can be supported by showing how King Midas's ability to turn things to gold made life difficult for him.

A last type of unsupportable focus is a topic sentence that <u>leads to support of the topic rather than support of the controlling idea.</u> Consider the following:

Some famous twentieth-century American writers were alcoholics.

What is the controlling idea? If you think you can support *alcoholics* by naming some famous authors who were alcoholics, you would be supporting the topic, *Some famous twentieth-century American writers,* not the controlling idea, *alcoholics.* If you focus on *alcoholics,* you will see that it is a fact, not a controlling idea, so once again, you must either modify or replace the controlling idea. Consider these two possible corrections:

Some famous twentieth-century American writers were <u>charming</u> alcoholics.

Some famous twentieth-century American writers were <u>self-destructive</u>.

Editing Unsupportable Focuses

DIRECTIONS In each of the following topic sentences, identify the unsupportable focus, tell why it is too narrow to support, and correct it by using one of the methods described in the previous section. Remember that a focus can be unsupportable because it is a statement of fact, it leads to a list, or it leads to support of the topic.

MODEL Topic sentence: Many doctors support the medical use of marijuana.

Unsupportable focus: <u>support the medical use of marijuana</u>

Why: <u>leads to support of the topic</u>

Correction: <u>Many doctors offer sound reasons for the medical use of marijuana.</u>

1. Topic sentence: Mantras are a part of chanting.

   Unsupportable focus: _____

   Why: _____

   Correction: _____

2. Topic sentence: Many athletes are spokespersons for exercise machines they have developed.

   Unsupportable focus: _____

   Why: _____

   Correction: _____

3. Topic sentence: Chemistry I requires students to memorize the chemical elements chart.

    Unsupportable focus: _____

    Why: _____

    Correction: _____

4. Topic sentence: Some financial practices are illegal.

    Unsupportable focus: _____

    Why: _____

    Correction: _____

5. Topic sentence: Many current Broadway musicals are really revivals of classic shows.

    Unsupportable focus: _____

    Why: _____

    Correction: _____

Editing Overly Subjective Focuses

A controlling idea that describes the writer's feelings about the topic rather than the topic itself is an overly subjective focus. Consider the following topic sentence:

   The quadratic equations the math teacher gave us to solve were depressing.

What is the controlling idea? Can the equations themselves really be *depressing,* or is that the effect they have on the writer? Can you think of an attitude or opinion that describes the equations themselves? Consider this edited topic sentence:

   The quadratic equations the math teacher gave us to solve were difficult.

   Here is a list of attitudes or opinions that are too subjective to be controlling ideas:

good	bad	pretty	handsome	ugly	interesting	special
weird	nice	dull	boring	exciting	different	unique
great	terrific	terrible	outstanding	okay	fabulous	dreadful

Can you see that all of these words express your like or dislike for someone or something without describing the person or thing itself?

Editing Overly Subjective Focuses

DIRECTIONS   In each of the following topic sentences, identify the overly subjective focus and correct it.

MODEL   Topic sentence: Beat poetry of the 1960s is very interesting.

Overly subjective focus: interesting

Correction: Beat poetry of the 1960s is unconventional poetry.

1. Topic sentence: Elton John's rewrite of his song "Candle in the Wind" to immortalize Princess Diana was great.

    Overly subjective focus: _____

    Correction: _____.

2. Topic sentence: The Alaskan oil spill created by the *Exxon Valdez* was terrible.

    Overly subjective focus: _____

    Correction: _____.

3. Topic sentence: DKNY fashions for women are truly unique.

    Overly subjective focus: _____

    Correction: _____.

4. Topic sentence: Some people still think "computer nerds" are weird.

    Overly subjective focus: _____

    Correction: _____.

5. Topic sentence: The annually televised Christmas music program featuring Kathleen Battle, Fredericka von Stade, Andre Previn, and Branford Marsalis is really special.

    Overly subjective focus: _____

    Correction: _____.

Editing Overly Complicated Focuses

A controlling idea that goes too far by including support for the attitude or opinion in the topic sentence is an overly complicated focus. Consider the following topic sentence:

Dogs are life-enhancing for several reasons, including their loyalty.

What is the controlling idea? Can you see that *loyalty* is one of the *several reasons* that *Dogs are life-enhancing,* so *loyalty* is really a primary detail? Now consider this edited topic sentence:

Dogs are life-enhancing for several reasons.

Exercise Five **Editing Overly Complicated Focuses**

DIRECTIONS In each of the following topic sentences, identify the overly complicated focus and correct it.

MODEL Topic sentence: Disregarding ski patrol warnings is a dangerous practice because it can lead to tragedy.

Overly complicated focus: dangerous practice because it can lead to tragedy

Correction: Disregarding ski patrol warnings is a dangerous practice.

1. Topic sentence: The early shoe industry in Massachusetts had long-term effects on the ecology of the region by dumping pollutants in nearby rivers.

    Overly complicated focus: _____

    Correction: _____

2. Topic sentence: The Upper Peninsula of Michigan is an economically depressed region because its iron ore was depleted by mining.

    Overly complicated focus: _____

    Correction: _____

3. Topic sentence: The independent spirit of New Hampshire residents shows up in many ways, such as in the motto on their license plate, which says *Live Free or Die!*

    Overly complicated focus: _____

    Correction: _____

4. Topic sentence: For a state with many isolated areas, Wyoming has initiated some socially advanced policies, including women's right to vote.

    Overly complicated focus: _____

    Correction: _____

5. Topic sentence: Taos, New Mexico, is a mecca for many different kinds of artists, such as turquoise and silver craftsmen.

Overly complicated focus: _____

Correction: _____

Editing Primary Details

As you recall from Chapter Six, primary details are parts of the whole expressed in the controlling idea of your topic sentence. If they are not equal parts of the same whole and are not expressed in parallel language, you have probably made one or more of the following errors:

1. non-parallel primary details

2. off-focus primary details

3. redundant primary details

4. vague primary details

5. unsupportable primary details

Editing Non-parallel Primary Details

Non-parallel primary details are the result of not asking the same focusing question to come up with each part of the whole or not expressing the primary details in parallel language. Consider the following topic sentence and four primary details:

Topic sentence: Nikita Khrushchev was a manipulative politician.

Primary detail 1: First, he threw tantrums.

Primary detail 2: Second, he was controlling.

Primary detail 3: Third, he pounded his shoe at United Nations Council meetings.

Primary detail 4: Finally, making threats was another way he was manipulative.

Do you see that each of the primary details above either answers a different focusing question or is expressed in non-parallel language? Primary detail 1 answers the focusing question *What did Nikita Khrushchev do that was manipulative?* Primary detail 2 answers the focusing question *What was Nikita Khrushchev like?*, so it is the same level of generality as the controlling idea in the topic sentence; in fact, it expresses the same controlling idea and is, therefore, redundant. Primary detail 3 answers the focusing question *What did Nikita Khrushchev do when he threw a tantrum?*, so it, too, is the wrong level of generality; it is really a secondary detail supporting primary detail 1. Finally, primary detail 4 answers the focusing question *What did Nikita Khrushchev do that was manipulative?*, so it does answer the right question, but it expresses that answer in language that is not parallel to the language in primary detail 1, which answers the same focusing question. Consider the edited topic sentence and primary details:

Topic sentence: Nikita Khrushchev was a manipulative politician.

Primary detail 1: First, he threw tantrums.

Primary detail 2: Second, he made threats.

Exercise Six   **Editing Non-parallel Primary Details**

DIRECTIONS   In each of the items below, identify the non-parallel primary details, tell why they are not parallel, and correct them. Remember the reasons for non-parallel details are wrong level of generality, redundancy, and non-parallel language.

MODEL   Topic sentence: Heart attacks are usually preceded by warning signals.

Primary detail 1: Sharp pain in the arms is a warning signal.

Primary detail 2: Circulatory problems are a warning signal.

Primary detail 3: Respiratory difficulties are a warning signal.

Non-parallel primary detail(s): 1 _____

Why: *wrong level of generality* _____

Correction: *Sharp pains are a warning signal.* _____

1. Topic sentence: In the 1990s, a number of professional athletes ran afoul of the law.

   Primary detail 1: Some athletes threatened officials.

   Primary detail 2: Some athletes got involved in illegal drug use.

   Primary detail 3: Gambling got some athletes in trouble with the law.

   Non-parallel primary detail: _____

   Why: _____

   Correction: _____

2. Topic sentence: Treatments for eye problems are diverse.

   Primary detail 1: Some treatments involve medication.

   Primary detail 2: Some treatments involve surgery.

Primary detail 3: Some treatments involve herbal infusions.

Primary detail 4: Some treatments involve strengthening exercises.

Non-parallel primary detail: _____

Why: _____

Correction: _____

3. Topic sentence: Electronic mail offers several benefits.

   Primary detail 1: It promotes letter-writing skills.

   Primary detail 2: It delivers the letter within seconds.

   Non-parallel primary detail: _____

   Why: _____

   Correction: _____

4. Topic sentence: Over the years, many dangerous consumer goods have been recalled.

   Primary detail 1: Hair-munching dolls have been recalled.

   Primary detail 2: Automobiles have been recalled.

   Primary detail 3: One kind of consumer good that has been recalled is toys.

   Primary detail 4: Electronic equipment has been recalled.

   Non-parallel primary detail: _____

   Why: _____

   Correction: _____

   Non-parallel primary detail: _____

   Why: _____

   Correction: _____

5. Topic sentence: Throughout history, many novels have been unreasonably censored by public schools.

   Primary detail 1: *The Adventures of Huckleberry Finn* was censored for its interracial relationships.

   Primary detail 2: *The Catcher in the Rye* was censored for its narrator's raw language.

   Primary detail 3: *The Catcher in the Rye* was censored for its narrator's swearing.

Primary detail 4: *Lady Chatterly's Lover* was censored for graphic sexual material.

Non-parallel primary detail: _____

Why: _____

Correction: _____

Editing Off-focus Primary Details

An error that results from not asking the <u>full</u> focusing question for each primary detail is an off-focus primary detail. Consider the primary details for the following topic sentence:

Topic sentence: Chinese cooking reflects a belief in the balance of opposites, or yin and yang.

Primary detail 1: Some dishes balance sweet and sour.

Primary detail 2: Other dishes balance crunchy and smooth.

Primary detail 3: Yet other dishes are more spicy than bland.

Can you see that primary details 1 and 2 answer the focusing question *What are some opposites that are balanced?,* but primary detail 3 answers only *What are some opposites?* What does the incomplete focusing question leave out? How would you edit primary detail 3 so that it answers the full focusing question?

Exercise Seven

Editing Off-focus Primary Details

DIRECTIONS

In each of the folloiwng items, identify the full focusing question and the primary details that answer it, the incomplete focusing question, what's missing from it, and the off-focus primary detail, and then correct it.

MODEL

Topic sentence: Judges pro tem perform many of the same functions real judges perform to help you.

Primary detail 1: They may perform your marriage ceremony.

Primary detail 2: They may issue a bench warrant for your arrest.

Primary detail 3: They may grant you custody of your children after your divorce.

Full focusing question: <u>What are some functions judges pro tem perform to help you?</u>

Primary details that answer it: <u>1 and 3</u>

Incomplete focusing question: <u>What are some functions judges pro tem perform?</u>

What's missing from it? <u>to help you</u>

Off-focus primary detail: 2 _____

Correction: <u>They may issue a bench warrant for your trespassing neighbor's arrest.</u>

1. Topic sentence: There are several physical reasons a young child may fail to thrive.

   Primary detail 1: Someone in his environment may be harming the child.

   Primary detail 2: The child may have allergies to certain foods.

   Primary detail 3: The child may have allergies to certain pollutants in the air.

   Full focusing question: _____

   Primary details that answer it: _____

   Incomplete focusing question: _____

   What's missing from it? _____

   Off-focus primary detail: _____

   Correction: _____ _____

2. Topic sentence: Renting an apartment has several financial advantages over owning your own home.

   Primary detail 1: You do not have to pay for landscaping.

   Primary detail 2: You do not have to pay property taxes.

   Primary detail 3: Your neighbors can watch your dwelling more easily when you are away.

   Full focusing question: _____

   Primary details that answer it: _____

   Incomplete focusing question: _____

   What's missing from it? _____

   Off-focus primary detail: _____

   Correction: _____

3. Topic sentence: Some home appliances can present dangers for children.

   Primary detail 1: Out-of-service refrigerators can be dangerous for children.

   Primary detail 2: Light sockets can be dangerous for children.

   Primary detail 3: Stoves can be dangerous for children.

Full focusing question: _____

Primary details that answer it: _____

Incomplete focusing question: _____

What's missing from it? _____

Off-focus primary detail: _____

Correction: _____

4. Topic sentence: Good students contribute positively in the classroom.

Primary detail 1: They keep class discussions going.

Primary detail 2: They share their notes with students who have returned from an absence.

Primary detail 3: They use instructors' office hours when they have questions.

Full focusing question: _____

Primary details that answer it: _____

Incomplete focusing question: _____

What's missing from it? _____

Off-focus primary detail: _____

Correction: _____

5. Topic sentence: Despite the male-dominated society he lived in, Shakespeare created some female characters who accomplished some powerful things.

Primary detail 1: Portia in *The Merchant of Venice* influenced a courtroom.

Primary detail 2: Desdemona in *Othello* tried unsuccessfully to reason with her jealous husband.

Primary detail 3: Lady Macbeth in *Macbeth* incited her husband to bloody deeds to further his ambition.

Primary detail 4: Katarina in *The Taming of the Shrew* frightened an entire town with her temper.

Full focusing question: _____

Primary details that answer it: _____

Incomplete focusing question: _____

What's missing from it? _____

Off-focus primary detail: _____

Correction: _____

Editing Redundant Primary Details

Redundant primary details, like a redundant controlling idea in the topic sentence, sound different from each other but really say the same thing twice. Consider the following topic sentence and three primary details:

Topic sentence: Tours provide many advantages for travelers.

Primary detail 1: They provide economic advantages.

Primary detail 2: They provide social advantages.

Primary detail 3: They provide financial advantages.

Which two primary details are really the same? If you said that *economic* in primary detail 1 and *financial* in primary detail 3 mean the same thing, you are right. You may replace either of these two details with a third detail that is different, like *They provide safety advantages,* or you may stop after the first two details. As you recall from Chapter Six, a minimum of two primary details is sufficient for a paragraph.

Exercise Eight

Editing Redundant Primary Details

DIRECTIONS   In each of the following items, identify the two details that say the same thing, and eliminate one or replace it, as necessary.

MODEL   Topic sentence: Open adoptions can help the adoptee.

Primary detail 1: They can put him in touch with his medical history.

Primary detail 2: They can provide additional emotional support.

Primary detail 3: They can provide more people to love him.

Primary details that say the same thing: 2 and 3

Correction: Replace Primary detail 2 with "They satisfy his curiosity about his roots."

1. Topic sentence: The failure of a national economy can have serious repercussions.

    Primary detail 1: It puts people out of work.

    Primary detail 2: It creates an employment crisis.

    Primary details that say the same thing: _____

    Correction: _____

2. Topic sentence: Some people have raised objections to the scientific practice of cloning.

   Primary detail 1: They have raised ethical objections.

   Primary detail 2: They have raised medical objections.

   Primary detail 3: They have raised moral objections.

   Primary detail 4: They have raised social objections.

   Primary details that say the same thing: _____

   Correction: _____

3. Topic sentence: Literary satire, making fun of society's weaknesses, can bring positive changes.

   Primary detail 1: It can change the way merchants deal with customers.

   Primary detail 2: It can change the way people do business.

   Primary detail 3: It can change the way doctors deal with patients.

   Primary detail 4: It can change the way police deal with suspects.

   Primary details that say the same thing: _____

   Correction: _____

4. Topic sentence: Besides providing fun, children's games often teach useful skills.

   Primary detail 1: They teach manual dexterity.

   Primary detail 2: They teach critical thinking.

   Primary detail 3: They teach cooperation.

   Primary detail 4: They teach logical analysis.

   Primary details that say the same thing: _____

   Correction: _____

5. Topic sentence: The eighteenth-century British painter Thomas Gainsborough made varied contributions to the art world.

   Primary detail 1: His portraits left a record of his time.

   Primary detail 2: His landscapes romanticized reality.

   Primary detail 3: His paintings immortalized important people in eighteenth-century London.

Primary details that say the same thing: _____

Correction: _____

Editing Vague Primary Details

Primary details are vague when they are too broad. In other words, a vague primary detail is the wrong level of generality for a primary detail; it is really broad enough for a topic sentence. Consider the following topic sentence and three primary details:

Topic sentence: Patrick Henry, Governor of Virginia in 1776, voiced several objections to the Constitution of the United States.

Primary detail 1: He thought it usurped the rights of the individual states.

Primary detail 2: He thought the Constitution's lack of a Bill of Rights created several problems.

Primary detail 3: He objected to the language used in it.

Which of the primary details is broad enough to set up a paragraph of its own? If you said primary detail 2, you are right. What is the controlling idea in the topic sentence? What words in primary detail 2 are on the same level of generality as that controlling idea? Can you see that the words *several problems* in primary detail 2 are the same level of generality as the words *several objections* in the topic sentence?

Exercise Nine

Editing Vague Primary Details

DIRECTIONS In each of the following items, identify the controlling idea in the topic sentence and the words in the vague primary detail that are the same level of generality as that controlling idea.

MODEL Topic sentence: Although all fish are cold-blooded animals with a backbone, that live in water, are covered with scales, breathe through gills, and have fins in place of limbs, all five groups of fish have exceptions within these characteristics.

Primary detail 1: There are several variations in gills.

Primary detail 2: There are several variations in skeletons.

Primary detail 3: All five groups have various adaptive behaviors.

Controlling idea in topic sentence: *exceptions within these characteristics*

Vague primary detail: *3*

Words on wrong level of generality: *various adaptive behaviors*

1. Topic sentence: Each of the ways hearing-impaired children can gather information has its own problems.

   Primary detail 1: Sign language presents isolation problems.

   Primary detail 2: Lipreading presents comprehension problems.

   Primary detail 3: The ways hearing-impaired children gather information sometimes are flawed.

   Controlling idea in topic sentence: _____ _____

   Vague primary detail: _____

   Words on wrong level of generality: _____

2. Topic sentence: Earthworms help gardeners in several ways.

   Primary detail 1: Earthworms condition the soil.

   Primary detail 2: Earthworms have ways of regenerating themselves.

   Primary detail 3: Earthworms process decaying matter.

   Controlling idea in topic sentence: _____

   Vague primary detail: _____

   Words on wrong level of generality: _____

3. Topic sentence: Some translators of literary works encounter various problems.

   Primary detail 1: Some translators present problems to readers.

   Primary detail 2: Some translators encounter problems of accuracy.

   Primary detail 3: Some translators encounter problems of style.

   Controlling idea in topic sentence: _____

   Vague primary detail: _____

   Words on wrong level of generality: _____

4. Topic sentence: Even in modern times, people have used caves for different purposes.

   Primary detail 1: Some people have used caves for storage.

   Primary detail 2: Some people have used different methods to explore caves.

   Primary detail 3: Some people have used caves for religious purposes.

   Controlling idea in topic sentence: _____

Vague primary detail: _____

Words on wrong level of generality: _____

5. Topic sentence: Most bacteria are beneficial to humans.

   Primary detail 1: Some bacteria turn garbage into rich soil.

   Primary detail 2: Some bacteria create foods through fermentation.

   Primary detail 3: Some bacteria are harmful to humans.

   Controlling idea in topic sentence: _____

   Vague primary detail: _____

   Words on wrong level of generality: _____

Editing Unsupportable Primary Details

If vague primary details are too broad, unsupportable primary details are too specific. In other words, they are the same level of generality as secondary details, or development. They cannot be supported because they already <u>are</u> support for a primary detail. Consider the following topic sentence and three primary details:

Topic sentence: Material from Web sources can reflect excessive bias.

Primary detail 1: Material on the Holocaust can reflect bias against certain ethnic groups.

Primary detail 2: Material on Islamic fundamentalism can reflect bias against some countries.

Primary detail 3: Material on abortion can show a chat line subscriber's angry condemnation of a clinic in his town that provides abortions on demand for teenaged girls without the consent of their parents.

Can you see that primary detail 3 is too specific to be a primary detail for this topic sentence? It is an example, or secondary detail, that would support a primary detail like *Material on abortion can reflect bias against pro-choice practitioners.* Did you notice also that primary detail 3 is longer than the other primary details? That is because a specific example requires more words to express it than a generalization does.

Exercise Ten

Editing Unsupportable Primary Details

DIRECTIONS   In each of the following items, identify the unsupportable primary detail and correct it by making its level of generality broader.

MODEL   Topic sentence: The wolves that were reintroduced to Yellowstone National Park in the mid-1990s have had positive effects on the ecosystem.

Primary detail 1: They have eaten the sick and old in the overbred elk population, thereby strengthening the herd.

Primary detail 2: They have controlled the numbers of other predators.

Primary detail 3: They have left food for scavengers.

Unsupportable primary detail: _Primary detail 1_

Correction: _They have culled overbred herds of various large mammals._

1. Topic sentence: General anesthesia falls into several categories.

   Primary detail 1: One kind of gaseous general anesthesia is nitrous oxide, or "laughing gas."

   Primary detail 2: Another category is solids that can be swallowed or liquified and then injected.

   Unsupportable primary detail: _____

   Correction: _____

2. Topic sentence: Shakespeare's character Hamlet, though the hero of his play, was sometimes cruel.

   Primary detail 1: One way he tried to trick people was to arrange for actors to present a play to the royal court that showed his uncle murdering his father in order to get his uncle to confess to murder.

   Primary detail 2: He verbally abused women.

   Unsupportable primary detail: _____

   Correction: _____

3. Topic sentence: Modern mainstream journalism shares some characteristics with tabloid journalism.

   Primary detail 1: Both rely heavily on photographs.

   Primary detail 2: Both attract attention through sensational headlines.

   Primary detail 3: The story that appeared in Colorado newspapers in the winter of 1997 about a stray dog who saved the life of a nine-year-old girl lost overnight in a national forest by keeping her warm is one illustration of the kind of human interest story both mainstream journalism and tabloids publish.

   Unsupportable primary detail: _____

   Correction: _____

4. Topic sentence: Despite Sir Isaac Newton's shy nature, he took part in several public controversies.

   Primary detail 1: He disputed German scientist G. W. Leibnitz's claim of having invented the calculus.

   Primary detail 2: He took part in an educational controversy.

   Primary detail 3: He took part in a political controversy.

   Unsupportable primary detail: _____

   Correction: _____

5. Topic sentence: Water safety for small crafts involves several areas of concern.

   Primary detail 1: One area of concern is having communication devices in working order.

   Primary detail 2: One should have a dry, snugly-fitting life vest with easy-to-fasten straps for each passenger.

   Primary detail 3: One area of concern is a survival plan for abandoning ship in emergencies.

   Unsupportable primary detail: _____

   Correction: _____

Editing Conclusions

Since your conclusion is the last thing your reader sees, you want it to be effective. As you recall from Chapter Seven, there are three types of errors you might make in your conclusion:

1. change of direction

2. exaggeration

3. failure to answer the conclusion question *So what?*

A change of direction error gives a conclusion that has nothing to do with the focus of the paragraph as expressed in the topic sentence. An exaggeration error gives a conclusion that overstates the main point of the paragraph. A conclusion that fails to answer the question *So what?* simply repeats the topic sentence exactly. If you need examples of these errors, look at Chapter Seven again before doing the following exercise.

Editing Conclusions

DIRECTIONS
Read the following paragraph. Then examine the ten suggested conclusions. Leave the effective conclusions alone. Identify the error in each flawed conclusion. Then write one effective conclusion of your own.

> My first meeting with my prospective in-laws was a terrifically embarrassing experience (topic sentence). First, I made a fool of myself entering their home (primary detail 1). In my eagerness to express my pleasure at meeting him, I enunciated violently when I said to Mr. Gordon, "I'm SO pleased to meet you!" The result was that I hurled my breath mint directly into his beard where it stuck like Velcro (secondary detail 1). Then, while trying frantically to extricate the glob from his startled face, I tripped over the threshold and came crashing down on a priceless Ming vase in the entryway, shattering it to confetti (secondary detail 2). Next, I mortified myself at dinner (primary detail 2). I was anxious to compliment Mrs. Gordon's cooking, so I inhaled a ladle-sized spoonful of her famous onion soup, which was so hot that I sprayed it back over my dining companions like an incontinent garden hose (secondary detail 1). Thoroughly shaken at that point, I began to fiddle with the border on Mrs. Gordon's damask lace tablecloth, obviously an heirloom. By the time I realized what I was doing, I had unraveled a half-inch of the bottom border (secondary detail 2). Finally, I sealed my humiliation with my awkward exit (primary detail 3). Alternately bowing and nodding as I backed out the front door, I tripped on the same door sill I had sailed in on, skinning my knees and leaving blood on the clean walkway (secondary detail 1). The capper was the angry gouge I left in the Gordons' antique TR4 parked in their driveway as I lurched to my feet, stumbling against it and scraping my jacket zipper along the passenger side door (secondary detail 2).

Suggested conclusions:

1. It should not be hard to imagine how embarrassed I was after this meeting.

   Flaw: _____

   Correction: _____

2. I must be the clumsiest person in the world.

   Flaw: _____

   Correction: _____

3. Not surprisingly, it was three weeks before I could get over my embarrassment enough to send a combined thank-you note and apology to the Gordons, who now lovingly refer to me as "The Terminatrix."

Flaw: _____

Correction: _____

4. Fortunately, I have had time in my ten years of marriage to recover from my embarrassment at that first meeting, and my in-laws and I laugh about it all now.

Flaw: _____

Correction: _____

5. Even though I am clumsy, my friends think I have some very good qualities.

Flaw: _____

Correction: _____

6. No one in history has ever made a clumsier first impression.

Flaw: _____

Correction: _____

7. Imagine my surprise when my fiance said, "I think that went well, don't you?" That's when I knew he *really* loved me.

Flaw: _____

Correction: _____

8. On the other hand, my in-laws probably have some embarrassing experiences of their own to tell.

Flaw: _____

Correction: _____

9. Meeting my in-laws certainly was a terrifically embarrassing experience.

Flaw: _____

Correction: _____

10. However, now that I think about it, I have had more embarrassing experiences than this.

Flaw: _____

Correction: _____

Your own conclusion: _____

_____

Review Questions

Answer the following questions to help you review the material you have learned in this chapter.

1. The process of correcting errors is called _____. (p. 217)

2. What's wrong with the subject in a topic sentence that has an unfocused topic? (p. 218) _____

3. A topic sentence has a split focus when it introduces _____
_____. (p. 219)

4. What are the three kinds of unsupportable focuses in a topic sentence? (p. 221–222)

_____   _____   _____

5. Instead of describing the topic itself, an overly subjective focus describes
_____. (p. 223)

6. List five descriptive words that are too subjective to be controlling ideas. (p. 223)

_____   _____   _____   _____

_____

7. What does an overly complicated focus include that it should not? (p. 224)

_____

8. What are the two errors that result in non-parallel primary details? (p. 226)

_____

_____

9. How do you get an off-focus primary detail? (p. 229) _____

_____

10. What is a redundant primary detail? (p. 232) _____

11. A vague primary detail is on the same level of generality as _____
_____. (p. 234)

12. An unsupportable primary detail is on the same level of generality as
_____. (p. 236)

13. What are three conclusion errors? (p. 238) _____

_____ _____

Writing Exercises

Look back at the three paragraphs you rewrote for Writing Exercise III in Chapter Eleven. Look for errors in topic sentences, primary details, and the conclusion. If you find any of the errors you learned about in this chapter, correct them, and if necessary rewrite the paragraphs to support your corrections.

Looking Back and Looking Forward

In this chapter, you have reviewed the structure of a paragraph and the structural errors that you need to look for as you edit. In the next chapter, you will review development and learn to edit errors of development in your secondary details.

Chapter thirteen · Errors in Development

In the last chapter, you learned to identify and correct specific errors in the structure of your paragraph. In this chapter, you will do the same for the secondary support of your paragraph.

Editing Secondary Details

Editing secondary details means correcting the following errors:

1. not enough secondary details
2. underdeveloped secondary details
3. off-focus secondary details
4. repetitive secondary details
5. vague secondary details

Editing Not Enough Secondary Details

In Chapter Eight, you learned that each primary detail needs at least two secondary details to support it. Sometimes you may use all of the techniques to develop a secondary detail that is lively and specific. Then if that detail is more than one sentence long, you may forget that you still need another secondary detail. When you edit secondary details, do not forget to count them. Consider this example:

Topic sentence: The mapping of the world globe has undergone a dizzying number of changes in the twentieth century.

Primary detail 1: Some changes have been geographical.

Secondary detail 1: The ethnic populations of Serbs, Croats, and Muslims in the former country of Yugoslavia exploded into violence in the 1990s. Ethnic minorities in small villages were completely purged by roving gangs who shot mothers and fathers and used machetes to butcher even small children. The country was carved into separate strongholds for the Serbs and Croats, leaving the Muslims in danger wherever they were found. What was once a unified Yugoslavia became Montenegro, Slovenia, Croatia, and Bosnia-Herzegovina, among others.

This secondary detail looks like a small paragraph all by itself because it has so much information and uses four sentences; yet, it is still only a single secondary detail because it describes a change in one geographical area. However, the primary detail it supports refers to geographical changes. Now you must supply an additional secondary detail with a second example of a geographical change. Consider the following:

Secondary detail 2: In addition, the Middle East is still experiencing changes that began directly after World War II when Great Britain partitioned the state of Israel as a Jewish homeland from what was formerly Arab lands called Palestine. To this day, Arabs and Jews still wage war with words and guns to define borders that are acceptable to both sides in the West Bank and the Sinai.

Exercise One — Editing Not Enough Secondary Details

DIRECTIONS   Read each of the following items carefully. For each item that does not contain enough secondary details, add at least one more fully developed secondary detail. Remember that it does not matter how long or how many sentences your secondary detail runs; if all the information is on the same example, you have only one secondary detail. Notice that in this exercise the topic sentence, primary detail, and secondary details are not identified for you.

MODEL   Humor can be used for different purposes. First, it can defuse anger. Imagine how difficult it would be to stay angry with a sales manager if when you brought back the toaster he had sold you because it started a fire when you plugged it in, you said to him, "Do you know how maddening it is when something doesn't work?," and the sales manager replied, "Do I ever! Just take a look at my employees!"

Number of secondary details: _one_

Additional secondary detail: Also, what highway patrolman could hold an angry expression after stopping a speeding driver on her birthday, who responds, after he hands her the ticket, "Gee, didn't you have time to get me a real present?"

1. Museum-goers can rely on readily-observable traits in order to understand the art they see there. First, they can understand the use of color. When they see a painting of a field of yellow daisies and orange poppies, they will be able to associate emotional heat or physical warmth with these colors, which should make them think of sunlight and fire. When they see a portrait that has a light-colored face against dark-colored clothes, they will sense that the face is being emphasized, even if they do not know that this technique is called *chiaroscuro,* or contrast of light and shadow.

   Number of secondary details: _____

   Additional secondary detail: _____

2. Despite whatever versatility they may possess as actors, many Hollywood stars have been typecast almost their entire careers. Some have been typecast as "tough guys." Arnold Schwarzenegger gained fame in the *Terminator* movies, in which he played a robotic killer of legendary strength who annihilated villains with both automatic weapons and his mechanically enhanced hands. Schwarzenegger carried through his tough-guy image even in movies like *Kindergarten Cop* and *True Lies,* in which he tempered justice with morality.

   Number of secondary details: _____

   Additional secondary detail: _____

3. Surface wounds can be treated in a number of ways. First, they can be treated surgically. One of the newest methods involves the use of an adhesive like Super Glue that holds the edges of the wound together for ten to fourteen days under a flexible cap with the texture of a soft contact lens. Then the glue dissolves.

   Number of secondary details: _____

   Additional secondary detail: _____

4. People learn in various ways. Some people learn by doing. When they need to learn how to use their new computer with its icons signifying functions like print and save, these people throw the user's manual aside, stick paper in the printer, turn the computer on, and learn all the functions of their computer by pushing every key and clicking every icon on the machine. When they want to program their VCR to tape the annual *Dr. Seuss Christmas Special,* they don't rely on the operating instructions. Instead, they turn on their television, take the remote control in hand, and, pointing it at the TV, examine every item on the menu until they get to the commands for recording television programs. Then they program the machine by following those commands.

Number of secondary details: _____

Additional secondary detail: _____

5. In United States history, the courts have made some legal decisions that violated human rights. Some of these decisions favored states rights over the individual. In the *Munn* vs. *Illinois* decision of 1877, the court ruled that states could regulate businesses in the event that "public interest" was a consideration. Theoretically, this meant that during World War II, a state could prevent businesses from advertising with lighted signs. This was to conserve energy and to prevent the enemy from easily identifying a target, even though this law hurt individual businesses. In the *Plessy* vs. *Ferguson* case of 1896, the Supreme Court ruled that racial segregation enforced by state law was constitutional so long as the accommodations provided to African Americans and whites were equal, even though forced separation violated the rights of individuals.

Number of secondary details: _____

Additional secondary detail: _____

Editing Underdeveloped Secondary Details

As you recall from Chapter Eight, a secondary detail puts flesh on the bones of your structure. In order to make a secondary detail a specific example, you must make it longer than a primary detail, frequently using more than one sentence. If you rely on a vague generalization, you may write a secondary detail that is long but still underdeveloped. If your reader cannot see, hear, taste, feel, smell and/or understand your secondary detail, then it is underdeveloped, no matter how long it is. Consider the following portion of a paragraph, including a topic sentence, the first primary detail, and the underdeveloped secondary detail that supports it.

Topic sentence: Potential jurors can be excused from serving on a jury for several reasons.

Primary detail 1: They can be excused for hardship.

Secondary detail 1: Some can be excused because their income is affected.

If you wonder how the potential jurors' income is affected, then you recognize that this secondary detail is not as specific as it should be. To make a secondary detail specific, use the techniques in Chapter Eight for developing secondary details: strong verbs, specific nouns, modifiers when necessary, and comparisons. Now consider the edited version of the preceding secondary detail.

Secondary detail 1: Some potential jurors can be excused because their jobs will not pay their salaries while they serve on a jury beyond ten days. They still have to pay their mortgages and their electric or gas bills, buy groceries, pay for child care, and make their credit card payments, even while they are on jury duty. Thus, serving longer than ten days might leave them sinking like helpless swimmers in a sea of debt.

Can you tell which techniques were used to develop this secondary detail? Can you see how the active verbs *will not pay, serve, buy, pay, make,* and *leave* in the edited version are all stronger than the passive voice verb *is affected* in the original secondary detail? What are the specific nouns in the edited version? Can you find several necessary modifiers in the edited version? What is the comparison that makes the edited secondary detail more specific and easier to understand? Also, do you see that the edited example really has two parts that are both necessary to support the primary detail? The second sentence of this secondary detail describes the jurors' personal financial responsibilities. The third sentence describes how serving more than ten days on jury duty might affect the jurors' ability to meet those responsibilities. While the second sentence gives necessary related information, it does not by itself support the primary detail. It needs the addition of the last sentence.

Exercise Two

Identifying and Editing Underdeveloped Secondary Details

DIRECTIONS   In the items that follow, identify the underdeveloped secondary detail and rewrite it, using strong verbs, specific nouns, modifiers that are truly necessary, and comparisons.

MODEL   Topic sentence: Many cultures have foods that serve several purposes.

Primary detail 1: One purpose is convenience.

Secondary detail 1: Pasties, cubes of beef and potatoes sealed in a hearty pastry crust, can be easily carried into the mines by Cornish miners because they fit into one hand.

Secondary detail 2: Jewish knishes, a portable food that contains different fillings in a crust, are a popular item at different celebrations because they are easy to pick up.

Underdeveloped secondary detail: *Secondary detail 2*

Revision: *Jewish knishes are an hors d'oeuvre packed with either a savory potato or meat filling completely encased in a flaky crust folded over like a tart, so they are convenient finger food for guests who can carry them easily on a cocktail napkin while they mingle with other people at weddings and*

bar mitzvahs.

1. Topic sentence: Air travel time has increased in the past decade because of additional safety measures.

   Primary detail 1: Safety measures for baggage add travel time.

   Secondary detail 1: All travelers and well-wishers accompanying travelers to the departure and arrival gates must pause at X-ray machines to have purses and carry-on luggage examined for weapons. If a packed item looks like a gun, a knife, or a bomb to the X-ray machine, the traveler must wait while an official searches the luggage by hand.

   Secondary detail 2: All travelers are questioned several times about their luggage by various personnel, which takes additional time.

   Underdeveloped secondary detail: _____

   Revision: _____.

2. Topic sentence: Psychologists often recommend several kinds of activities for relieving stress.

   Primary detail 1: One kind of activity that relieves stress is physical.

   Secondary detail 1: Playing a team sport can calm frayed nerves by providing a physical outlet for stress.

   Secondary detail 2: Swimming fifty laps or more in an Olympic-sized pool can relieve stress because it uses all the muscles of the arms and shoulders, as well as those of the back, abdomen, legs, and feet, leaving the swimmer pleasantly tired and as relaxed as the elastic in an old pair of gym shorts.

   Underdeveloped secondary detail: _____

   Revision: _____.

3. Topic sentence: Many people with living-space limitations use furniture that can be adaptable for their needs.

   Primary detail 1: Some beds can be adapted to the user's needs.

   Secondary detail 1: In limited space, a futon, a folded mattress on a flexible frame, can serve as a sofa by day and open into a bed at night.

Secondary detail 2: Trundle beds can be hidden away.

Underdeveloped secondary detail: _____

Revision: _____ .

4. Topic sentence: Many popular movies have a premise that is far-fetched.

   Primary detail 1: Some successful movies have strained belief with men posing as women.

   Secondary detail 1: *Tootsie* asks us to believe that an insensitive male actor, who forgets dates with his girlfriend and argues with his agent about being too good an actor to take a role in a commercial as a tomato, could accurately portray a sensitive middle-aged actress who auditions for and wins a role as a sympathetic hospital administrator on a popular soap opera.

   Secondary detail 2: *Mrs. Doubtfire* asks us to believe an irresponsible father could fool people into believing he is a responsible female nanny.

   Underdeveloped secondary detail: _____

   Revision: _____ .

5. Topic sentence: Several foods are known for their ability to masquerade as other foods.

   Primary detail 1: Some fish can masquerade as more expensive shellfish.

   Secondary detail 1: Monkfish tastes a lot like lobster. Its texture is also like that of lobster.

   Secondary detail 2: Pollock is a firm-fleshed white fish that can be made to look and taste like crab meat by the addition of reddish food coloring and crab-flavored brine.

   Underdeveloped secondary detail: _____

   Revision: _____ .

Editing Off-focus Secondary Details

After the edited instructional model of the underdeveloped secondary detail for Exercise Two, you were told that this secondary detail has two parts that are both essential to support the primary detail. This is true of many secondary details. If you do not include both parts of a two-part secondary detail, the detail will be off-focus because it will be incomplete. Consider again the topic sentence, the primary detail, and the first part of that secondary detail, which when given alone is off-focus:

Topic sentence: Potential jurors can be excused from serving on a jury for several reasons.

Primary detail 1: They can be excused for hardship.

Secondary detail 1: Some potential jurors can be excused because their jobs will not pay their salaries while they serve on a jury beyond ten days. They still have to pay their mortgages and their electric or gas bills, buy groceries, pay for child care, and make their credit card payments, even while they are on jury duty.

This detail is certainly specific about the financial responsibilities of the potential jurors. However, it is incomplete. It should support the primary detail, which is about hardship, and these responsibilities do not become hardships unless the potential jurors are unable to meet them. Therefore, the second part of the secondary detail, which is found in the third sentence, is necessary to complete the connection between the financial responsibilities of the potential jurors and how jury duty can turn those responsibilities into hardships. Now consider this detail with the second part added:

Secondary detail 1: Some potential jurors can be excused because their jobs will not pay their salaries while they serve on a jury beyond ten days. They still have to pay their mortgages and electric and gas bills, buy groceries, pay for child care, and make their credit card payments, even while they are on jury duty. Thus, serving longer than ten days might leave them sinking like helpless swimmers in a sea of debt.

Exercise Three / Identifying and Editing Off-focus Secondary Details

DIRECTIONS Each item below contains a topic sentence, a primary detail, and one secondary detail. Tell whether each secondary detail is focused or off-focus because it is incomplete. If it is an off-focus detail, tell what part of the primary detail is not supported, and add what is necessary to support it.

MODEL Topic sentence: The kind of violence in many of the nation's urban grammar schools, which used to be found mainly at the high school level and above, has resulted in the kinds of punishment that are usually reserved for adults.

Primary detail 1: Bringing weapons to school can result in legal action.

Secondary detail 1: Even while we are still shocked over news stories of high school and college students carrying guns to campus and using them against classmates and teachers, we are beginning to hear even more shocking tales of third- and fourth-graders being caught in class with handguns in their knapsacks which they have taken without permission from parents who keep them for protection against crime.

Secondary detail focused or off-focus: <u>off-focus</u>

Part of primary detail not supported: <u>can result in legal action</u>

Addition: <u>These grammar school students are being arrested for carrying con-</u>

<u>cealed weapons and sometimes stand trial in juvenile court, where they</u>

<u>can be sentenced to serve time in a youth detention center.</u>

1. Topic sentence: Some hospitals are starting to offer patients both standard medical techniques and alternative techniques for certain conditions.

   Primary detail 1: Some hospitals use standard and alternative techniques to treat bone conditions.

   Secondary detail 1: For people who have stenosis, which is a painful narrowing of the spinal column, the standard treatment ultimately involves surgery that cleans the column internally of arthritic bone growth that obstructs the spinal column and presses painfully on surrounding nerves. An alternative technique to surgery is acupuncture, where small needles are inserted in related areas of the body by certified practitioners of Eastern medicine. Once inserted, the needles are twirled to stimulate healing electrical impulses in the body and then left in place for anywhere from five to sixty minutes.

   Secondary detail focused or off-focus: _____

   Part of primary detail not supported: _____

   Addition: _____

2. Topic sentence: Some television advertisements are misleading because in trying to be funny, they do not include information about the product itself.

   Primary detail 1: Some television ads for food products are more funny than informative.

   Secondary detail 1: One sandwich spread product ad portrays a man watching television with his dog beside him. When the man praises a dog on television, saying, "Now *that's* a dog!," his own dog, feeling hurt, jumps off the couch and trots into the kitchen where he surveys the contents of the refrigerator, tossing lettuce, tomatoes, and ham onto the counter. Then he begins making a colossal sandwich. When he looks back into the refrigerator for the particular brand of sandwich spread being advertised, he sees with obvious horror that the bottle is empty. Depressed, he plops the sandwich into the cat's bowl and returns to the living room to lie dejectedly on the couch again. As he sighs, the man reaches out to pat him comfortingly, while the announcer tells us that a sandwich without this spread is not worth eating.

Secondary detail focused or off-focus: _____

Part of primary detail not supported: _____

Addition: _____

3. Topic sentence: A number of educational trends that have briefly enjoyed widespread favor in America's schools eventually lost favor because they created problems for students.

Primary detail 1: Some trends in the teaching of English composition were widely accepted as effective innovations until they proved otherwise.

Secondary detail 1: The portfolio approach to teaching English composition involves assigning six to eight essays a semester, which the instructor corrects in rough-draft form. Near the end of the semester, each student selects three or four of those corrected drafts to rewrite and submit for a grade. While this approach was intended to give the student more control over his writing choices and the editing process, students and instructors both found it counterproductive. It left developmental-level students, who often need to write more than one draft for correction, without sufficient guidance and feedback. In addition, by the time the students had chosen which essays they wanted to revise for final grades, most had forgotten what the instructors' comments meant. Finally, because no grades were assigned to essays before the end of the semester, students had less control than intended because they had little idea how they were doing in the class and, therefore, could not make informed decisions about staying in or withdrawing from the class before the last day to drop.

Secondary detail focused or off-focus: _____

Part of primary detail not supported: _____

Addition: _____

4. Topic sentence: Prom customs are noticeably different from what they used to be.

   Primary detail 1: One way prom customs are different from what they used to be involves the amount of money spent on personal grooming.

   Secondary detail 1: Today, girls go all out just to have their nails done. They can invest as much as $60 to have acrylic nails painted on top of their own and then hardened either under a fan or a heat lamp, filed, and polished. Then they may spend up to an additional $50 just for ornamentation. For instance, they may have a small jewel, like a diamond chip, embedded in one nail, or they may have intricate swirl and curlicue patterns transferred by decal or even painted on freehand by a nail artist, who may charge even more than $50 to paint the design in costly gold leaf. The total charge for just these fake nails can run as high as $300.

   Secondary detail focused or off-focus: _____

   Part of primary detail not supported: _____

   Addition: _____

5. Topic sentence: For every official version of the death of an important person, there are several unofficial theories.

   Primary detail 1: In addition to the official explanation of President John F. Kennedy's assassination, several conspiracy theories continue to circulate.

   Secondary detail 1: The Warren Commission officially reported that a single gunman, Lee Harvey Oswald, acting on his own initiative, shot the President on November 22, 1963. However, a number of people still believe that a second shooter fired at the President that day, and that both assassins were acting on the orders of the military-industrial complex, which did not want Kennedy to end American involvement in the Vietnam War.

   Secondary detail focused or off-focus: _____

   Part of primary detail not supported: _____

   Addition: _____

Editing Repetitive Secondary Details

While you probably would not intentionally use the same secondary detail twice, you might accidentally write two secondary details so similar that they are repetitive. Consider the following topic sentence, primary detail, and two secondary details, one of which is repetitive:

Topic sentence: Ancient sailors who were superstitious created wild stories to explain odd phenomena they saw at sea.

Primary detail 1: Odd-looking sea creatures gave rise to some tales.

Secondary detail 1: The tentacles of the octopus gave rise to tales of evil giant creatures capable of grabbing human beings in their many "arms" and holding them under water until they drowned.

Secondary detail 2: The tentacles of squid caused similar fears in ancient sailors.

Can you see that secondary detail 2 is essentially the same detail as secondary detail 1? Even though a squid is not an octopus, they both have tentacles, and they created similar fears in the ancient sailors. In fact, the octopus and squid could be mentioned together in secondary detail 1.

To avoid being repetitive when you write your second secondary detail, do not use the first secondary detail as a model. Instead, re-examine your primary detail. It will help you refocus on what you need to support. Consider this edited secondary detail 2:

Secondary detail 2: The manatee, or sea cow, led to tales of longhaired mermaids because they sometimes surfaced with their heads strewn with the long sea grasses they fed upon.

Exercise Four

Identifying and Editing Repetitive Secondary Details

DIRECTIONS   In each of the following items, examine the two secondary details. If they are essentially the same, replace one.

MODEL   Topic Sentences: Different flowers have different associations for many people.

Primary detail 1: Some flowers are associated with certain events.

Secondary detail 1: Lilies are often associated with death because they are often used in funeral arrangements.

Secondary detail 2: Chrysanthemums are also associated with death, and authors use them as a symbol for it.

Repetitive secondary detail: _yes_

Revision: <u>Roses, especially red roses, are a symbol of romance so they are often given on Valentine's Day.</u>

1. Topic sentence: Many people are drawn to certain carnival rides because they like the extraordinary physical sensations.

   Primary detail 1: They like the physical sensation of being held motionless by centrifugal force.

   Secondary detail 1: Some people enjoy the Tilt-a-Whirl, a tilted platform with small open gondolas for riders to sit in, which twirl them around a track fast enough to keep them securely against the backs of their seats.

   Secondary detail 2: Some people like The Scrambler, rectangular metal cages in a blade-like configuration extending from a central post that twirl the riders in the same way but even faster than the Tilt-a-Whirl does.

   Repetitive secondary detail: _____

   Revision: _____.

2. Topic sentence: Even though life was harsh in the Middle Ages, some forms of entertainment existed.

   Primary detail 1: Troupes of traveling entertainers often stopped to perform in castles and inns.

   Secondary detail 1: Some troupes were traveling players who performed Mystery Plays, which were enactments of Biblical stories, like the story of God speaking to Moses through the burning bush, instructing him to lead the people of Israel out of Egypt.

   Secondary detail 2: Some troupes were traveling dancers who performed the Sword Dance, in which dancers formed circles, holding their swords toward the center of the circle and maneuvering them over and under each other into a star pattern, which the lead dancer of each circle then hoisted over his head for all spectators to admire.

   Repetitive secondary detail: _____

   Revision: _____.

3. Topic sentence: Our knowledge of prehistoric animals comes from the pre-served remains of some these creatures.

   Primary detail 1: Some of these animals were land mammals.

   Secondary detail 1: The woolly mammoth was an elephant-like mammal with curved tusks and shaggy hair that fed upon the shoots of pine trees in what are now Siberia, Central Europe, England, and North America.

   Secondary detail 2: The mastodon was another elephant-like creature with thick skin and a woolly coat to protect it from the Arctic cold. It sported a considerable amount of ivory in its tusks and numerous teeth.

   Repetitive secondary detail: _____

   Revision: _____.

4. Topic sentence: In the last twenty-five years, deep cuts to educational funding have resulted in the elimination of many valuable school programs.

   Primary detail 1: Some budget reductions have affected extracurricular programs.

   Secondary detail 1: In many schools, the cost of uniforms and loaner instruments has necessitated the elimination of the marching band.

   Secondary detail 2: Likewise, the cost of loaner instruments and instruction has forced schools to do away with their orchestras.

   Repetitive secondary detail: _____

   Revision: _____.

5. Topic sentence: In addition to lending books, modern public libraries offer a variety of other services as well.

   Primary detail 1: Some libraries offer interactive services for people interested in literature.

   Secondary detail 1: Reading groups often meet monthly in some libraries to share their analyses of the fiction the members have read that month. Frequently, a librarian will guide the group in discussion of the style, content, and structure.

   Secondary detail 2: Writers' groups also meet regularly in some libraries to read aloud their poems, short stories, and novels, in order to have them criticized by fellow writers who may suggest ways to improve their work.

Repetitive secondary detail: _____

Revision: _____.

Editing Vague Secondary Details

If your secondary detail does not present a complete specific picture that the reader can experience with a least one of his senses (sight, hearing, touch, taste, smell), your secondary detail is vague. Consider the following topic sentence, primary detail, and secondary detail:

Topic sentence: Some study abroad programs that place students in local homes have had complaints from host families.

Primary detail 1: Some complaints have involved neatness.

Secondary detail 1: Host families have complained that American students leave their clothes lying around everywhere.

Does this secondary detail use generalizations or specific detail? Do you know exactly what items of clothing the detail refers to? Do you know specifically where those clothes are lying? This secondary detail expects the reader to supply the specific details for these generalizations, so the generalizations make the reader do the writer's work. Consider the following edited secondary detail:

Secondary detail 1: Host families have complained that American students leave their Levis draped over the television in the living room and their pajamas balled up on the floor of the bathroom.

Exercise Five   Identifying and Editing Vague Secondary Details

DIRECTIONS   In each of the following secondary details, identify the generalizations, if any, and make them specific details.

MODEL   Computers help writing students by allowing them to produce papers more efficiently.

Generalization: produce papers more efficiently

Revision: Computers help writing students by allowing them to add specific examples to vague description, by allowing them to correct grammar errors like run-ons and fragments, and by allowing them to move paragraphs around for better organization without having to retype the whole paper.

1. Secondary detail: Birthday cake decorations can involve writing specialized messages and creating ornamentation out of frosting.

Generalizations: _____ and _____

Revision: _____

2. Secondary detail: Spouses can experience marital difficulties when they treat each other disrespectfully.

   Generalizations: _____ and _____

   Revision: _____ .

3. Secondary detail: Even pothos and dracena palms, two of the hardiest house plants, can be subject to devastating infestations.

   Generalization: _____

   Revision: _____ .

4. Secondary detail: One way the canals in Venice, Italy, are used is as avenues and streets. Since the buildings in Venice rest on wooden piles that are driven into the mud of many islands, sea water that flows around those piles creates nearly two hundred canals. The traffic of the city must traverse these canals, either by footbridges over the canals or by boats upon them.

   Generalization: _____

   Revision: _____ .

5. Secondary detail: One thing that influences depth perception is atmospheric conditions. Moisture particles in the air, as well as dust, can make even close objects look fuzzy.

   Generalization: _____

   Revision: _____ .

Review Questions

Answer the following questions to help you review the material you have covered in this chapter.

1. How many secondary details are enough to support each primary detail? (p. 243) _____

2. When might you think you have enough secondary details when you really don't? (p. 243) _____

3. What should a developed secondary detail help your reader do? (p. 246)

   _____

4. What are the four techniques that help you develop secondary details? (p. 246)

   _____ _____ _____ _____

5. What is an off-focus secondary detail? (p. 249) _____

6. Why is an off-focus secondary detail incomplete? (p. 249)

   _____

7. When is a secondary detail repetitive? (p. 254) _____

8. How do you avoid writing a repetitive secondary detail? (p. 254)

   _____

9. What is the error called when a secondary detail does not present a complete, specific picture? (p. 257) _____

10. What must be corrected in a vague secondary detail? (p. 257) _____

Editing Exercises

For the last time, look at the three paragraphs you rewrote for the Writing Exercise in Chapter Twelve. Look for errors in secondary details. If you find any of the errors you learned about in this chapter, correct them.

Looking Back and Looking Forward

In the two chapters of this fourth section, you have learned to identify errors in structure and development in your paragraph and to edit those errors. In the next section, you will learn to apply what you have learned about writing a single paragraph to writing a multi-paragraph college essay. In Chapter Fourteen, you will see how the structure of a paragraph can provide the foundation for the structure of an essay.

Section four review *Editing*

I. Rewriting for Structure and Development

Remember what you have learned in Chapters Twelve and Thirteen about editing the structure and development of your paragraph. Read the following paragraphs on historical mysteries. Rewrite, correcting any of the following errors you find:

Topic Sentence Errors

unfocused topic sentence
split focus in topic sentence
unsupportable focus in topic sentence
overly subjective focus in topic sentence
overly complicated focus in topic sentence

Primary Detail Errors

off-focus primary details
vague primary details
non-parallel primary details
redundant primary details
unsupportable primary details

Conclusion Errors

change of direction
exaggeration
failure to answer *So what?*

Secondary Details Errors

underdeveloped secondary details
repetitive secondary details
not enough secondary details
off-focus secondary details
vague secondary details

Grammar Errors

fragments
subject–verb agreement errors
verb tense agreement errors
parallelism errors
pronoun agreement errors

Famous Disappearances

Several of history's unexplained disappearances are terrific and fascinating, one of which involves the famous American aviatrix Amelia Earhart who disappeared in 1937 while attempting to fly around the world from east to west. First, we are fascinated by reports that she disappeared while on a spying mission for the American government. Because tension was building toward World War II. The timing of her mission may have looked suspicious to America's enemies, who might have kept her prisoner after her plane ran out of fuel and crashed somewhere in the Pacific, according to one theory. Another theory that fascinates us is the possibility that Earhart and her naviga-tor, Fred Noonan, simply crashed in the Pacific. Even though no wreckage nor remains has ever been found at the coordinates given in Earhart's last radio transmission. Secondly, the kidnapping of aviator Charles Lindbergh's two-year-old son, Charles Augustus, Jr., happened in 1932 and fascinates us still. Although a body was eventually found. There have been speculation that the body identified as the Lindbergh baby was actually another child. This speculation is fueled by the claim many years later by an adult who claimed to be Charles Lind-bergh, Jr. Furthermore, there were theories concerning the falsifica-tion of evidence at the hands of local authorities. Moreover, there has been speculation of a different sort concerning the guilt or innocence of Bruno Hauptmann, the German immigrant carpenter who was exe-cuted for the murder of the Lindbergh baby. Hauptmann and his wife both maintained his innocence, which is also supported by people who claimed that Lindbergh misidentified Hauptmann's voice as that of the man who accepted the ransom and that the police had manu-factured evidence in order to solve this highly emotional, publicly scrutinized case quickly. Not surprisingly, these two disappearances have proved to be the most fascinating history has ever known.

Suspicious Deaths

Suspicious deaths of famous people have been explained to the pub-lic. First, there are several explanations for the death of actress Mari-lyn Monroe. The official explanation for her death is that she took an accidental overdose of barbiturates. She may have been taking the barbiturates for depression caused by insomnia and recent profes-sional problems. On the other hand, the conspiracy theory of her death points fingers at high-ranking political figures. Who were known to have had intimate relations with her which could have proved em-barrassing to him if made public. Second, Mary Jo Kopechne's drown-ing death off Chappaquiddick has also been explained in several ways. The official version states that Kopechne, who was in the company of Massachusetts Senator Ted Kennedy, drowned when Kennedy's vehi-cle plunged accidentally off the Chappaquiddick Bridge. Senator Kennedy, according to the official report, was dazed and disoriented and unable to free Kopechne from the submerged vehicle and was barely able to swim to safety himself. There is, however, those who feel that Kennedy and Kopechne may have a deeper relationship than that of politician and staff member, which may have played a role in the tragedy. Finally, the death of Diana, Princess of Wales. Officially, her death is listed as the result of a car crash caused by the driver's drinking and that he was traveling at high speed in order to avoid pursuing paparazzi. Police are also investigating the possibility that a small, white car played a role in the crash. Regardless of the ways they died, all of these women should be remembered for the ways they lived.

II. Rewriting with Structure and Development

Choose one or more of the following assignments and write a paragraph on it. Pay attention to the elements of structure and the development of your secondary details. Do not forget to use the grammar skills you have learned to edit the paragraph. You will notice that these assignments reflect a variety of college courses.

1. Trace the development of the steam engine.
2. Make a case for or against the minimum wage law.
3. Describe how vegetation migrates from one land mass to another.
4. Describe a mythical beast.
5. Describe what secondary details do in a college composition.
6. Describe the types of movements in a symphony.
7. Describe how we can protect endangered species.
8. Choose a traitor in history and defend him or her against the charge of treason.
9. Discuss the characteristics of or treatments for clinical depression.
10. Describe yoga as both an athletic pursuit and a relaxation technique.
11. Take and support a stand on whether or not air traffic controllers should strike.
12. Describe how to set up a household budget.
13. Contrast either a film with a television series based on it or a film with the novel it was based on.

III. Editing for Structure and Development

Once more reread the two paragraphs you edited for style in III of Section Three Review. This time, review them for structure and development. Find and correct any of the errors identified in Chapters Twelve and Thirteen, including the grammar errors covered in those chapters.

Writing Essays

Chapter fourteen

From Paragraph to Essay

For the past thirteen chapters, you have learned how to structure and develop a single paragraph. Within that paragraph are also the main elements of a multi–paragraph essay. The following is a multi–paragraph essay based on a paragraph you read in Chapter Twelve. Each of the structural and developmental elements in that original paragraph was labeled. Can you tell what these elements have become in the following essay?

Most of us have had a moment when we wished the earth would open up and swallow us, and I am no exception (preliminary statement). My first meeting with my prospective in-laws was a terrifically embarrassing experience (thesis). I embarrassed myself entering their home, having dinner, and leaving (blueprint).

First, I made a fool of myself entering my prospective in-laws' home (topic sentence). In my eagerness to express my pleasure at meeting Mr. Gordon, I enunciated violently when I said to him, "I'm SO pleased to meet you!" I expelled my breath with gale-force wind when I said "SO." The result was that I hurled my breath mint directly into his bushy beard, where it stuck like Velcro. There it hung securely, taunting me (secondary detail 1). Then, while trying frantically to extricate the glob from his startled face, I missed my footing, tripped over the threshold, and, still clutching at Mr. Gordon's beard, came crashing down on a priceless Ming vase in the entryway. Mr. Gordon also fell to his knees on the shards of the vase, which had shattered to brittle confetti. My father-in-law-to-be moaned a pitiful "Ow, ow, ow." My agony was compounded by not knowing which hurt him the most: the sharp pottery embedded in his knees, my fingers yanking on his beard, or the thought that this dangerously clumsy stranger was joining the family (secondary detail 2).

Next, I mortified myself at dinner (topic sentence). I was anxious to compliment Mrs. Gordon's cooking, so just after telling her that she was the Julia Child of Springfield, Illinois, I inhaled a ladle-sized spoonful of her famous onion soup, which was so hot that I sprayed it back over my dining companions like an incontinent garden hose. The only one I left dry was the family dog, cowering from me under my fiance's chair (secondary detail 1). Once everyone at the table had mopped up sufficiently and settled down to a tense, silent attention to the pot roast, I let my nerves get the best of me. Thoroughly shaken at that point, I began to fiddle with the border on Mrs. Gordon's damask lace tablecloth, obviously an heirloom. By the time I realized what I was doing, I had unraveled a half inch of the bottom border. A sizable mound of crinkled thread filled my lap, and the bottom of the tablecloth looked like the fringe on a Victorian lamp (secondary detail 2).

Finally, I sealed my humiliation with an awkward exit (topic sentence). I was still trying to appear unfailingly agreeable, as my nervous hosts walked my fiance and me to the door. Doing my impression of an apologetic Columbo, alternately bowing and nodding as I backed out the front door, I tripped on the same door sill I had sailed in on, clutching the air as I crumbled in a heap on the pavement, skinning my knees and leaving blood on the clean walkway (secondary detail 1). I'm sure the Gordons hoped the worst was over, but I had one more humiliating *faux pas* left in me: The capper was the angry gouge I left in the Gordons' cream-colored antique TR4 parked in their driveway as I lurched to my feet, stumbling against it and scraping my jacket zipper along the passenger side door. The metallic scar glinted wickedly in the bright sun. It nearly blinded me as I slunk toward my fiance, who was already gunning the motor of my car in a frantic attempt to remove me from the scene of my crimes (secondary detail 2).

If it had not been for my excrutiatingly clumsy entrance, dining, and exit, I am sure I would have made a terrific first impression on my future in-laws instead of one that totally humiliated me (summary sentence). Not surprisingly, it was three weeks before I could get over my embarrassment enough to send a combined thank-you note and apology to the Gordons, who now lovingly refer to me as "The Terminatrix" (so what? statement).

In the preceding multi-paragraph essay, as in any multi-paragraph essay, the first paragraph is an *introduction*, the last paragraph is a *conclusion*, and all the paragraphs between are *main body paragraphs*. Did you notice that the *topic sentence* in the original paragraph became the *thesis* in the introduction of the essay? Did you also see that the three *primary details* in the original paragraph became the *topic sentences* of three main body paragraphs? Did you notice that the *secondary details* in the original paragraph were expanded for support? Finally, the part that is a *conclusion* in a single paragraph becomes a *so what? statement* in the concluding paragraph of an essay.

Note that the introductory paragraph and the concluding paragraph of the essay each had structural elements that were not in the original paragraph. What is each of those elements called?

In the introduction, a **preliminary statement,** which comes before the thesis, introduces the general subject and makes it relevant to the reader. One way to make a topic relevant to the reader is to make a statement about that topic that is true for *many people.* In the essay about meeting prospective in-laws, *a moment when we wished the earth would open up and swallow us* is another way of introducing an embarrassing experience, which is the general subject. The general subject is different from and broader than the specific topic of the essay which is, in this case, a specific embarrassing experience, meeting prospective in-laws. Stating that *most of us* have experienced such a moment makes the general subject relevant to the reader by including the reader in that experience.

Another way of writing a preliminary statement that is true for many people is to state an opposite for the thesis to "push against." For example, the thesis under discussion could have been introduced by the preliminary statement *Many people remember their first meeting with their prospective in-laws as being a thoroughly comfortable experience.* Can you see how this would provide a contrast for the thesis which would now begin with a contrasting word like *however?* Notice that when you write this kind of preliminary statement, you are introducing the specific topic of the thesis rather than the general subject to which the thesis belongs, as in the first type of preliminary statement, which is illustrated in the preceding essay.

Then, after the thesis in the introductory paragraph, the **blueprint** provides a plan of development for the essay. It is formed by breaking the thesis into subcategories, the same way you worked with structural "pies" throughout Chapter Six, carving your topic into primary details. You will notice that each of the points in the blueprint, along with the controlling idea from the thesis, is repeated in a topic sentence for a main body paragraph. In the essay about meeting the in-laws, the embarrassing experience was subdivided into *entering their home, having dinner,* and *leaving.* Each subcategory becomes the subject of a main body paragraph, and these main body paragraphs in the essay follow the same order as the subcategories in the blueprint.

In the conclusion, a **summary sentence** restates the controlling idea from the thesis and all the subcategories in the blueprint. Although you should follow the same order of subcategories in your summary sentence as in your blueprint, you should try to find a fresh way of presenting the information. In the preceding essay, the blueprint says, *I embarrassed myself entering their home, having dinner, and leaving.* However, the summary sentence says, *If it had not been for my excrutiatingly clumsy entrance, dining, and exit, I am sure I would have made a terrific first impression on my future in-laws instead of one that totally humiliated me.* Even though the summary sentence repeats the thesis opinion *embarrassing* in the word *humiliated,* which means the same, as well as the blueprint subcategories *entering their home, having dinner,* and *leaving,* the summary sentence finds a new way to give the same information.

Introductory Paragraphs

Notice that everything you plan to do in your essay is set out in the introductory paragraph. If you follow this plan as you write, you will never get to the middle of an essay and wonder, *Where do I go from here?* Likewise your reader will always know where you are headed and what points you are supporting. In fact, your thesis and your blueprint give the reader a basis for evaluating your paper. If you do in your essay what your thesis and blueprint promise you will do, you will provide your instructor with an objective basis for grading your paper.

Even though an introductory paragraph begins with a preliminary statement, it is easier to write the thesis and blueprint before the preliminary statement because once you write your thesis and blueprint, you will know exactly what you need to introduce in the preliminary statement, and then you can go back to the beginning of the paragraph to do it.

Exercise One

Writing a Blueprint from a Thesis

DIRECTIONS   To divide each of the following theses into a blueprint, use the focusing questions you used in Chapter Six to subdivide a topic into primary details (Who? What? Which one(s)? When? Where? Why? How? How much?). Remember to ask the same focusing question for each subdivision of the thesis in a single blueprint so that your blueprint subcategories will be parallel. You may write two, three, or even four subdivisions for each blueprint. Do not forget to make your blueprint a complete sentence.

MODEL   Thesis: Although most weight-reducing diets try to limit fat intake, different diets emphasize eating one type of food more than others.

Focusing question: What type of food?

Blueprint: Some diets emphasize eating proteins, others emphasize eating carbohydrates, and still others emphasize eating fruits and vegetables.

1. Thesis: Alcohol abuse frequently leads to antisocial behavior.

   Focusing question: _____ ?

   Blueprint: _____ .

2. Thesis: There are several objections to the clear-cutting of forest areas.

   Focusing question: _____ ?

   Blueprint: _____ .

3. Thesis: Some people avoid family reunions for several reasons.

   Focusing question: _____?

   Blueprint: _____.

4. Thesis: Speech therapy can treat several kinds of speech impediments.

   Focusing question: _____?

   Blueprint: _____.

5. Thesis: Flowers serve different purposes in people's lives.

   Focusing question: _____?

   Blueprint: _____.

Now that you have practiced writing a blueprint from a thesis, you are ready to introduce that thesis and blueprint with a preliminary statement. Do not forget that a preliminary statement either introduces the general subject and makes it relevant to the reader or introduces the specific topic in the thesis by setting up an opposite for that thesis to push against.

Exercise Two

Writing a Preliminary Statement for a Thesis and Blueprint

DIRECTIONS For each of the five preceding thesis statements and blueprints, determine the general subject, and then write two preliminary statements for each. Make the first preliminary statement introduce the general subject for the specific topic in the thesis; make the second preliminary statement present an opposite for the specific topic in the thesis to push against.

MODEL Thesis: Different diets emphasize eating one type of food more than others.

Blueprint: *Some diets emphasize eating proteins, others emphasize eating carbohydrates, and still others emphasize eating fruits and vegetables.*

General subject: *food intake*

Preliminary statement 1: *For many reasons, people these days are concerned about what they eat.*

Preliminary statement 2: *Most weight-reducing diets are based on limiting what the dieter eats.*

1. Thesis: Alcohol abuse frequently leads to antisocial behavior:

   Blueprint: _____.

General subject: _____

Preliminary statement 1: _____.

Preliminary statement 2: _____.

2. Thesis: There are several objections to the clear-cutting of forest areas.

   Blueprint: _____.

   General subject: _____

   Preliminary statement 1: _____.

   Preliminary statement 2: _____.

3. Thesis: Some people avoid family reunions for several reasons.

   Blueprint: _____.

   General subject: _____

   Preliminary statement 1: _____.

   Preliminary statement 2: _____.

4. Thesis: Speech therapy can treat several kinds of speech impediments.

   Blueprint: _____.

   General subject: _____

   Preliminary statement 1: _____.

   Preliminary statement 2: _____.

5. Thesis: Flowers serve different purposes in people's lives.

   Blueprint: _____.

   General subject: _____

   Preliminary statement 1: _____.

   Preliminary statement 2: _____.

Exercise Three   **Putting Introductions Together**

DIRECTIONS   For each of the following assignments, write a complete introduction, including preliminary statement, thesis, and blueprint. Remember that repeating specific language from an assignment in your thesis helps you focus that thesis. As the model in Exercise Two illustrates, a preliminary statement can be written two ways. Finally, as explained earlier in this chapter, your blueprint can have two, three, or four subdivisions.

MODEL   Assignment: Discuss the value of studying history.

Preliminary statement: Many students believe that the study of history is no more than memorizing dates;

Thesis: <u>however, the study of history has several practical benefits for society.</u>

Blueprint: <u>It helps society avoid repeating mistakes, and it helps society prepare</u>

<u>for the future.</u>

1. Assignment: Discuss the drawbacks of traveling alone.

    Preliminary statement: _____ .

    Thesis: _____ .

    Blueprint: _____ .

2. Assignment: Give reasons for or against the existence of life elsewhere in the universe.

    Preliminary statement: _____ .

    Thesis: _____ .

    Blueprint: _____ .

3. Assignment: Many animals and insects find unusual ways to protect themselves from danger. Discuss some of these adaptive techniques.

    Preliminary statement: _____ .

    Thesis: _____ .

    Blueprint: _____ .

4. Assignment: Discuss the ways a fictional character becomes known to a reader.

    Preliminary statement: _____ .

    Thesis: _____ .

    Blueprint: _____ .

5. Assignment: Describe several ways a new business can market itself to attract customers.

    Preliminary statement: _____ .

    Thesis: _____ .

    Blueprint: _____ .

Main Body Paragraphs

As discussed in the explanation and model at the beginning of this chapter, each of the main body paragraphs in an essay is introduced by a topic sentence that repeats the controlling idea from the thesis along with a subcategory from the blueprint. As you recall, the topic sentences present the subcategories in the same order as the blueprint.

Exercise Four

Writing Topic Sentences from Introductions

DIRECTIONS   Use the thesis and blueprint from each of the introductions you wrote in Exercise Three to create at least two topic sentences for main body paragraphs. Notice in the following model that the introduction is written out more like a paragraph, even though the structural elements are still identified for you in parentheses at the end of each sentence.

MODEL   Introduction: Many students believe that the study of history is no more than mem-orizing dates (preliminary statement); however, the study of history has several practical benefits for society (thesis). It helps society avoid repeating mistakes, and it helps society prepare for the future (blue-print).

Topic sentence 1: One practical benefit of studying history is that it helps society avoid repeating mistakes.

Topic sentence 2: Another practical benefit of studying history is that it helps society prepare for the future.

1. Introduction: _____.

   Topic sentence 1: _____.

   Topic sentence 2: _____.

2. Introduction: _____.

   Topic sentence 1: _____.

   Topic sentence 2: _____.

3. Introduction: _____.

   Topic sentence 1: _____.

   Topic sentence 2: _____.

4. Introduction: _____.

   Topic sentence 1: _____.

   Topic sentence 2: _____.

5. Introduction: _____.

    Topic sentence 1: _____.

    Topic sentence 2: _____.

Concluding Paragraphs

As the explanation and model essay at the beginning of this chapter illustrate, the conclusion of your essay begins with a summary sentence that restates the controlling idea from the thesis along with the whole blueprint. In order to present that material in a way that does not sound repetitive, you can do several things: You can reverse the order, restating the blueprint before the controlling idea from the thesis; also, you can use synonyms, or words that mean the same thing, in place of key words. Then the paragraph ends with a *so what?* statement that can be the same as the concluding sentence in a single paragraph. This *so what?* statement examines the greater implications (possible results) of the subject of the essay, or it can be another broad generalization about the general subject, like the preliminary statement that introduced the essay.

Exercise Five

Writing Summary Sentences from a Thesis and Blueprint

DIRECTIONS   Use the thesis and blueprint from each of the items you wrote in Exercise Three to create a summary sentence. Try to present that material from your introduction in a new way in the summary by reversing the order of the blueprint and the controlling idea from the thesis and/or using synonyms for key words.

MODEL   Thesis: however, the study of history has several practical benefits for society.

Blueprint: It helps society avoid repeating mistakes, and it helps society prepare for the future.

Summary sentence: Whether it is helping society not to make the same errors it has made in the past or it is helping society pave the way for what is to come, the study of history provides people with practical benefits.

1. Thesis: _____.

   Blueprint: _____.

   Summary sentence: _____.

2. Thesis: _____.

  Blueprint: _____.

  Summary sentence: _____.

3. Thesis: _____.

  Blueprint: _____.

  Summary sentence: _____.

4. Thesis: _____.

  Blueprint: _____.

  Summary sentence: _____.

5. Thesis: _____.

  Blueprint: _____.

  Summary sentence: _____.

Exercise Six

Writing *So What?* Statements

DIRECTIONS Examine the summary sentence from each of the items in Exercise Five. Now add a *so what?* statement. It should present the greater implications or results of the general subject or make a generalization about the general subject, the same way the preliminary statement of an essay does.

MODEL Summary sentence: Whether it is helping society not to make the same errors it has made in the past or it is helping society pave the way for what is to come, the study of history provides people with practical benefits.

So what? statement 1: Clearly, what we learn from history's lessons can help us live in peace and prosperity with our neighbors, avoiding a repeat of such tragedies as Hiroshima and the Holocaust. (implications)

So what? statement 2: Despite what reluctant students think about the study of history as being nothing more than the memorization of historical data, it can teach us how to control our own destiny. (generalization)

1. Summary sentence: _____.

  So what? statement: _____.

2. Summary sentence: _____.

   So what? statement: _____.

3. Summary sentence: _____.

   So what? statement: _____.

4. Summary sentence: _____.

   So what? statement: _____.

5. Summary sentence: _____.

   So what? statement: _____.

Exercise Seven	**Putting Conclusions Together**

DIRECTIONS Examine the introductions you completed with preliminary statements in Exercise Two. Now write a complete conclusion for each one, including a summary sentence and a *so what?* statement.

MODEL Introduction: Most weight-reducing diets are based on limiting what the dieter eats (preliminary statement); however, some diets emphasize eating one type of food more than others (thesis). Some diets emphasize eating proteins, others emphasize eating carbohydrates, and still others emphasize eating fruits and vegetables (blueprint).

Conclusion: Eating mainly proteins, eating mainly carbohydrates, or eating mainly fruits and vegetables are ways of dieting that concentrate on the specific kinds of food we eat (summary sentence). Perhaps a more reasonable way of dieting is to consume a wider variety of foods in moderation rather than to deprive the body of the nutrients that variety can provide (so what? statement).

1. Introduction: _____.

   Conclusion: _____.

2. Introduction: _____.

   Conclusion: _____.

3. Introduction: _____.

   Conclusion: _____.

4. Introduction: _____ .

   Conclusion: _____ .

5. Introduction: _____ .

   Conclusion: _____ .

Review Questions

Answer the following questions to help you review the material you have learned in this chapter.

1. What is the first paragraph in a multi-paragraph essay called? (p. 266)

   _____

2. What is the last paragraph in a multi-paragraph essay called? (p. 266)

   _____

3. What are the paragraphs between the first and last paragraphs in a multi-paragraph essay called? (p. 266) _____

4. What structural element in a single paragraph becomes a thesis in a multi-paragraph essay? (p. 266) _____

5. Where do topic sentences for main body paragraphs come from? (p. 266)

   _____

6. In a multi-paragraph essay, what happens to the secondary details from a single paragraph? (p. 266) _____

7. What part of a single paragraph becomes a *so what?* statement in a multi-paragraph essay? (p. 266) _____

8. Where does a preliminary statement belong in an essay? (p. 267)

   _____

9. What two things does a preliminary statement accomplish? (p. 267)

   _____ and _____

10. Give two ways it accomplishes this. (p. 267)

    _____ and _____

11. What does the blueprint provide for an essay? (p. 267) _____

12. How is the blueprint formed? (p. 267) _____

13. What order do the main body paragraphs in an essay follow? (p. 267)

    _____

14. What goes into a summary sentence in the conclusion of an essay? (p. 267)

    _____

15. What is new about a summary sentence? (p. 267) _____

16. Why is it easier to write the thesis and blueprint before writing the preliminary statement even though the preliminary statement comes first in the essay?

    (p. 268) _____

17. What are the two parts of a topic sentence for a main body paragraph? (p. 272)

    _____ and _____

18. What is one way you can repeat the controlling idea from your thesis along with the whole blueprint in your summary sentence without sounding repetitive? (p. 273) _____

19. What is the other way? (p. 273) _____

20. What can the *so what?* statement in the conclusion examine? (p. 273)

    _____

21. What kind of generalization can a *so what?* statement be? (p. 273)

    _____

Writing Exercises

I. Setting Up Structures: Paragraph to Essay

Choose three of the following assignments. First, set up an outline for a paragraph following the first model format. Then expand it into an outline for a complete essay following the second model format.

1. Describe the characteristics of the weather phenomenon known as El Niño.

2. Discuss several methods that farmers and gardeners use to restore nutrients to soil.

3. Describe some nonverbal techniques speakers can use to convey meaning.

4. As the English Restoration playwright William Congreve said, "Music has charms to soothe a savage breast." Describe several qualities in music that you find soothing.

5. Describe several ways of establishing or re-establishing financial credit.

6. Describe the advantages or disadvantages of meeting someone through the Internet.

Model for Paragraph Outline:

  I. Topic sentence: _____.

 II. Support

   A. Primary detail 1: _____.

   B. Primary detail 2: _____.

   C. Primary detail 3: _____.

   D. Primary detail 4: _____.

III. Concluding sentence: _____.

Model for Essay Outline:

  I. Introduction

   A. Preliminary statement: _____.

   B. Thesis: _____.

   C. Blueprint: _____.

 II. Main Body Paragraphs

   A. Topic sentence for main body paragraph 1: _____.

      _____.

   B. Topic sentence for main body paragraph 2: _____.

      _____.

   C. Topic sentence for main body paragraph 3: _____.

      _____.

D. Topic sentence for main body paragraph 4: _____.

_____.

III. Conclusion

    A. Summary sentence: _____.

    B. *So what?* statement: _____.

II. Writing the Structural Essay

Choose any two topics from Exercises One and Three in this chapter, and write a multi-paragraph essay on each. Do not worry about expanding secondary details at this point, but do edit for style and grammar as you learned to do in Chapters Twelve and Thirteen.

III. Writing an Essay from a Single Paragraph

Turn the two paragraphs you wrote for Section Two Review into full essays. Make sure your essay contains all the structural elements of a multi-paragraph essay: preliminary statement, thesis, blueprint, main body topic sentences, summary sentence, and *so what?* statement. Do not worry about expanding secondary details yet, but do edit for style and grammar as you learned to do in Chapters Twelve and Thirteen.

IV. Revising the Starter Essay

Look back at the starter essay you wrote at the beginning of this book. Does your essay have four paragraphs that are each indented? Does the first paragraph have a preliminary statement, a thesis, and a blueprint? Does each main body paragraph begin with a topic sentence that refers back to one of the two parts of the blueprint? Does the concluding paragraph have a summary sentence that restates the thesis and blueprint? Does it end with a *so what?* statement? Revise the structure of this essay wherever necessary.

Looking Back and Looking Forward

In this chapter, you have learned how to expand the structure of a single paragraph into the structure of a multi-paragraph essay. Now you are ready to build on that foundation. In the next chapter, you will learn how to develop secondary details even more than you have already done because a larger framework calls for more developed support to convince the reader that your thesis is true.

Chapter fifteen
Expanding Secondary Details

In Chapter Fourteen, where you learned to expand the structure of a paragraph into the structure of an essay, you saw that an essay is not just longer than a paragraph but more complex. In this chapter, you will learn techniques for making the support for the structure of your paragraphs or essays more complex.

When you learned to develop secondary details for a single paragraph in Chapter Eight, you used strong verbs, specific nouns, necessary modifiers, and comparisons. Now you will learn to support the larger framework of an essay by adding more sophisticated techniques:

1. expanded details

2. additional examples

3. anecdotes

Expanded Details

In the last chapter you read an essay-length version of a paragraph you first read in Chapter Twelve. You may have noticed that expanding the structure from paragraph to essay also requires that the details be expanded. In the following examples, compare the secondary details of the paragraph to the supporting details of the corresponding main body paragraphs:

First secondary detail 1: In my eagerness to express my pleasure at meeting him, I enunciated violently when I said to him, "I'm SO pleased to meet you!" The result was that I hurled my breath mint directly into his beard where it stuck like Velcro.

Main body paragraph 1 / supporting detail 1: In my eagerness to express my pleasure at meeting <u>Mr. Gordon,</u> I enunciated violently when I said to him, "I'm SO pleased to meet you!" <u>I expelled my breath mint with gale-force wind when I said "SO."</u> The result was that I hurled my breath mint directly into his *bushy* beard where it stuck like Velcro. <u>There it hung securely, taunting me.</u>

First secondary detail 2: Then while trying frantically to extricate the glob from his startled face, I tripped over the threshold and came crashing down on a priceless Ming vase in the entryway, shattering it to confetti.

Main body paragraph 1 / supporting detail 2: Then while trying frantically to extricate the glob from his startled face, I <u>missed my footing,</u> tripped over the threshold, and, <u>still clutching Mr. Gordon's beard,</u> came crashing down on a priceless Ming vase in the entryway. <u>Mr. Gordon also fell to his knees on the shards of the vase, which</u> shattered to <u>brittle</u> confetti. <u>My father-in-law-to-be moaned a pitiful "Ow, ow, ow." My agony was compounded by not knowing which hurt him most: the sharp pottery embedded in his knees, my fingers yanking on his beard, or the thought that this dangerously clumsy stranger was joining the family.</u>

Second secondary detail 1: I was anxious to compliment Mrs. Gordon's cooking, so I inhaled a ladle-sized spoonful of her famous onion soup, which was so hot that I sprayed it back over my dining companions like an incontinent garden hose.

Main body paragraph 2 / supporting detail 1: I was anxious to compliment Mrs. Gordon's cooking, so <u>just after telling her that she was the Julia Child of Springfield, Illinois,</u> I inhaled a ladle-sized spoonful of her famous onion soup, which was so hot that I sprayed it back over my dining companions like an incontinent garden hose. <u>The only one I left dry was the family dog, cowering from me under my fiance's chair.</u>

Second secondary detail 2: Thoroughly shaken at that point, I began to fiddle with the border on Mrs. Gordon's damask lace tablecloth, obviously an heirloom. By the time I realized what I was doing, I had unraveled a half-inch of the bottom border.

Main body paragraph 2 / supporting detail 2: <u>Once everyone at the table had mopped up sufficiently and settled down to a tense, silent attention to the pot roast, I let my nerves get the best of me.</u> Thoroughly shaken at that point, I began to fiddle with the border on Mrs. Gordon's damask lace tablecloth, obviously an heirloom. By the time I realized what I was doing, I had unraveled a half-inch of the bottom border. <u>A sizable mound of crinkled thread filled my lap, and the bottom of the tablecloth looked like the fringe on a Victorian lamp.</u>

Third secondary detail 1: Alternately bowing and nodding as I backed out the front door, I tripped on the same door sill I had sailed in on, skinning my knees and leaving blood on the clean walkway.

Main body paragraph 3 / supporting detail 1: <u>I was still trying to appear unfailingly agreeable as my nervous hosts walked my fiance and me to the door. Doing my impression of an apologetic Columbo,</u> alternately bowing and nodding as I backed out the front door, I tripped on the same door sill I had sailed in on, <u>clutching the air as I crumbled in a heap on the pavement,</u> skinning my knees and leaving blood on the clean walkway.

Third secondary detail 2: The capper was the angry gouge I left in the Gordons' antique TR4 parked in their driveway as I lurched to my feet, stumbling against it and scraping my jacket zipper along the passenger side door.

Main body paragraph 3 / secondary detail 2: <u>I'm sure the Gordons hoped the worst was over, but I had one more humiliating *faux pas* left in me:</u> The capper was the angry gouge I left in the Gordons' <u>cream-colored</u> antique TR4 parked in their driveway as I lurched to my feet, stumbling against it and scraping my jacket zipper along the passenger side door. <u>The metallic scar glinted wickedly in the bright sun. It nearly blinded me as I slunk toward my fiance, who was already gunning the motor of my car in a frantic attempt to remove me from the scene of my crimes.</u>

If you examine the underlined print in the preceding examples, you will see how much interesting development can be added to the support of an essay. There are four techniques for adding development to your supporting details:

1. expanded transitions

2. more specific details

3. allusions

4. results

Expanded Transitions

In Chapter Nine, you learned that transitions help ideas flow smoothly from sentence to sentence. In a single paragraph, your transitions were single words or phrases, like *First, Next,* and *however.* In the main body paragraphs of an essay, transitions can often be full sentences. Expanded transitions frequently look back at the last idea and forward to the next. For instance, consider the transition between the two supporting details in the third main body paragraph *I'm sure the Gordons hoped the worst was over, but I had one more humiliating <u>faux pas</u> left in me:* Do you see that the first independent clause refers to what has already happened while the second independent clause prepares the reader for what is to come? Can you identify the other expanded transitions in the preceding underlined text?

More Specific Details

More specific details simply add modifiers to describe important people, places, and objects. As you learned in Chapter Three, a string of modifiers is not as effective as one or two carefully chosen modifiers. Consider the modifier *cream-colored* which is added to the description of the Gordons' antique TR4 in the second supporting detail of the third main body paragraph. Do you see how the addition of this adjective helps the reader form a more vivid picture of the elegance of the car that was damaged? Can you identify other more specific details added in the preceding underlined text?

Allusions

Allusions are references to well-known persons, places, objects, and events in history, literature, arts, or religion that are instantly recognized by most people and, thereby, help the reader to form a more complete picture in his mind because of the associations he makes. Consider the allusion to *Columbo* in the first supporting detail of the main body paragraph 3. Can you identify another allusion added in the underlined text?

Results

Results take a supporting detail beyond the example itself and show what happens as a result of it. Consider the result of the breath mint's sticking to Mr. Gordon's beard, *There it hung securely, taunting me.* Can you identify other results added in the underlined text?

Exercise One **Supplying Expanded Transitions**

DIRECTIONS Read the following underdeveloped essay. Add expanded transitions where appropriate.

Studying for the Big Exam

Many people fall apart when dealing with stressful situations. However, we could all take a lesson from those students, who, faced with the stress of studying for the Big Exam, often find the most creative ways for avoiding the disaster they anticipate. Some of those students avoid studying by dealing with alternate realities while others conjure up unrealities.

First of all, some students creatively avoid studying for "The Big One" by dealing with pressing needs in their lives. For instance, some admirably tidy people suddenly notice at 11:30 P.M. that the bathroom grout situation has gotten out of hand. They must clean, all night if necessary, before they can open a book. Other students of the male persuasion are compelled by curiosity to phone all of the numbers in their dating Rolodex to see whatever happened to old What's-her-name.

Second, some students hope and plan for the worst. A common daydream for the truly desperate involves mental preparation for the unlikely chance that he might manage to catch his writing arm in the permit machine at the student parking lot, rendering himself unable to hold a pen. Other ecologically-minded students, even those who live in the Midwest, watch the weather channel, hoping that an offshore earthquake will send a tsunami coursing toward campus.

Whatever their grasp on reality, alternate or otherwise, these students eventually arrive at a common ground—the realization that nothing will save them, and they must ultimately start cramming. Teachers can only hope that this realization hits before, rather than after, the exam.

Exercise Two	## Supplying More Specific Details
DIRECTIONS	Read the expanded essay you wrote for Exercise One. Now add more specific details by using modifiers where appropriate.
Exercise Three	## Supplying Allusions
DIRECTIONS	Read the expanded essay you wrote for Exercise Two. This time add some allusions where appropriate.
Exercise Four	## Supplying Results
DIRECTIONS	Read the expanded essay you wrote for Exercise Three. Now add results where appropriate.

Additional Examples

Until now, you have been using two supporting details in each main body paragraph. There are times, however, when a main body paragraph in your essay calls for more than two examples to support its topic sentence.

One time you should use more than two specific examples to support a topic sentence in a main body paragraph is when you are reporting material from research sources like a book, a magazine, a newspaper, an essay, or a movie. If your source material offers more supporting details than two, you should represent the totality of the source material.

Another time you should use more than two examples is when your thesis is <u>controversial,</u> so you need to be especially persuasive in order to convince the reader of your point of view. A controversial thesis may or may not involve a controversial subject like abortion, gun control, or euthanasia, but it is what you say about the subject and/or how you state your thesis that makes it truly controversial. If your thesis is controversial, then certainly your blueprint and topic sentences will also be controversial, for they are the thesis broken down into parts. The controlling idea of the thesis and/or the language used to express the thesis are what you need to consider.

1. A Controversial Controlling Idea

   A controlling idea is controversial when it is unlikely that a single viewpoint will ever be accepted by everyone. Consider the thesis *Abortions for the poor should be funded by the state.* Can you see that the controlling idea *should be funded by the state* is the controversial part of the thesis? This is an opinion that both sides of the abortion issue will never agree on.

2. Controversial Language

   The language of the thesis is controversial when any part of the thesis is stated in an inflammatory way. There are several ways to be inflammatory. One way is name-calling. Consider the thesis *People who have opposed government funding for abortions for the poor must accept responsibility for a portion of the child abuse that occurs in this country.* Can you see that while there may be some correlation between child abuse and the forced birth of unwanted children, accusing people who oppose government funding for abortion of being, in effect, child abusers is name-calling, no matter how restrained the language is?

   Another way of being inflammatory is using emotional language. Consider the thesis *Abortion is murder.* The word *murder* is an emotional word. Since the crux of the whole abortion issue hinges on when life begins, using this emotional word intensifies the controversy.

Exercise Five — Identifying Controversial Theses

DIRECTIONS   Decide whether each of the theses below is controversial or not. If it is, tell why. Remember that the reasons a thesis is controversial are (1) its viewpoint is unlikely to be accepted by everyone and/or (2) its language is inflammatory.

MODEL   Thesis: The practice of American companies of building factories in Third World nations where labor costs are lower is bad business.

Is thesis controversial? <u>Yes</u>

Reason: <u>The viewpoint is unlikely to be accepted by everyone.</u>

1. Thesis: The metric system of measurement has been unsuccessful in America for several reasons.

   Is thesis controversial? _____

   Reason: _____.

2. Thesis: Zoos are not good for animals.

   Is thesis controversial? _____

   Reason: _____.

3. Thesis: In any year when a number of film actors have given outstanding performances in a variety of roles, singling out one as "best" actor is an artificial distinction.

   Is thesis controversial? _____

   Reason: _____.

4. Thesis: In any year when a number of film actors have given outstanding performances in a variety of roles, singling out one as "best" actor is stupid.

   Is thesis controversial? _____

   Reason: _____.

5. Thesis: Euthanasia is the only merciful release for a terminally ill person whose continued existence is a living hell.

   Is thesis controversial? _____

   Reason: _____.

Exercise Six

Identifying and Supplying Additional Examples for Controversial Theses

DIRECTIONS   For each of the following items, decide whether or not the thesis is controversial. If it is controversial, tell why and add another supporting example for the topic sentence. If it is not controversial, you do not need to add another example. Remember that a thesis is controversial if its viewpoint is unlikely to be accepted by everyone or if its language is inflammatory.

MODEL   Thesis: Human error was more responsible for the *Titanic* tragedy than the iceberg that pierced the ship's hull.

Blueprint: Arrogance and ignorance were the two major human errors.

Topic sentence 1: First, arrogance contributed significantly to the tragedy.

Supporting detail 1: The owners of the ship arrogantly believed it was unsinkable, so they failed to equip it with a sufficient number of lifeboats to accommodate the total number of passengers and crew aboard, thus resulting in the loss of over 1,500 lives.

Supporting detail 2: Some representatives of the owners aboard for the maiden voyage persuaded the captain to sail at dangerous speed in order to effect a New York arrival in record time. Their concern for publicity over safety made it difficult for the crew on watch to sight the iceberg in time to alter the ship's course.

Is thesis controversial? Yes

Reason: The viewpoint is unlikely to be accepted by everyone.

Additional supporting detail: Some of the commanders in the lifeboats did not return to pick up drowning passengers after the ship sank even though those lifeboats were only half full. Some of these commanders thought that many of the people still in the water were from steerage and not as important as first-class passengers.

1. Thesis: The first week of college can be frustrating.

   Blueprint: Registering, adjusting to dorm mates, and learning one's way around campus are processes fraught with frustration.

   Topic sentence 1: First, registration can be frustrating.

   Supporting detail 1: Widespread budget cuts have resulted in fewer classes being offered; consequently, students cannot always get the courses they need to graduate or transfer the semester they need them.

   Supporting detail 2: When the children of the baby boomers reached college age, they added to the number of registering students; as a result, students spend hours in several different lines just securing class cards before they wait in yet another line to pay their fees.

   Is thesis controversial? _____

Reason: _____

Additional supporting detail: _____.

2. Thesis: Reasons to support the existence of life after death are compelling.

Blueprint: Some reasons are based on anecdotes or personal accounts while others are based on science.

Topic sentence 1: First, there are strong anecdotal reasons to believe in life after death.

Supporting detail 1: Some people who have had near-death experiences uniformly report the same phenomenon, walking through a long tunnel toward a brilliant light and being met by loved ones who have already died.

Supporting detail 2: Other people who have been pronounced dead in an operating room also report a common experience. Upon being revived, they have repeated the conversations of doctors and nurses who were present in the operating room after these patients had been pronounced dead.

Is thesis controversial? _____

Reason: _____

Additional supporting detail: _____.

3. Thesis: Snails are not merely garden pests; rather, they are remarkable creatures.

Blueprint: Snails have remarkable powers and strength.

Topic sentence 1: First, snails have impressive powers.

Supporting detail 1: Snails can regenerate a body part. If a snail loses one of the two stalks on its head that is topped by an eye, it simply grows a new one.

Supporting detail 2: To protect itself from ants and other predatory insects, snails can form a vacuum, sealing themselves to the pavement with the mucus they produce for movement.

Is thesis controversial? _____

Reason: _____

Additional supporting detail: _____

_____.

4. Thesis: Symbols provide a shorthand form of communication between people.

   Blueprint: Both literary symbols and road symbols help people understand each other quickly.

   Topic sentence 1: To begin with, literary symbols quickly add depth to a reader's understanding of a work of literature.

   Supporting detail 1: For example, in Hemingway's short story "Hills Like White Elephants," the barren, dry landscape of rural Spain is symbolic of the sterile relationship between the two main characters.

   Supporting detail 2: In addition, in Kurt Vonnegut's short story "Harrison Bergeron," the physical handicaps, such as the heavy weights graceful people have to wear to make them ordinary, symbolize political systems, like communism, that are intended to minimize the uniqueness of the individual.

   Is thesis controversial? _____

   Reason: _____

   Additional supporting detail: _____

   _____ .

5. Thesis: The outrageous practice in some states of erasing a juvenile offender's criminal record when he or she becomes an adult should be abolished.

   Blueprint: This policy has harmful psychological and sociological effects.

   Topic sentence 1: First, erasing a juvenile offender's criminal record has harmful psychological effects.

   Supporting detail 1: For instance, it sends the wrong message to victims and their families. It says that no matter how horrible the crime was, after a certain time, the crime will be treated as if it never happened. For survivors this is hurtful because it devalues the loved one who was victimized.

   Supporting detail 2: It also sends the wrong message to the criminal, allowing him to feel that any and all crimes are forgivable after enough time has gone by. This message reinforces a dangerous belief in the criminal mind that "anything goes."

   Is thesis controversial? _____

Reason: _____
Additional supporting detail: _____

_____.

Anecdotes

Some supporting details can take the form of an **anecdote,** which is a short incident that is relevant to the topic sentence you use to support your thesis. Consider the following topic sentence and the anecdote that supports it:

Topic sentence: Truth is stranger than fiction.

Supporting anecdote: Matthew Gregory "Monk" Lewis, a writer of Gothic fiction in the late eighteenth century, was often criticized for his use of supernatural elements; however, his own burial at sea seems stranger than anything he ever wrote. According to biographers, he died while making a sea voyage, and, although his casket was properly weighted before being lowered into the sea, the casket rose to the surface after initially sinking. The weights dropped off, the canvas that was wrapped around the body filled with wind, and the casket was last seen bobbing off toward Jamaica on a voyage all its own.

Exercise Seven

Supplying Anecdotes

DIRECTIONS   For each of the following topic sentences, write at least one anecdote for support. You may use your own personal experience or that of someone you know. You may also use experiences you have read about or seen in the media. Be sure to mention the source of your anecdote if it is not from your own experience, as the model does when it refers to Lewis's biographers.

1. Topic sentence: Some of the rudest behavior people encounter these days comes from people in service jobs.

    Supporting anecdote: _____

    _____.

2. Topic sentence: Sometimes the media go too far in reporting graphic details.

    Supporting anecdote: _____

    _____.

3. Topic sentence: Many people have unreasonable fears.

   Supporting anecdote: _____

   _____ .

4. Topic sentence: Learning a skill by jumping in and trying it without prior prep-
      aration can be foolish.

   Supporting anecdote: _____

   _____ .

5. Topic sentence: Extraordinary circumstances can turn ordinary people into he-
      roes.

   Supporting anecdote: _____

   _____ .

Review Questions

Answer the following questions to review the material you have covered in this chapter.

1. What are the four techniques for expanding secondary details? (p. 282)

   _____ _____ _____ _____

2. What do expanded transitions do? (p. 282) _____

3. How do you make a detail more specific? (p. 283) _____

4. What are allusions? (p. 283) _____

5. What do results do to a supporting detail? (p. 283) _____

6. When are two times you use additional examples? (p. 284–285) _____

   _____

7. What are the two things that make a thesis controversial? (p. 285)

   _____ _____

8. What is inflammatory language? (p. 285)

   _____ _____

9. What is an anecdote? (p. 290) _____

Writing Exercises

I. Writing the Completely Developed Essay

Choose two of the three essay outlines you constructed for Writing Exercise I in Chapter Fourteen and write a completely developed essay from each, using any or all of the techniques you have learned in this chapter for developing supporting details.

II. Writing the Completely Developed Essay: The Sequel

Take the two essays you wrote in response to Writing Exercise III in Chapter Fourteen and expand the supporting details, using any or all of the techniques you have learned in this chapter.

III. Revising the Starter Essay

Look back at the starter essay you revised for structure in Writing Exercise IV in Chapter Fourteen. Do you have enough supporting details in the main body paragraphs? Do the supporting details really support the topic sentence in each main body paragraph? Now add more development to your supporting details, using all of the techniques you learned in this chapter: expanding transitions, making details more specific, adding allusions, and adding results. You may also use additional examples and anecdotes where appropriate.

Looking Back and Looking Forward

In this section, you have learned to expand the structure and development of a single paragraph into a multi-paragraph essay. In the final section of this textbook, you will learn to apply that structure and development to write a multi-paragraph summary.

Chapter sixteen

Summary

In the last section, you learned how to expand the structure and development of a single paragraph paper into a multi-paragraph essay. In college, the essay is used to respond to ideas presented in materials you are assigned to study, like literature and film. In order to make your essay effective, you will need to refer to this source material by summarizing it.

A **summary** reduces a source to its main ideas. That is why a summary is always shorter than the original material. In college essays, summaries are presented as *background* or *supporting details,* rather than a whole essay, so they usually require only a few sentences. You should assume your reader is not familiar with your source material, so you must give just enough information in your summary for the material to make sense. Consider this essay that you read at the beginning of Chapter Fourteen. Notice that it now has a title and author, which are then repeated in the first sentence of the summary in order to identify the source material.

My "Terrorist" Attack

by Barbara Dahlgren-Gordon

Most of us have had a moment when we wished the earth would open up and swallow us, and I am no exception. My first meeting with my prospective in-laws was a terrifically embarrassing experience. I embarrassed myself entering their home, having dinner, and leaving.

First, I made a fool of myself entering my prospective in-laws' home. In my eagerness to express my pleasure at meeting Mr. Gordon, I enunciated violently when I said to him, "I'm SO pleased to meet you!" I expelled my breath with gale-force wind when I said "SO." The result was that I hurled my breath mint directly into his bushy beard, where it stuck like Velcro. There it hung securely, taunting me. Then, while trying frantically to extricate the glob from his startled face, I missed my footing, tripped over the threshold, and, still clutching Mr. Gordon's beard, came crashing down on a priceless

Ming vase in the entryway. Mr. Gordon also fell to his knees on the shards of the vase, which had shattered to brittle confetti. My father-in-law-to-be moaned a pitiful "Ow, ow, ow." My agony was compounded by not knowing which hurt him most: the sharp pottery embedded in his knees, my fingers yanking on his beard, or the thought that this dangerously clumsy stranger was joining the family.

Next, I mortified myself at dinner. I was anxious to compliment Mrs. Gordon's cooking, so just after telling her that she was the Julia Child of Springfield, Illinois, I inhaled a ladle-sized spoonful of her famous onion soup, which was so hot that I sprayed it back over my dining companions like an incontinent garden hose. The only one I left dry was the family dog, cowering under my fiance's chair. Once everyone at the table had mopped up sufficiently and settled down to a tense, silent attention to the pot roast, I let my nerves get the best of me. Thoroughly shaken at that point, I began to fiddle with the border on Mrs. Gordon's damask lace tablecloth, obviously an heirloom. By the time I realized what I was doing, I had unraveled a half-inch of the bottom border. A sizable mound of crinkled thread filled my lap, and the bottom of the tablecloth looked like the fringe on a Victorian lamp.

Finally, I sealed my humiliation with an awkward exit. I was still trying to appear unfailingly agreeable, as my nervous hosts walked my fiance and me to the door. Doing my impression of an apologetic Columbo, alternately bowing and nodding as I backed out the front door, I tripped on the same door sill I had sailed in on, clutching the air as I crumbled in a heap on the pavement, skinning my knees and leaving blood on the clean walkway. I'm sure the Gordons hoped the worst was over, but I had one more humiliating faux pas in me: The capper was the angry gouge I left in the Gordons' cream-colored TR4 parked in their driveway as I lurched to my feet, stumbling against it and scraping my jacket zipper along the passenger side door. The metallic scar glinted wickedly in the bright sun. It nearly blinded me as I slunk toward my fiance, who was already gunning the motor of my car in a frantic attempt to remove me from the scene of my crimes.

If it had not been for my excrutiatingly clumsy entrance, dining, and exit, I am sure I would have made a terrific first impression on my future in-laws instead of one that totally humiliated me. Not surprisingly, it was three weeks before I could get over my embarrassment enough to send a combined thank-you note and apology to the Gordons, who now lovingly refer to me as "The Terminatrix."

Now consider this summary of the essay:

In her essay "My 'Terrorist' Attack," Barbara Dahlgren-Gordon writes about her disastrous first meeting with her in-laws. First, she describes her disastrous arrival, when she got her breath mint stuck in Mr. Gordon's beard and then tripped him in his doorway, turning an expensive vase that she fell on into "brittle confetti." Next, she tells about her disastrous dinner, when she spit out hot soup and then unraveled an imported tablecloth. Last, she describes her disastrous exit, when she scraped her knees and scratched the Gordons' sports car.

Did you notice that the first sentence of the summary acts as a **summary introduction?** It includes the *title*, the *author's name*, and the *topic of the source material*. This information tells the reader that you are writing a summary of someone else's ideas. Did you notice also that each of the three remaining sentences in the summary condenses a main body paragraph from the essay, including the information from the topic sentence and both supporting details? For instance, the sentence that follows the summary introduction sentence condenses the topic sentence from the first main body paragraph in the original essay to *First, she describes her disastrous arrival.* In addition, it condenses the first supporting detail to *she got her breath mint stuck in Mr. Gordon's beard.* Moreover, it condenses the second supporting detail to *then tripped him in his doorway, turning an expensive vase that she fell on to "brittle confetti."* Notice that the summary combines all of this information in a single sentence, using coordination and modification, which you learned about in Chapter Eleven. Do you see that each of the last two sentences summarizes a topic sentence and its two examples in the same way?

Sometimes a summary might give just one supporting detail as an example; however, in this case, all of the supporting details are necessary to prove the author's point that the meeting was *disastrous* because it takes more than just a couple of embarrassing incidents to make a disaster. Finally, did you notice that the conclusion of the essay is not summarized? As you recall from Chapter Fourteen, the first part of a conclusion in an essay is a restatement of the thesis and blueprint. The summary has already included this information, so it does not need to be stated again. The last part of an essay's conclusion is also not necessary in a summary. That is because a *so what?* statement goes beyond the main points of the source material.

Exercise One **Summarizing**

DIRECTIONS Read the following passages and write a one-paragraph summary of each, beginning with a summary introduction sentence that gives the title, the author's name, and the topic. Use the preceding summary as a model.

1. Passage:

A Short History of Salt

by Dr. Sheldon Gaylord

Salt, one of our most valuable commodities, has both helped and harmed mankind. First, it has helped people by seasoning their food. The salt in our food provides our bodies with sodium and chlorine, elements in salt that are essential to our bodies, which do not naturally contain much of these elements. Seasoning our food with salt also brings out the flavor of food, the way it does when we sprinkle it on melons, like cantaloupe. Second, salt has also helped people by providing commercial value. Caravans in the Sahara Desert traded salt, as did early Italians who named one of their oldest trade routes the Salt Road, or Via Saleria. Furthermore, because it is so valuable, people used salt as money in some areas of the world. In fact, Roman soldiers received money that they used to buy salt, so they called it *salarium*, or *salt money*, which is where we get the term *salary*, as well as the saying someone is *worth his salt*. On the other hand, people have fought wars over salt. For instance, the British salt monopoly helped to spark India's struggle for independence from Great Britain. Furthermore, unreasonable taxes on salt contributed to the French Revolution. Clearly, the history of humankind would be vastly different without salt.

Summary:

2. Passage:

The Birth of the Boycott

by Mavis Ryan

Everyone has a way to show his or her disapproval of someone else's product, position, or behavior. One way is a *boycott*. A boycott is a refusal to deal with or support an individual or a company. The term comes from Captain Charles C. Boycott, who was the first victim of a boycott, in County Mayo, Ireland, in the mid-1800s. Captain Boycott was a harsh landlord to his tenants. He charged unreasonable rent and made no adjustments for poor harvest years, so his tenants and neighbors responded by shunning him. His neighbors refused to speak with him or include him in social events. They also made it difficult for him to get food deliveries, and they persuaded his servants to quit. This boycott continued until Captain Boycott finally left the country. Today, people boycott for many reasons. For instance, many people boycott grapes by not buying them since Cesar Chavez told the public about the miserable working and living conditions of migrant farm workers who harvest the grapes. In addition, many people refuse to buy razors, shaving cream, and other toiletries by the Gillette Company because the company refuses to completely end product testing on animals. Everyone should realize that he or she has a voice that can be heard.

Summary:

3. Passage:

Foolish King Midas

retold by
Miriam Kohane

One of the most misguided characters in Greek mythology is King Midas of Phrygia, the land of roses. King Midas was not a cruel man but merely foolish, and he proved it with two foolish choices. First, he entertained an inebriated, old follower of Bacchus, the Greek god of wine and drunken revelry, who stumbled into his rose garden. When King Midas returned the old man, a grateful Bacchus granted Midas a wish, and the foolish king wished that everything he touched would turn to gold. He overlooked the consequences until he touched his dinner that evening, and it turned to gold, leaving him hungry and unable to feed himself. Even though Bacchus eventually took pity on King Midas and told him where to wash away the golden touch, King Midas persisted in his foolishness when he was one of the judges at a musical competition between Apollo, the god of music and poetry, and Pan, a lesser god of shepherds, who was famous for playing pretty songs on his reed pipe. Even though Apollo was the better musician and won the contest, King Midas foolishly cast his vote for Pan. He should have known that powerful gods make powerful enemies. Apollo proved this when he gave King Midas the ears of an ass in retaliation. Apollo said the ears reflected King Midas's taste in music. From then on, King Midas hid his ears under a special hat, but the servant that cut his hair felt so burdened by the secret that he dug a hole in a field and whispered the secret into it before filling the hole back up. Consequently, the plants that grew there in the spring whispered the secret each time the wind blew and told all men how foolish King Midas was.

Summary:

4. Passage:

Open Adoption Records: Yes or No?

by Andrew Wilson

One place where the individual's right to privacy and the individual's right to know collide is in the area of adoption. Many people object to adult adoptees getting help in finding their birth parents, either by private investigators or sympathetic court officials, who make available legally sealed biographical information. Some of these objectors are women who surrendered children for adoption many years ago with the promise of lifelong secrecy. They live in fear that the unexpected arrival of that now grown-up child will shatter their lives and current families. Other objectors include adoption agencies who fear they will lose clients if they cannot guarantee secrecy. Yet another group who feels threatened by the release of information about birth parents is the adoptive parents, who fear losing the love, loyalty, and sometimes even custody of the child they consider their own. On the other side of the debate are adult adoptees who claim the right to know their origins for different reasons. Many adult adoptees need to know the biological histories of their birth parents for their own health or that of their children. Some even need to locate a biological relative for an organ transplant. Other adult adoptees seek a relationship with their birth family in order to feel emotionally complete. Most adoptees simply want to know their "roots" because they feel entitled to know what non-adoptees take for granted: who they are and where they come from. Because feelings on both sides run high, a resolution to the issue of opening sealed records and revealing formerly secret information is not likely in the near future.

Summary:

5. Passage:

The Myth of Daphne

retold by
Khoi Dang

Greek mythology presents a bleak picture of beautiful women whom the gods loved. These women were the equivalent of today's mistresses of powerful men: Their children were in danger from the angry wives of the gods, and their own position was never secure nor legal. The young huntress Daphne knew this very well and, consequently, was terrified of the god Apollo's amorous attention. Daphne, daughter of a river god named Peneus, wanted no lover at all, mortal or immortal. When her father tried to convince her to marry, she begged to remain free and hunt like the goddess Diana in her beloved woods, and her adoring father gave in to her. The greatest threat to Daphne's freedom was Apollo, who saw her hunting and desired her. When he pursued her, she ran through the woods, calling out to her father for help. As she reached the river where her father lived, she felt bark and leaves sprouting on her body. Her father turned her into a laurel tree to protect her. Then Apollo sadly made the laurel his sign of victory so that song and story would forever link him with Daphne.

Summary:

Verb Tenses for Summary

In Chapter Six you learned to recognize the present, past, and future verb tenses. In a summary, you may need to use all of these verb tenses but especially the present and past tenses.

Attribution Verbs

Did you notice that each sentence in the summary of "My 'Terrorist' Attack" gives credit to Dahlgren-Gordon by introducing the information in that sentence with *Dahlgren-Gordon writes about, she describes,* or *she tells about*? An introduction to borrowed material is necessary because it helps you avoid **plagiarism,** the unauthorized repetition of someone else's ideas or words. When you introduce borrowed material by crediting the source, you are giving an **attribution.** The attribution is usually made up of the person's name or a pronoun referring to that person, like *he* or *she,* and a verb that means the words or ideas came from that person, like *says* or *writes.* The **attribution verb** is in the present tense. That is because each time you look at a source, the author *speaks* to you again. Here are some verbs commonly used in attributions:

says	tells about	describes	relates	asserts	confirms
emphasizes	details	states	tries to	compares	notes
explains	implies	suggests	persuade us	traces	contrasts
claims	demonstrates	classifies	explores	evaluates	defends
defines	clarifies		lists		summarizes
argues			discusses		
tells how					

As you learned in Chapter One, many of these verbs mean to *describe* something in <u>different</u> ways. That is why they are not interchangeable. In other words, you would not use *discusses* in an attribution if you really mean *defends* because *discusses* means the author covers all parts of the subject while *defends* means the author supports his or her point of view against a differing point of view.

Non-attribution Verbs

Non-attribution verbs are the verbs in the material being summarized, rather than the verbs that introduce that material. They may be in past tense or present tense.

Did you notice in the summary that the verbs which describe the events that took place in the meeting that Dahlgren-Gordon writes about are in the past tense?

These verbs are *got, tripped, fell, spit, unraveled, scraped,* and *scratched.* They describe factual events that occurred in the past, before the author tells us about them. If you are summarizing facts or events that are happening now or are currently true, your non-attribution verbs must be in the present tense.

If, however, you are summarizing literature or film rather than a factual essay, like Dahlgren-Gordon's, you are summarizing fiction. The non-attribution verbs for a summary of fictional events are in the present tense, just like the attribution verbs, because the story happens again each time you read it.

Exercise Two

Correcting Summaries for Verbs

DIRECTIONS Examine the summaries you wrote for Exercise One. First, check each summary for attribution verbs. Make sure that all sentences with borrowed material include an attribution verb in the present tense. Next, identify the remaining verbs in each summary. If the summarized material is factual, make sure your non-attribution verbs are in the past tense; if the summarized material is fictional, make sure your non-attribution verbs are in the present tense.

Using Quotations in Summaries

Sometimes your source material may contain information or images that grab your attention when you read them. If you cannot present the same information as effectively in your summary using your own words, then you may wish to quote the original source. A **quotation** is an idea, a phrase, an image, or a thought expressed in the original author's own words.

A quotation has three characteristics:

1. it contains striking language and/or important information

2. it is introduced by an attribution

3. it is enclosed by quotation marks

Look back at the quotation in the summary of "My 'Terrorist' Attack." Can you see that *brittle confetti* is striking language that brings a vivid picture to mind? If you tried to express the same idea in your own words, you probably would not be as effective. Now look for the attribution. Do you see that the quotation is in a sentence that begins with *She describes?* Finally, notice that only Dahlgren-Gordon's exact words *brittle confetti* are enclosed in quotation marks. The ideas in the summary that are not expressed in the author's exact words are not in quotation marks, even though they are introduced by attributions that tell you these ideas are borrowed, but the exact language is not.

Two ways to put a quotation in your sentence are:

1. separated
2. non-separated

A **separated quotation** is separated from the attribution that introduces it by a comma. Consider this example: *The ancient Greek philosopher Heraclitus said, "Nothing endures but change."* A **nonseparated quotation** is not separated by a comma from the attribution that introduces it. Consider this example: *The ancient Greek playwright Aeschylus believed that death was preferable to tyranny because it was "a milder fate."* A separated quotation is usually in the form of a whole sentence, so it begins with a capital letter; however, a nonseparated quotation is usually a single word or phrase, so it begins with a small letter.

Finally, you should use quotes sparingly. Notice that the summary of "My 'Terrorist' Attack" includes only one quotation. A well-chosen quotation goes a long way while too many get in the way of your own writing. A summary, after all, should reflect your understanding of the source material. Therefore, you should never quote something you do not understand.

Exercise Three

Adding Quotations to Summaries

DIRECTIONS Examine the summaries you rewrote for Exercise Two. Then go back to the source material those summaries are based on and look for striking language and important information that you think you should quote in your summaries. Add those quotations, making sure that each quotation is introduced by an attribution and that you have punctuated correctly for both separated and nonseparated quotations. Remember to choose your quotations carefully, since you should use them only when necessary.

Long Quotations

If your summary is relatively short, a few sentences, your quotations will also be short. You will quote single words and phrases or perhaps a complete sentence. After all, a quotation is not an end in itself. Rather, it is a tool that you can use to support your own point. Although you must limit the number of quotations you use in a long summary just as you do in a short summary, you may find some long quotations that you feel are necessary. When you find a quotation that runs three or more typewritten lines and cannot be broken up without losing its effect, you may use it in your summary as a **block quotation.** A block quotation has three characteristics:

1. it is introduced by an attribution that is a complete sentence ending in a colon

2. it is indented ten spaces from the left-hand margin

3. it does not have quotation marks around it

Can you identify two block quotations in the following long summary of the movie *Titanic?*

Summarizing a Movie in an Essay

In this chapter, you have summarized relatively brief passages. Now you are ready to summarize a longer work. Read the following summary of the movie *Titanic.*

A Summary of *Titanic*

The movie *Titanic,* written and directed by James Cameron and starring Kate Winslet and Leonardo DiCaprio, is about the fate of the luxury liner of the same name, which everyone thought was unsinkable, and her passengers on her first and final voyage. The central characters Rose and Jack, played by Winslet and DiCaprio, become involved in a romance that is finally overpowered by complications. First, complications arise from Rose's engagement to another passenger and Jack's and Rose's opposite backgrounds and social standings; then further complications arise when the couple begins to fall in love; and finally, nature provides insurmountable complications to the couple as the ship strikes an iceberg and ultimately sinks.

First, Jack and Rose's romance is complicated by Rose's engagement and the social differences between Rose and Jack. When they first meet, Rose's dissatisfaction with her engagement to John Hockley has driven her to the point of near suicide. Hockley is a wealthy but domineering snob, who refers to the Picasso paintings Rose has bought in Europe as "finger paintings" and "a waste of money." He offers Rose a life consisting mainly of endless society parties that she finds numbing. When Jack saves Rose from plunging into the ocean, they fall onto the deck, with Jack falling on top of Rose. Rose's fiance, who has been searching for her, finds them in this compromising position and whisks Rose away. Then, shamed by Rose into rewarding Jack with something more substantial than money, Hockley invites Jack to dine with them in the main dining salon the next evening. He is hoping to embarrass Jack, who is a steerage passenger, by placing him among important society people. However, Jack, manages to borrow a tuxedo and appears appropriately dressed at dinner, where he charms his dinner companions when he expresses his *carpe diem* philosophy:

> I love waking up in the morning not knowing what's going to happen or where I'm going to wind up. Just the other night I was sleeping under a bridge, and now here I am on the grandest ship in the world, having champagne with you fine people. I figure life's a gift, and I don't intend on wasting it.

When his dinner companions toast Jack with "to making it count," Hockley's hope to discredit Jack in Rose's eyes is ruined.

Second, complications arise when Jack and Rose begin to fall in love. After Jack shows Rose his sketches of Parisian models and teaches her the fine art of spitting, Rose's mother snatches her away, selfishly reminding Rose that if she does not want her mother to take in sewing to make ends meet, she will refrain from endangering her engagement to Hockley by any further association with Jack. Later, Jack secretly arranges to meet Rose and escort her to a rollicking party in steerage, where they enjoy each other's company so much that they stay the rest of the evening. When Hockley's servant reports that Rose spent the night dancing wildly in public with Jack, Hockley is enraged. Over coffee with Rose the next morning, he shouts, "You will honor me the way a wife is required to honor her husband because I will not be made a fool of!" Consequently, Rose wavers and tells Jack that she cannot see him again, despite their obvious feelings for each other.

Finally, the most devastating complications arise for Rose and Jack as *Titanic* strikes an iceberg and sinks. To begin with, Hockley frames Jack for stealing the Coeur de la Mer diamond that he had given Rose as an engagement present. As a result, Jack is arrested and led below deck, where he is shackled to a pipe by Hockley's servant and left to drown as the ship sinks. After Rose has freed Jack, they must struggle against rising water and the prejudice of crew members, who keep passageways to the upper decks locked against the steerage passengers, while first-class passengers board lifeboats. Later, when Rose leaps out of a lifeboat, refusing to leave Jack, she tells him, "You jump; I jump," echoing the words he used when he saved her from jumping overboard at their first meeting. Hockley then loses control and shoots at the couple, forcing them to a lower deck that is rapidly filling with water. When the ship at last goes down, Jack saves Rose from a hysterical passenger who forces her under water to keep himself afloat. Then, when the floating debris that Jack helps Rose climb onto will not hold both of them, Jack remains in the water, holding onto the raft and Rose's hand. When Rose tells him she loves him, as if she is preparing to die, he commands her to live:

> Don't you do that! Don't you say your good-byes! Not yet. Do you understand me? Listen, Rose, you're going to get out of here. You're going to go on, and you're going to make lots of babies, and you're going to watch them grow. You're going to die an old, an old lady, warm in her bed, not here, not this night, not like this!

Soon the frigid water and the tardy rescue efforts contribute to Jack's death, the only insurmountable complication to Rose and Jack's relationship.

As a result of all the complications at the beginning, middle, and end of their relationship, Jack and Rose's physical connection is broken apart, even as *Titanic* breaks apart in the North Atlantic. However, their spiritual connection survives a lifetime through Rose, who, at 101 years of age, returns the Coeur de la Mer to the wreck of Titanic after she has told her story to the salvage crew that discovered the pictures that Jack had drawn of her while she was wearing the jewel.

Did you notice that the last paragraph of this multi-paragraph summary of *Titanic* is a conclusion? If your summary is a full-length essay, it must have the same kind of conclusion every essay should have with a summary sentence and a *so what* statement; however, if you write a single-paragraph summary or even a single-sentence summary in a longer essay, you will not need a conclusion for the summary.

Summarizing a Movie in a Single Paragraph

Sometimes you may find it useful to summarize a movie or other source more briefly in order to support a claim in your essay or to use as background material so the reader can understand other parts of your essay. In those cases, a paragraph-length summary, like the one of "My 'Terrorist' Attack," is appropriate. As you recall, that summary begins with a summary introduction sentence, which includes the title of the essay being summarized, the author's name, and the topic of the source material. Then it condenses each body paragraph's topic sentence and supporting details into a single sentence, each using coordination and modification. Now consider this example of a single-paragraph summary of the movie *Titanic*:

> The movie *Titanic,* written and directed by James Cameron and starring Kate Winslet and Leonardo DiCaprio, tells the story of Rose and Jack, whose romance is overwhelmed by complications. First, Rose and Jack are divided by Rose's engagement to another man, John Hockley, and by Jack's lower-class background. Furthermore, as the two fall in love, Rose and Jack are separated by Rose's mother's financial objections to Jack and Rose's fiance's vehement objections to Rose's association with another man, which makes him look foolish. Finally, Jack and Rose are divided temporarily by Hockley's treacherous attempt to discredit and then kill Jack, and then irrevocably by the sinking of the *Titanic,* which Rose survives but Jack does not.

Summarizing a Movie in a Single Sentence

Sometimes you may find it useful to summarize a movie or other source in a single sentence. This usually happens when your assigment tells you to tell about a theme or idea that is shared by the movie, book, or other source. For instance, if your assignment tells you to contrast the people who are able to overcome obstacles with those people who cannot overcome obstacles, you might compare and contrast the stories of famous lovers like Romeo and Juliet, in the play of the same name; Jack and Rose, in *Titanic;* and Nicky and Terry in the movie *An Affair to Remember.* You might condense each of these stories to a single-sentence summary to serve as background before you contrast the characters to show the first couple do not overcome obstacles, one member of the second couple survives obstacles while the second member does not, and the third couple triumphs together over obstacles. Now consider the following one-sentence summary of *Titanic:*

> The movie *Titanic,* written and directed by James Cameron and starring Kate Winslet and Leonardo DiCaprio, tells the story of Rose and Jack, who are lovers thwarted by the complications of differences in their social status and by natural disaster.

Did you notice in both the single-paragraph summary and single-sentence summary of *Titanic* there are no quotations? This is because the shorter the summary, the more general the content must be. Since quotations are very specific details, they are usually inappropriate for short summaries.

Review Questions

Answer the following questions to help you review the material you have covered in this chapter.

1. What does a summary do? (p. 293) _____

2. How are summaries used in college essays? (p. 293)

   _____ and _____

3. What is the purpose of the first sentence of a summary? (p. 295)

   _____

4. What three things does the first sentence of a summary include? (p. 295)

   _____ _____ _____

5. What does the information in the first sentence of a summary tell the reader? (p. 295) _____

6. Why does a summary not include the first part of the conclusion of an essay? (p. 295) _____

7. Why does a summary not include the last part of the conclusion of an essay? (p. 295) _____

8. Why is an introduction to borrowed information necessary? (p. 299)

   _____

9. What is the introduction to borrowed material called? (p. 299) _____

10. What is an attribution usually made up of? (p. 299)

    _____ _____ _____

11. What is always the tense of the attribution verb? (p. 299) _____

12. Why? (p. 299) _____

13. What do you use the past tense of a non-attribution verb in a summary for? (p. 300) _____

14. What do you use the present tense of a non-attribution verb in a summary for? (p. 300) _____ _____

15. What is a quotation? (p. 300) _____

16. What are the three characteristics of a quotation? (p. 300)

   _____   _____   _____

17. What are the two ways to put a quotation into your sentence? (p. 301)

   _____   _____

18. How is a separated quotation separated from its attribution? (p. 301) _____

   _____

19. When does a quotation begin with a capital letter? (p. 301) _____

20. When does a quotation begin with a small letter? (p. 301) _____

21. Why do you use quotations sparingly? (p. 301) _____

22. What should you never quote? (p. 301) _____

23. What is a long quotation called? (p. 301) _____

24. How long must a block quotation be? (p. 301) _____

25. What are the three characteristics of a block quotation? (p. 302)

   _____   _____   _____

26. What are the two uses for a single-paragraph summary? (p. 304)

   _____   _____

27. When is it useful to write a single-sentence summary? (p. 305)

   _____

28. Why are quotations usually inappropriate for short summaries? (p. 305)

   _____

Writing Exercises

I. Summarizing a Movie in a Multi-Paragraph Essay

See the movie of your choice, and write a summary of it in the academic essay form you have learned, using the summary of *Titanic* as a model. Since most movies are about people in conflict, your thesis, like the thesis of the model summary of *Titanic,* can say that there are several complications in the movie that you are summarizing. Then your blueprint should identify those complications. The rest of your essay will follow the structure set out in your blueprint. Your summary should include quotations where appropriate.

When you revise, make sure your summary begins with a summary introduction sentence. Also, make sure each of your quotations begins with an attribution. Then, make sure you have punctuated correctly for separated, nonseparated, and block quotations. Make sure your verb tenses are appropriate. Finally, if possible, rent the movie so that you may watch it several times. Repeated viewings will help you make sure your quotations are accurate.

II. Summarizing a Movie in a Single Paragraph

Condense the multi-paragraph summary essay you wrote for Writing Exercise I into a single-paragraph summary.

III. Summarizing a Movie in a Single Sentence

Condense the single-paragraph summary you wrote for Writing Exercise II into a single-sentence summary.

Looking Back and Looking Forward

In this chapter, you have learned how to summarize source material and to present some of that material in the form of quotations. This is the beginning of a process that will culminate with your ability to write a full-length research paper for any college class. In this book, you have learned how to construct an academic essay from an assignment. You have gone from understanding the assignment; to narrowing the focus of your subject matter to a topic; to structuring your essay with an introduction, main body paragraphs, and a conclusion; to developing your support; to editing for structure, development, and grammar; and finally, to summarizing source material that may include quotations.

As you continue the writing process in your college studies, you will learn to discuss what borrowed material implies, as well as what it says directly. This is called **analysis,** and careful analysis relies upon more critical thinking skills that you will learn. Once you can analyze your source material, you will discover over and over again how analysis affects other areas of your life. Before you choose a product in a store, you will be able to analyze and evaluate the advertising for the product. Before you choose a candidate to vote for, you will be able to analyze and evaluate his or her campaign promises. Before you enter into any written agreement, like a rental agreement or a marriage contract, you can analyze what you are getting yourself into! In short, the writing process will help you make informed choices in your life. These informed choices are the signs of an educated person.

Section five review *Writing Essays*

I. Expanding Paragraphs into Essays

Go back to the paragraph you wrote in response to Writing Exercise II at the end of Chapter Ten and write a fully developed multi-paragraph essay from it.

II. Writing Essays

Reread the topics in Section Four Review under "II. Rewriting with Structure and Development" and choose two that you did not write paragraphs on previously. Now write a fully developed multi-paragraph essay for each.

III. Writing a Multi-Paragraph Summary

Choose a chapter in *From Thought to Word,* and write a multi-paragraph summary of it using short or block quotations where appropriate.

IV. Writing Essays that Use Summaries

Choose one of the following three topics and write a multi-paragraph essay that includes summarized material with appropriate quotations.

1. Discuss how some movies glorify violence.

2. Some television critics say that child characters in sitcoms are unrealistic. Write an essay in which you agree or disagree, using specific examples from episodes you have seen.

3. Many talk show hosts seem to encourage the worst behavior in their guests. Using specific examples, write an essay that proves or disproves this claim.

INDEX

Abstract nouns, 23
accept, 161
Action verbs
  in commands, 14
  explanation of, 9
  helping verbs with, 11
Active voice, 153, 154
Adjectives
  beginning with relative pronouns, 42
  coordinate and noncoordinate, 187–188
  explanation of, 36, 186
  guidelines for recognizing, 37
  participles as, 38
Adverbial conjunctions, 180–181
Adverbs
  function of, 40, 129, 186
  placement for single-word, 191
advise, 161
affect, 161
Agreement
  parallelism as, 104
  primary details and, 108
  pronoun-antecedent, 92–97
  in structure, 98–103
  verb-subject, 85–88
  verb-tense, 90
all ready, 161
allusion, 162
Allusions, 283
almost, 191
already, 162
Analyze, 14
and
  split focus and, 219
  use of, 176
Anecdotes, 290
Antecedents, 92–97
Appositive phrases, 196
Appositives, 189
are, 162
Assignments
  broken into topics, 55
  commands as, 14–15

with controlling ideas, 78
modifiers in, 46–47
nouns and pronouns in, 31
with partial controlling ideas, 80
questions as, 13
verbs in, 13–17
without controlling ideas, 79
Attitudes
  editing overly complicated, 224–225
  editing overly subjective, 223
Attribution, 299
Attribution verbs, 299

barely, 191
because of, 159
"The Birth of the Boycott" (Ryan), 296
Block quotations, 301–302
Blueprints
  function of, 267
  from theses, 268–269
  writing preliminary statements from, 269–270
  writing summary sentences from, 273
Brainstorming
  by clustering, 16
  focused, 15
  with focusing questions, 56
  by listing, 15–16
brake, 162
break, 162
but
  split focus and, 219
  use of, 176

can, 159
Capitalization, 22
Cause and effect, 184
choose, 162
chose, 162
Clarify, 14
Classify, 14
Clause modifiers
  explanation of, 201
  punctuation and placement of, 202–206

311